THE STORY

Murray Watts grew up on Merseyside, where he began his career writing for Radio Merseyside. He studied English Literature and the History of Art at Emmanuel College, Cambridge, and Theology at St John's College, Nottingham. He was a founding director of Riding Lights Company in York and has written many scripts for theatre, radio, TV and film.

He is the author of a number of books, including the novel *The Miracle Maker*. He also wrote the screenplay for the acclaimed animated feature film *The Miracle Maker*, which was released in the year 2000. He is the director of the arts charity The Wayfarer Trust at Freswick Castle in Caithness, Scotland.

For more information about Murray, go to:
www.freswickcastle.com

THE
STORY

BY

MURRAY WATTS

**For my two best friends,
my sons Fionn and Toby,
with love forever.**

A Lion Book
an imprint of
Lion Hudson plc
Mayfield House, 256 Banbury Road,
Oxford OX2 7DH, England
www.lionhudson.com
ISBN 13: 978-0-7459-5251-2
ISBN 10: 0-7459-5251-8

First published in 2002 under the title *The Lion Bible for Children*
This revised edition 2006
10 9 8 7 6 5 4 3 2 1 0

A catalogue record for this book is available
from the British Library

Typeset in 12/15 Berkeley Old Style Book BT

Printed and bound in the UK
by Cox and Wyman Ltd

The text paper used in this book has been made from
wood independently certified as having come from sustainable forests

CONTENTS

THE OLD TESTAMENT

THE NEW TESTAMENT

INTRODUCTION

An introduction marks the beginning of a journey for the reader, but the end of one for the writer. This is the last page to be written and, for me, the hardest of all. How can I describe the joys, fears, challenges and surprises of such an exhilarating journey? I can only hope that some of this experience will shine through my retelling of the Bible story. Writing this book has been an adventure for me, and I hope that it will be the same for anyone who reads it.

I have frequently been moved by the struggles and failures of the characters in these narratives, as well as by the many heart-warming examples of courage and nobility. The men, women and children of the Bible are so like us, and the themes of the Bible do not become dated. This is a love story, the moving tale of God's love for the world in all its wonder and all its brokenness. It is full of beauty and hope but it is also very realistic about people and the consequences of their actions.

The Bible is not simply one book but a library of great works, written over hundreds of years, recording the experiences of many different personalities and their times. In *The Story*, I have tried to reflect the magnificent breadth of this material, expressed in a rich variety of history, story-telling and song. The unique archive which makes up the Bible also shows how people's knowledge of God deepened and developed over centuries – there is a vast difference between the harsh and sometimes warlike world of some books of the Old Testament and the love and forgiveness we see in the life of Jesus, many generations later. However, there is a strong sense of continuity throughout the Bible and a deep unity, which has influenced my retelling.

Perhaps the greatest virtue of the original biblical material is its simplicity. There is an economy in the language of the Bible and a directness which can be inspiring as well as devastating in the accuracy of its aim. The truth is like an arrow which can pierce the armour of our modern sophistication and our intellectual pretensions. It is a mistake to see the Bible simply as a supreme achievement of literature – which it is – or as a "great religious work". It is only sublime literature, and spiritually so profound, because it speaks sympathetically to our common humanity and is concerned with universal truths which are available to all men, women and children, whatever their age, background, education, culture, nationality, faith – or lack of it. The Bible speaks to the human heart and, in the words of the Psalmist, "deep calls to deep".

In writing *The Story* I have tried to do justice to the unadorned language of the Bible so anyone – anywhere in the world – can truly appreciate "the greatest story ever told". Of course, the use of the word "story" emphasizes the unity of many stories which are rooted in history, memory, deep personal experience and – far beyond human imagination and creativity – divine inspiration. This is neither a work of fiction, nor faction, nor basic historical fact. *The Story* is responding to a mystery which is not so much about words or a book, but about love – about a God who is Love.

Researching and writing *The Story* over several years has had a deep effect on me, for this reason, and has greatly increased my awe and respect for the beautiful work which is simply known as "The Book" (Bible) or "The Writings" (Scriptures) or, to many faithful believers, "The Word of God". However, Jesus himself had stern words for those who saw no further than the text: "You search the Scriptures because you think that in them you will find eternal life, yet you will not come to me." This not only refers to the Pharisees but to modern day religious readers. As so often, the Bible challenges and cautions us just at the moment when we are beginning to feel comfortable.

The Bible is so much more than a book, but in writing *The Story* I recognize that there are many different levels of appreciation along the way, and it is certainly impossible to arrive finally at a place of imagined security or worse, superiority, claiming "I understand all this". Every reader is on their own journey and God alone knows where each of us is wandering, perhaps meandering, along our pathway in life.

For some readers, *The Story* will appear to be a valuable introduction to great themes, teaching and stories that have influenced two millennia of human history. For others, *The Story* may prove for a while to be a source of personal inspiration at a stage in their experience quite apart from any religious beliefs. For others, it may simply be a wonderful and classic story to be enjoyed with fresh interest, curiosity and delight. I will be content if there is such a diversity of responses but I will be truly rewarded in my struggles if there are some readers at least who discover that *The Story* is much more significant than any "story" or epic tale in the history of the world.

I hope that for these readers, young and old, *The Story* will open a window into paradise and fill their hearts with the fragrance of the divine lover.

Murray Watts
Freswick, Caithness
August, 2006

God said,
"Let there be light."

Genesis 1:3

THE OLD TESTAMENT

THE CREATION

GENESIS 1, 2

In the beginning, God created the heavens and the earth.

The earth was formless and empty, darkness lay over the deep oceans, and God's Spirit was moving over the surface of the waters.

Then God spoke: "Let there be light!" And there was light. God saw that the light was good. He divided the light from the darkness. And so God named the light Day and the darkness Night. There was evening and morning, the very first day.

And God said, "Let there be a space above the oceans, to separate the heavens from the earth." And it was so, and God named this space Sky. There was evening and morning again, and that was the second day.

And God said, "Let dry ground appear from the deep waters." And it was so. God named the dry ground Land and the waters he named Seas. God looked at what he had made and saw that it was good.

Then God said, "Let the land produce plants and crops and fruit trees of every kind." And it was so. There was evening and morning, and that was the third day.

And God said, "Let there be lights in the sky to divide the day from the night, marking the days, the seasons and the turning of the years, and let the lights shine down on the earth." And it was so. God made the sun to shine in the day and the moon to shine at night. Then God made the stars. And God saw that all that he had made was good. So evening and morning came again, and that was the fourth day.

God said, "Let the waters breed life and swarm with living creatures, and let birds wing their way through the sky." So God created the huge sea-creatures and every living being that glides through the waters and all species of fish, and he made every kind of bird that flies through the air. And God saw that all that he had made was good. He blessed the creatures and said, "Be fruitful and multiply, fill the seas, fill the air!" So evening and morning came again, and that was the fifth day.

And God said, "Let the earth produce every type of animal, all species of living creatures, cattle and reptiles and wild beasts of every kind." And it was so. And God saw that it was good.

Then God said, "I shall make human beings in my image, in my own likeness. Let them rule the animal kingdom and be responsible for the whole earth."

So God created human beings. He made them in his own image, creating both male and female.

God blessed the human race and said, "Fill the earth with your descendants and look after everything I have created."

And God saw all that he had made, and it was very good. So evening and morning came again, and that was the sixth day.

In this way, the heavens and the earth were completed in all their magnificence.

By the seventh day, God had finished all his work of creation, so he rested on that day. He blessed the seventh day, because it was the special day of his rest.

THE GARDEN OF EDEN

This is how God made man. He took the dust of the earth,
formed his body and then breathed into his nostrils the breath
of life. So man became a living being.

Then God planted a beautiful garden in the east, in the land
of Eden, and he put the man there to tend the garden. God
planted every kind of tree there, trees with rich blossom and
delicious fruit to eat, and bright, fragrant flowers and bushes –
a garden that was a delight to the eyes. And in the middle of
the garden he planted two trees, the tree of life and the tree of
the knowledge of good and evil.

God told the man, "You may eat of every tree in the garden,
but you must not eat of the tree of the knowledge of good and
evil. The day you do that, you will be doomed to die."

The man was all alone in the Garden of Eden, so God
brought all the animals to him. The man gave names to all
the different creatures that came to him. He named every
kind of animal, from the cattle and the wild beasts on the
land to the birds in the sky. But there was no special
companion for him.

"It is not good for man to be alone like this," God said, and
he laid the man down and put him into a deep sleep. And
while the man was sleeping soundly, God took one of his ribs
and healed up the wound, and from the rib he made a woman.

God woke the man from his sleep, and there before him was
the woman.

The man was filled with wonder and he cried out, "Here

at last is one of my own kind, bone from my bone and flesh from my flesh!"

And so in the perfect happiness of Eden, among the glorious trees and the fragrance of the flowers, the man and the woman walked together. They were naked, but they were not ashamed. They lived together in harmony with each other and their world.

CREATION IS SPOILED

GENESIS 3

Now the snake was the most cunning of all the animals that God had made. He saw the woman sitting by herself and came sliding through the grass towards her.

"Has God really said, 'You must not eat from any of the trees in the garden?'"

The woman looked at him with her wide eyes, curious that this creature had the power of speech, but each day in Eden was full of new discoveries.

"Well?" said the snake, curling around the roots of a tree and gazing at her steadily.

"We may eat of any tree in the garden," said the woman, "but God did say that we must not eat the fruit of that tree…"

She pointed at a tree with a deep, dark radiance, far in the depths of the garden.

"That tree?" asked the snake, pretending to be astonished.

"Oh yes," said the woman. "God said, 'If you eat the fruit of that tree – if you even touch it – you will die!'"

"No, no," said the snake, "you will not die. God knows

that when you eat fruit from that tree you will become like him."

The snake uncurled himself from the tree, sped through the grasses and climbed swiftly up the tree of the knowledge of good and evil.

The woman followed. The fruit hung down, rich and luscious, enticing her. She stretched out her hand. She hesitated. She looked around her.

"Go on," said the snake. "Try a little."

And the woman seized the fruit suddenly and bit deeply.

The snake disappeared into the undergrowth as her husband approached. The man was puzzled to see the woman by the tree – the forbidden tree of the knowledge of good and evil – but she handed him the fruit, and he saw how delicious it looked. He put his tongue to it and tasted.

Immediately, they both knew they were naked. Suddenly, everything in Eden seemed to be different, as if a dark shadow had fallen, and they tied together fig leaves to make themselves clothes.

Then they heard the voice of God as he was walking in the cool of the evening. They ran and hid themselves among the trees.

"Where are you?" said God.

The man peered out from the darkness, ashamed.

"I heard you in the garden," he said, "but I was afraid because I was naked, so I hid myself."

"Who told you that you were naked?" said God. "Have you eaten of the fruit of the tree?"

"The woman," stammered the man, "the woman, she gave some of the fruit to me and so I ate it."

"Why did you do that?" God asked the woman, who

walked out of the bushes slowly, not daring to lift her face from the ground.

"The snake," she said. "It was his fault. He tempted me, so I ate it."

Then God turned to the snake, who was lurking in the depths of the garden, and said, "Because you have done this, you will be cursed among animals."

He turned to the man and woman and told them that, through their disobedience, pain had come into the world. From now on, their lives would be marked by hardship and suffering.

The man and the woman stood there trembling, in bitter sorrow. And God took pity on them and made them clothes out of animal skins to keep them warm. Yet they were banished from the garden forever, and angels guarded the entrance with a sword of fire.

A FAMILY TRAGEDY

GENESIS 4

The man became known as Adam and his wife was named Eve.

Adam and Eve made their home in the land beyond Eden. Life was very hard for them but they found joy in their sorrow. Eve gave birth to two sons – the first she named Cain and the second she named Abel.

Abel grew up to be a shepherd, looking after his flocks. He spent his life in the hills, watching over his sheep in all weathers, keeping them safe in the harsh storms that thundered in the sky, or protecting the lambs in the spring from the wolves that came prowling.

Cain was a farmer who dug the earth and planted crops. He worked on the plains far below, digging and hacking the earth. He sweated and sighed at his work. Sometimes it was so tough he scarcely raised his eyes from the hoe. It seemed as if all he ever did was break up the earth and sow seeds, then dig and hack and sow more seeds.

Time passed and Cain and Abel decided to make a special offering to God. Cain chose some of his crops, a few vegetables and some fruit. His offering might not be the best of all he had grown that year, but it was a fair choice. After all, God had the whole world, so what was one little offering to him?

Abel thought differently. He believed that everything he had belonged to God, so he chose as his offering the finest sheep from the whole flock.

God was pleased with Abel's gift, and Cain became jealous. He felt anger burning inside him. He shouted at his younger brother and poured scorn on his offering. God saw what happened and said to Cain, "Why are you angry? If you do what is right, then you will win my approval too."

God knew that Cain resented giving even his small offering and that he hated his brother bitterly.

"Cain," whispered God, "sin is crouching at the door of your life like an animal, ready to attack you. But you must win the battle against the evil in your heart."

Cain refused to listen. He found Abel and said to him, "Why don't we go for a walk in the fields?" When they were alone together, Cain turned on his brother, Abel, in a fury and killed him.

Cain quickly dug a hole in the ground and buried Abel. He

covered the grave with stones and soil, but God called out to him, "Cain! Where is your brother, Abel?"

"How should I know?" Cain shrugged his shoulders. "Am I my brother's keeper?"

"What have you done?" asked God sorrowfully, and his voice was like the wind raging across the wild plains. "Your brother's blood is crying to me from the earth!"

Cain sank down to his knees. His terrible crime could not be hidden from God, who told him, "Now you are under a curse. You must leave the land which will never be fruitful for you again. From today, you will be a restless wanderer through the earth."

Cain trembled in fear at the thought of this punishment, but God took pity on him. "I will protect you wherever you go," he promised. So Cain left his home forever and journeyed far away.

A FLOOD AND A RAINBOW

GENESIS 6–9

In the centuries that followed the time of Cain and Abel, the human race multiplied. Many followed the example of Cain and turned to violence – so much so that when God looked down upon the earth, he was filled with pain and sorrow.

"I should never have made humankind," God said. "All they can think about is doing terrible evil." The whole world had become corrupt and full of wicked people. God was angry at the ruin of his creation and said, "I will remove the people from the face of the earth – I will destroy this wickedness forever."

But there was one man – one alone – who pleased God. His name was Noah, and he lived an honest life. He was different from everyone else. He walked with God each day on the journey of his life, and this is how God decided to save Noah and his family from the destruction of the world.

God spoke to Noah and said, "I am going to put an end to all the people on earth because of their violence and hatred. You must build an ark of cypress wood, a huge boat with many rooms and a roof. Then you must seal the whole vessel with tar."

Noah listened with great astonishment, for God was telling him to build a boat a long way from the sea.

God told Noah exactly how to build the ark, saying, "Put a great door in the side and build lower, middle and upper decks."

Noah nodded quietly. He would obey everything that God told him, to the last detail.

Then God said, "I am going to flood the whole earth and destroy every living creature. The waters will cover the world, and everything that breathes will perish. But I will make my promise to you, Noah, my covenant forever with you and your family. You will go into the ark and you will be safe. The floodwaters will not touch you."

Noah stood up, in fear and awe of the judgment that God was bringing on the earth. And God said, "You must take with you two of every living creature, every kind of bird and every kind of animal, males and females. Take them by pairs into the ark. And take food for all the living creatures and for yourselves. In this way, you must take my creation with you."

So Noah did everything that God commanded him. He and his sons – Shem, Ham and Japheth – began to build the ark in the desert lands near where he lived. And Noah continued to build, although many people mocked and jeered and said that he was mad. At last, the massive floating box was ready, the strangest vessel on earth. But still there was no rain.

The sun shone in a cloudless sky. People who had no respect for God or for Noah continued to laugh. Although Noah warned them, they took no notice, and when Noah began to gather hundreds of animals, they were certain that he had gone mad.

But the animals came to Noah and his family eagerly. They sensed thunder in the sky long before it sounded, and smelled the floodwaters in the air. They hurried in their pairs towards safety, and Noah welcomed them into the ark, where they were fed and watered and housed in their stables, pens and hutches.

At last, when Noah and all his family – his wife, their three sons and their wives – and all the animals were gathered in the ark, God slammed the huge wooden door shut. And it began to rain.

It rained for forty days and forty nights. The floodgates of heaven opened, and the springs of the deep burst into the desert, and streams and rivers swelled and burst their banks. Rain pelted down like a cascading waterfall over the whole earth. The storm was terrifying. The world was engulfed in an endless darkness, and the wild seas rose to fantastic heights and buried the tops of mountains, so every single being outside the ark perished in the great flood. Only Noah, his family and all the creatures in the ark survived.

For one hundred and fifty days after the rain had stopped, the ark floated on the floodwaters that covered the earth, and there was no dry land in sight. But God had not forgotten his faithful servant Noah, and he sent a great wind which swept the waters back. Slowly, the floods began to go down.

There was still no sight of land, but the darkness had rolled away. The ark floated slowly on until suddenly Noah and his family felt a shudder. They sprang to their feet as the boat made a loud scraping sound, wobbled and then settled. The ark had come to rest on the tip of Mount Ararat.

Noah opened the window in the ark and gazed across the huge expanse of water. It gleamed like silver under the greyness of the sky. He could see no sign of life, nor could he hear anything. So he let out a raven to fly across the waters, to see if the bird could find anywhere to settle, but the raven returned to the ark.

Then Noah took a dove and released the bird into the air to see if she would find a place to perch. The dove circled in the sky, then flew to the far horizon and back. After a long while she returned. Noah held out his hand and brought her into safety.

He waited another seven days. Then he released the dove again, and this time she returned the same evening, carrying an olive leaf in her beak.

Noah knew that the waters were ebbing away from the earth at last, so he let the dove go once more. She did not return, so he released her mate. Then he opened the door and everyone saw that the waters had flowed back into the rivers and the seas, and all around them was dry land.

God said to him, "Come out of the ark, you and your wife, and your sons and their wives! Bring out all the animals, every living creature, and set them free on the earth. Be fruitful, increase and fill the earth with all your offspring!"

So the animals ran, jumped, slithered and scuttled to freedom, and the birds flew and swooped and dived in the sky, singing and calling to each other, and Noah and all his family knelt down to worship God on Mount Ararat.

Then God said, "I will make a promise to you and all your descendants, and to every creature that was in the ark. This is my promise: never again will I cover the earth with water, never again will I devastate the world with a flood that overwhelms every living creature. As long as the world lasts, so will the times and seasons of the year. There will be sowing and harvesting, there will be cold and heat, summer will turn into winter, and night will follow day. You will know that my promise is sure, because I will put my rainbow in the clouds."

At that moment, the most beautiful rainbow in all its shining array appeared and hung over the dark velvet of the sky. Noah and his family gazed up in wonder, tiny figures beneath the glorious arch of light.

"My rainbow," said God, "will remind you of my promise to you and every living creature. I will see it and I will remember the everlasting bond that I have made between me and all life on the earth."

In the years to come, Noah gazed up at rainbows in the heavens and remembered God's promise. He served God all the days of his very long life.

People gradually filled the earth again but, despite all that had happened, once more a time came when the human race became proud and did not remember or respect the power of God.

THE TOWER OF BABEL

GENESIS 11

After the great flood, there was an age when everyone in the whole world spoke the same language, and all the people on the earth could understand each other.

Now, as some tribes of people were journeying towards the east, they discovered a broad plain named Shinar. There they decided to build a magnificent city.

"Come on," they shouted, "let's make a great name for ourselves and create the most famous city on earth!"

"We'll dig the clay and make bricks."

"We'll bake them in the hottest ovens and use tar as mortar." They were confident of their skill.

"Let's build the tallest tower in the world, reaching up to the heavens!"

"Our tower will soar through the clouds and become a gateway to the gods!"

So they all gathered together in one place and began building.

God decided to pay their city a visit.

"Look at them now," he said. "All these people building their tower. Before long, they'll think they can do anything. Nothing will ever seem impossible for these people."

So God came among them, saying, "I will confuse their speech. From now on, they will not speak one language but many."

There was chaos. Suddenly, the tower-builders could not understand a word they were saying to each other. They ran to and fro, shouting wildly and waving their hands. They were utterly bewildered, stumbling and afraid.

God scattered them far and wide. They were forced to abandon all their great plans. The building was left unfinished forever, and the place became known as the Tower of Confusion or Babel.

It became famous, not as the tallest tower in the world, but as the place where the people of the earth were scattered in fear and turmoil.

ABRAHAM AND SARAH

The time came for God to show his love and kindness to one man, and through him to bless the whole earth.

Abraham lived in the city of Haran with his brother, and his nephew, Lot, and his family. He had many reasons to be happy – a loving and beautiful wife, Sarah, a comfortable home and a great many possessions and servants. But there was one precious thing he did not have. Abraham and Sarah longed to have a child.

As a young woman, Sarah often cried herself to sleep when the longing in her heart and the sadness were too great to bear. She would see other families with their many sons and daughters playing happily together or helping in the fields with the sheep, and each day she saw her husband, Abraham, walking home alone in silence.

"There is no future for us," she would say. "What will happen when we are dead and gone? There is no child to carry on your name."

For Sarah, there was only the wind stirring the dust in the street. Her life seemed of no more value than a leaf floating in the air, broken from its tree, useless. Abraham tried to console her. He was very fond of his nephew, Lot, and he used to say, "He is like a son to us." But the sight of Lot, who already had children of his own, only filled Sarah with despair.

"A son..." she said. "Oh, if only..."

And now, too many years had passed. Sarah and Abraham were getting older. Hope faded like the sun vanishing into the twilight over the roofs of Haran. Each day was like a step towards the bitterest disappointment, the end of all her dreams.

GOD SPEAKS TO ABRAHAM

GENESIS 12

One night, Abraham was returning from looking after his flocks in the pasture land around Haran.

"I have everything," he told himself, "so why do I feel I have nothing?" He talked to himself, musing for a while as the sunlight flared on the horizon, then flickered and sank into the blueness of a cold evening.

Still he reflected on the good fortune of his life, his wealth and comfort, and the security of his home in Haran. He was seventy-five years old. There was no point now in mourning a child who would never be born.

Then, as he sat there listening to his own thoughts and trying to reason with himself, it seemed that another voice was speaking to him. At first, it was so soft he thought it was in his imagination. Perhaps he had fallen asleep for a moment and was dreaming. Perhaps it was the wind shaking the date palms which arched over the ancient wells of Haran.

"Abraham." The voice was clearer. This was not inside his mind; it was outside. It was deep, strong, all around him and yet far up above him.

"I am the Lord, your God," said the voice. Now Abraham stood up, for fear had seized him. Who *was* this? In Haran, people believed in many gods; everywhere there were altars and idols and little temples to the many gods of the East. But this was the "Lord, your God" speaking!

"Abraham, leave your country," urged the mysterious voice.

Abraham looked around him, but he could see nothing, no one, only the night and the distant fires in the city, and the stars in the freezing darkness above.

"Leave?"

"You must leave everything – your people, your father's household – and go."

Abraham repeated the command to himself, whispering, already sensing that he had to obey.

"Go to the land that I will show you." And now the voice of God was singing in his heart, "I will make you into a great nation and I will bless you."

Sarah gazed out of the doorway, trembling. Where was her husband? Had something terrible happened? If she lost him, there would be nothing for her but sorrow and death. Suddenly, she saw a figure far down the street. He was running. He was waving.

"Sarah! Sarah! We must go!"

"Go?" She had no idea what he was talking about.

"Leave. We have to leave Haran."

"Leave our home? Why? What's happened? Why?"

Abraham was already in the house. "We must call the servants. We must tell them to get everything ready."

"What is this madness? Leave our home, our land, our families?"

"The Lord has spoken."

Sarah looked at her husband and he looked at her, and in that gaze between them was a whole world of understanding. She had known and loved him for fifty years, and in his eyes she saw a blazing fire, and she felt the presence of the Lord of heaven and earth. Sarah knew for herself that God had spoken.

A FAMILY QUARREL

GENESIS 13

So Abraham left Haran, just as God had commanded him, and he took with him his nephew, Lot, and Lot's family.

They journeyed south through the desert towards the land of Canaan. When they arrived in Canaan, Abraham's herdsmen and Lot's herdsmen began to quarrel over the best pasture.

"Soon it will be like two tribes at war!" said Abraham. "This should never happen between close families, all this fierce arguing and shouting. We have the whole land before us."

Lot nodded. He and Abraham were relatives. It was wrong for their men to fight over the land.

"Why don't we settle in different places?" said Abraham.

It seemed a good idea to Lot. He had dreamed of great lands and increasing his wealth, and now he could freely choose the best. So Lot looked around him. Abraham was offering him the first choice, and in the distance he could see the wide plains of Jordan. The land beside the river was very fertile, so green and lush it could have been the Garden of Eden.

"I'll take the plains of Jordan," said Lot, with a sweep of his arm.

"Very well," said Abraham unselfishly, turning towards the

steep paths and wild hills in the distance, "then I will move further on into the land of Canaan." And so it was that Lot and Abraham went their different ways.

GOD'S PROMISE TO ABRAHAM

Genesis 13, 15

As soon as Lot and all his company had left, God spoke to Abraham again.

Slowly, surely, Abraham was surrounded by the presence of God, and inside himself he could hear the voice ringing out so clearly, "Look up and see! Look to the north, to the south, to the east, to the west. Everything that you can see I will give to you and to your children and to your children's children. Your descendants will be like the dust upon the earth. When people succeed in counting every speck of that dust, they will have counted your descendants too!"

Abraham looked at his feet and the dust on his sandals, and he could not even count those tiny spots.

"Go on then!" said God. "Walk through the whole land, up and down, back and forth. I am giving it all to you and your descendants."

So Abraham journeyed on and finally settled near the oak trees of Mamre. Sarah and Abraham lived there for several years, but Sarah secretly wondered about all that was happening. They had a new land, their flocks were increasing. Their menservants and maidservants were having more children. But still Sarah had no son.

One day, God came to Abraham in a vision. Abraham heard the words ringing in the air.

"Do not be afraid, Abraham." The voice was strong, commanding him to obey, urging him to keep trusting, even though he struggled so hard. Sometimes Abraham felt he was just hanging on to hope. Year after year, and no child!

"Do not be afraid," said the voice. "I am your shield, and I will give you a very great reward."

But Abraham replied, "O sovereign Lord, what can you give me since I am still childless?"

He bowed his head to the ground, and said, "I have no son… There is no son to inherit my lands, my possessions… My only successor is my servant Eliezer."

The presence of God surrounded him, enfolded him and soothed his pain. "Abraham! This man will not be your heir. No, your heir will come from your own body. You *will* have a son…"

Abraham felt God leading him from his tent. Far above, the night sky was brilliant with stars, stretching forever, innumerable in the heavens.

"Can you count all these?" God said. Abraham shook his head in sheer amazement. "If you could count them all, then you would know the number of your own descendants who will one day walk the earth."

Abraham believed everything that God had said and, because of this, God delighted in his trust. He looked upon Abraham as a truly good man.

THE SLAVE AND HER SON

GENESIS 16

The years passed and still Abraham and Sarah had no son.

Sarah was troubled. Where was God? What about his promise to give them a son?

One day, she saw her maidservant Hagar kneeling down and washing some clothes outside Abraham's tent. The sight of the beautiful young woman gave her an idea.

"The Lord has kept me from having children," she said to Abraham, "so take Hagar instead of me. Perhaps this is the way we can have a family."

Abraham was astonished, but Sarah was determined. "Hagar is my servant, and so I can do what I like with her. She can have a child in my place!"

In time, Abraham agreed and took Hagar into his bed, and she became pregnant.

At first, Sarah was delighted that her plan had worked, but it soon began to go wrong.

Hagar could not hide her joy and her triumph that she – not Sarah – was going to have Abraham's child.

Suddenly, Sarah could stand it no more. She stormed into Abraham's tent and said, "This is your fault! You've done this to me by taking that woman into your arms and giving her a baby! Now she scorns me with every look and every word!"

"Sarah," Abraham stood up, reaching out to her, "Hagar is your servant. You must do with her what you think best."

Then Sarah began to treat Hagar so badly that the young woman ran away into the desert.

The sun blazed down upon Hagar. After many hours of walking, she collapsed, exhausted. Then she heard a voice.

"Hagar, servant girl of Sarah, where are you going?"

"I am running away from my mistress," she sobbed.

Hagar looked up. It was an angel sent by God. The angel spoke to her with such love that she no longer felt afraid. She brushed away her tears.

"You must go back to your mistress," he said. "And, although it is hard, you must obey her. Soon you will give birth to a son, and you shall name him Ishmael – which means 'God hears' – because the Lord has heard your misery. Ishmael will have many descendants who will become a great people."

So Hagar went back to Abraham and Sarah, and she gave birth to a son. Abraham named him Ishmael, just as the angel had said, and the old man held the baby in his arms with pride.

But Ishmael was not the child that God had promised to Abraham.

MYSTERIOUS VISITORS

GENESIS 18

After many more years had passed, it was nearly time for God to make his promise come true. When Abraham was ninety-nine years old, God appeared to him near the great oak trees of Mamre. It was noon and Abraham was sitting in the entrance to his tent, in the shadows, quietly waiting for the heat of the day to pass.

Abraham's eyes were closing in the stifling heat, but he thought he saw a figure. He blinked in the harsh light. Was he dreaming? He saw three figures standing nearby. He opened his eyes wider. In the glare of the midday sun, Abraham could not see their faces, but something told him that these visitors were no ordinary men. He got up hastily, walked up to them and bowed very low.

"My Lords," he said, "if you find me worthy of your company, then please do not travel any further. Stay here and let a little water be brought to wash your feet. Take some rest now in the shade."

As he looked at the figure in the middle of the three, Abraham sensed that he was in the presence of God himself. He bowed low again.

"Let me fetch you something to eat so you can be refreshed for your journey," he said.

"It is well," they replied. "Do as you say."

And the three figures sat down near the oaks of Mamre.

Abraham ran into Sarah's tent. "Quick!" he said. "Knead three measures of our finest flour. Bake some loaves for our guests!" Then Abraham ran to his herd of cows, chose the best calf and ordered his servant to prepare it for a meal.

While the three visitors ate, Abraham stood respectfully apart from them. He did not dare sit down in their company.

"Where is your wife, Sarah?" they asked him.

"She is in her tent," he replied.

Then God said to him, "This time next year I will come back to you, and your wife, Sarah, will have a son."

Now Sarah was standing at the entrance to her tent, and she heard what he said. She and Abraham were very old by then, and she laughed to herself when she heard this. Here I am, an

41

old wrinkled woman, she thought, so am I now going to have this great pleasure?

God heard the secret laughter in Sarah's heart. He turned to Abraham and said, "Why did Sarah laugh and say, 'How am I going to have a baby, now that I am so old?'"

Abraham had heard nothing. He gazed at his mysterious visitors in astonishment.

As they got up to go, God spoke quietly and firmly, saying, "Is anything too hard for the Lord? I will return to you at the same time next year, and Sarah will have given birth to a son."

Sarah was suddenly afraid as she stood in the shadows of her tent. She came forward hurriedly. "I did not laugh," she lied.

"Yes," said God, "you did laugh."

THE TWO SONS

GENESIS 21

God was good to Sarah and did everything that he had promised.

She became pregnant and the next year gave birth to Abraham's son. Abraham named his son Isaac – which means "he laughs" – and Sarah sang out for joy: "God has brought Isaac into my life, so I have good reason to laugh too. Everyone who hears about my baby will laugh with me!"

Abraham and Sarah loved their baby and delighted in everything he did. So Abraham held a great feast to celebrate. But when Sarah saw that Ishmael, Hagar's son, was playing with Isaac, she became angry.

"Get rid of that slave woman and her son," she said. "Don't let him come near Isaac!"

Furiously, she ordered Hagar and Ishmael out of her sight.

Abraham was very troubled because he loved Ishmael, who was now tall and strong. But God spoke to Abraham and told him to let Hagar and her son go. God promised to keep them both safe. So early the next morning, when the guests at the feast were still sleeping soundly and Isaac lay fast asleep in Sarah's arms, Abraham led Hagar and Ishmael to the edge of the desert. He gave them food and water.

Perplexed, the boy looked at Abraham, who held him close. Then Abraham turned away, slowly, painfully, and did not look back.

Hagar wandered for several days in the desert. This time, she knew she was leaving forever. The water Abraham had given her was all gone, and now she feared her son would die, for Ishmael was very weak and desperately thirsty. Hagar and her son began to cry.

At that moment, the angel of God called down from heaven, "Don't be afraid, Hagar! The Lord has heard your son crying. Lift him up and take him by the hand. For I am going to make him into a great nation!"

Hagar stood up slowly, rubbing her eyes, and then she saw, right in front of her, a deep well.

Immediately, she filled a skin with water and rushed over to Ishmael. She poured the clear, cold stream into his mouth and bathed his face. The boy smiled at her. She helped him up, and they walked on until they reached a place where they could stay in safety.

So Ishmael grew up in the desert lands. God was with him. He became an archer, a powerful man who survived in the wilderness and feared no one. Later, his mother found him a wife from Egypt, her own country. Ishmael had many children and, as God had promised, he became the father of a great nation.

Meanwhile, Isaac grew up with Abraham and Sarah, but before God's promise about Isaac and the future could come true, Abraham faced the greatest challenge of all.

GOD TESTS ABRAHAM

GENESIS 22

It was some years later that God tested Abraham.

"Abraham!" said a voice.

Abraham had heard the voice of God many times, soft as rain, powerful as the storm winds raging across the plain, still and clear beneath the night sky. But this time the voice was different.

The voice came from within, deep within. It came from the secret place in Abraham's heart, where all his hopes and fears lay, where he treasured his love for his son Isaac.

"Abraham!" The voice was insistent. It had to be obeyed.

"Here I am," said Abraham. He had obeyed at the beginning, in Haran. He had left everything and journeyed into an unknown land, and he had believed the incredible promise that he would be the father of a great nation.

"Take your only son, Isaac," said God, "and go to the land of Moriah. Sacrifice him there to me."

Sacrifice his son? Take his beloved son and bind him to an altar and kill him? That was what the heathens did. They offered up their little children to idols made of stone. But they were ignorant of God and his love.

Terror raged through Abraham's heart, wild confusion like a hurricane uprooting all he had ever known. At that moment, the whole world seemed to plunge into darkness.

But the voice was clear, and the command came from God himself.

So Abraham obeyed.

Very early in the morning, he saddled his donkey and loaded bundles of firewood onto it. He took two servants and his son, Isaac, and set out for the land of Moriah. Abraham told his companions he was going to worship God, but no one knew what was truly in his heart.

On the third day, they came within sight of the mountains of Moriah.

"This is the place," said Abraham. He turned to his servants. "Stay here with the donkey. Isaac and I will go on alone. We will worship God together and then…" He paused. He looked at the servants and then at his son, who was smiling up at him. "Then we will come back to you," he added.

He did not know how this would be possible. He did not know anything in the darkness of his own mind, but he trusted God. He gave the firewood to Isaac to carry, and he took a knife and a burning torch in his hand.

As the two of them set off, Isaac turned to his father. "Father?" he said.

"Yes, my son," said Abraham.

"We have the fire and the wood, but where is the lamb for the burnt offering?"

"God himself will provide the lamb for the burnt offering,

my son," said Abraham, and then he gazed ahead to the mountain in silence. They walked on.

They reached the top, and there they built an altar of stones and laid the firewood on it. Neither of them spoke. Then Abraham sat down. For a long time, he held the knife in his hand. He was crying out to God in his heart, but he did not say anything. Tears welled up in his eyes as he turned to his son.

"Isaac, my son…"

The way he said "son" so softly, with his voice breaking and the look of dread in his eyes, made Isaac realize why they had come and what God had commanded.

So Abraham tied Isaac to the altar, and the boy lay there, perfectly still.

Abraham looked around him. He looked up at the cloudless sky. Far below, the servants were tending the donkey, tiny figures in the blue haze. Father and son, they were alone on the mountain, under the empty heavens.

Abraham did not dare look at Isaac but took the knife and held it up high, preparing to strike.

Suddenly, a voice called out to him, "Abraham, Abraham!"

He turned. He knew that voice, the voice of the angel of the Lord, echoing all around. "Abraham!"

"Here I am," said Abraham.

The voice was clear and loud and commanded him, "Do not harm the boy, because now I know that you fear God."

Abraham sank to his knees. The knife clattered onto the stones beside the altar.

"You have not withheld your son from me, your only son!" the voice rang out.

Then Abraham looked up and he saw a ram, caught by its horns in a bush. So he took the ram and offered it up as a

sacrifice instead of his son. And Abraham named that place
The Lord Will Provide.

Then the angel of God spoke to Abraham again: "This is
what the Lord says to you: 'Because you have not refused to
give me your only son, your beloved son, I will shower
blessings on you. Your descendants will be like the stars in the
heavens and the grains of sand beside the sea, and through
them all the nations of the earth will be blessed, because you
have obeyed me.'"

And so Abraham and Isaac returned home.

IN SEARCH OF A WIFE

GENESIS 24

God showered blessings and wealth and happiness on
Abraham as he had promised, and Abraham watched his son,
Isaac, grow up into a strong and thoughtful young man.

After Sarah died, Abraham knew that soon his time would
come too. It was important for Isaac to get married and have a
family, so Abraham sent for his chief servant and told him to
find a wife for Isaac from his own people, not from the people
who lived in Canaan.

The servant took ten of his master's camels and, carrying
many precious gifts, set out for Haran, Abraham's former
home. He and the other servants with him arrived in the cool
of the evening when the women were coming out to draw
water from the well.

As they prepared the camels for rest, Abraham's servant

prayed quietly to God. "Lord God," he said, "please give me success today and show your faithful love to my master Abraham. When I say to a girl, 'Lower your jar so I can have a drink,' and she replies, 'Drink, and I will fetch water for your camels too,' let her be the one you have chosen."

Even as he was praying, a beautiful girl named Rebekah came towards him, carrying a jar on her shoulder. The servant ran to her and said, "Please give me a little water to drink."

"Drink, my Lord," she said, and she immediately lowered the jar from her shoulder. When he had finished drinking, she said, "Now let me draw water for your camels," and she ran down quickly to the well.

The servant watched her closely. He gazed at her every movement in silence, hardly daring to speak. When she had finished, he took out a gold ring and two gold bracelets and put them on her. She stared at him in wonder.

"Whose daughter are you?" he asked. "Please tell me if there is room for us to stay in your father's house tonight."

"Sir," she said gently and with great courtesy, "I am the daughter of Bethuel, who is the son of Milcah and Nahor."

"Nahor!" The servant breathed the name of Abraham's brother with astonishment. Tears came to his eyes. God had led him straight to his master's own family.

"Blessed be the Lord, the God of my master!" he cried out, overwhelmed with joy. "I praise God's name because he is still showing great kindness and love to my master, Abraham."

Rebekah had heard about her father's uncle Abraham, the one who had journeyed into the unknown, the one who had left everything to follow the command of God, long before she was born. It was a tale told by the fireside, by menfolk who sang songs beneath the stars. Abraham was a name that touched her heart.

THE QUEST IS ACCOMPLISHED

GENESIS 24

Rebekah hurried back to her family and told them everything. When her brother, Laban, saw the magnificent ring and the bracelets on his sister's arms and heard all that she said, he ran all the way to the well to fetch Abraham's servant.

When they arrived, food was set before them, but the servant of Abraham held up his hand.

"I will not eat," he said, "until I have told you what I have to say."

"Then speak!" said Laban.

"I am Abraham's servant," said the man, gazing at the throng of people, at Bethuel and Laban and all the men of the household. He looked across the room to where Rebekah stood silently in the shadows. "God has blessed my master, and he has become very wealthy. The Lord God has given him sheep and cattle, silver and gold, menservants and maidservants, camels and donkeys. And Sarah, my master's wife, had a son in her old age. His name is Isaac…"

The old man hesitated. How could he speak of one who was the greatest gift of all to Abraham, a blessing worth more than any wealth or success, too precious for words?

"Isaac," he said, "will inherit everything from his father. It is because of him that I have come."

There was silence as flames from the fire leaped and danced, their reflection burning in the eyes of Rebekah, who saw that the man's gaze was upon her whenever he mentioned the name of Isaac.

Abraham's servant told Bethuel and Laban everything that had happened; how he had prayed to the Lord for a sign, and how Rebekah had given him a drink and watered his camels. As he told his story, everyone looked at him with the greatest respect and in absolute silence.

When he had finished, Laban and Bethuel nodded at each other. They turned to him and said, "This is from the Lord. It is not for us to say yes or no. It is from the Lord himself, and he has chosen. Here is Rebekah…"

She stepped forward. Her eyes were steady, although her heart was beating fast. Her beauty was more radiant than ever.

"Take Rebekah and go," said Bethuel. "Let her become the wife of Isaac, for the Lord has spoken."

Then Abraham's servant gave thanks to the God of Abraham. He got up and went, along with the other servants, to the camel train and collected the gifts – gold and silver rings and richly decorated clothes for Rebekah, and expensive gifts for her family.

Then the feasting began.

A WIFE FOR ISAAC

GENESIS 24

The feast lasted long into the night. In the morning, Rebekah's brother, Laban, and her mother said, "We are happy for Rebekah to return with you to be Isaac's wife, but let her stay with us for ten more days, then you may take her."

"Please," said the old servant, "do not hold me back. The

Lord has given me success, and it is time for me to return to my master Abraham."

"We'll call the girl," they said. "We'll find out what she has to say."

Rebekah came to them, and they asked her, "Will you go with this man?"

"I will go," she replied.

So they let her go with their blessing.

Now Isaac was living in the Negev desert. One evening, he was walking in the fields, meditating alone and thinking of many things as the sun disappeared below the horizon. He looked up, and suddenly he saw the train of camels riding towards him.

Rebekah saw Isaac at that moment. She got down from her camel and asked the servant, "Who is that man walking through the fields towards us?"

"He is the son of my master," said the servant, "Isaac."

The name stirred her heart, the name of the husband she had never seen. She trembled for one moment, but then she called her maidservants to gather around her. She took her veil and covered her face.

Isaac greeted Abraham's servant, and the servant told him everything that had happened. So Isaac brought Rebekah into his tent and he took her to be his wife. And he loved her.

Soon after this, Abraham died peacefully, content in the knowledge that his beloved son Isaac had found a loving wife.

TWIN BROTHERS

GENESIS 25

For many years, Rebekah was unable to have children, but Isaac prayed to God for her.

God answered his prayer, and Rebekah became pregnant with twins. The two boys inside her struggled so much, she felt she was dying and cried out to God. He spoke to her and said, "There are two nations in your womb! Two rival tribes will descend from your sons. One people will be stronger than the other, and the elder child will serve the younger!"

At last, the babies were safely born. The first to arrive was Esau. Jacob followed, grabbing his brother's heel. The two rivals had entered the world. They were completely different characters – Esau was a man of action, a strong and skilled hunter who loved the open fields and Jacob was much quieter and thoughtful. He liked to stay at home, happy to be with Rebekah and the servants.

Their father, Isaac, loved Esau best. He was proud of his son's hunting, and he had a taste for wild game, and found his younger son hard to understand. It was Rebekah who loved Jacob.

One day, Jacob was cooking some thick soup when Esau came running in from the fields. He had been away for days and he was desperately hungry.

"Quick," he shouted, "give me some of that soup!"

"Wait…" said Jacob, holding up the ladle which was dripping with broth. "What will you give me?"

Esau was impatient with his brother's joking. "Just give me something to eat!"

"How about your birthright?" said Jacob. "Will you give me that for some soup?"

As the elder child, Esau would one day receive his father's special blessing and inherit the greatest part of his wealth. Jacob was playing a dangerous game, but Esau was so famished, he hardly knew or cared what he was doing.

"Look," he said, "can't you see I'm dying of hunger? What use is my birthright to me?"

So Jacob stepped forward, blocking the cauldron of soup, and said craftily, "Give me your word. Swear to me that you will give me your birthright."

Esau hastily swore the oath, pushed his brother aside and devoured the soup. He finished it all, ate some bread and drank his fill. Then he got up, satisfied, and walked away.

That was how little Esau cared about his birthright.

ISAAC IS TRICKED

GENESIS 27

When Isaac was an old man, he was weak and had begun to go blind. So he called his elder son to him.

"Esau, my son, listen to me! Any day now, I could die. So go out hunting one more time. Take your bow and arrow and bring back some game for me to eat, the kind of tasty food I love. Then I will give you my blessing before I die."

Isaac's wife, Rebekah, overheard all this. She waited till Esau had gone, and then she called her beloved son, Jacob, to her. "Do everything I tell you," she said, "and you will get the blessing of the firstborn child instead of Esau!"

Jacob looked at her and he could see a smile playing on her lips. He could see she was determined that he would come first and no one would stand in her way.

"Esau's gone hunting to fetch some food for your father," she said. "Now, you fetch two of the best goats from our flock so I can make a tasty stew. I know just how he likes it. And then you can take his food to him!"

"What if he recognizes me?"

"He won't!"

"He only has to touch me! My skin is smooth, but Esau is so hairy. My father will know, the moment he touches me!"

Rebekah took him firmly by the shoulders. "Quickly, before Esau returns!"

So Jacob ran and fetched the goats. Rebekah prepared the meal with the most delicious spices. She took Esau's best clothes and put them on Jacob. Then she took a goat skin and covered his neck and his arms.

At last, Jacob was ready. He took the food to his father, Isaac.

"Here you are, Father," he said, trying his best to sound like Esau.

"Who is it?" said Isaac.

"I am Esau, your firstborn child. Here's your special food."

Isaac was confused. Something was wrong. "How did you get here so quickly?" he asked.

"Oh," said Jacob, "the Lord gave me wonderful success today."

"Come near to me," said Isaac. "Let me touch you."

Jacob began to sweat. He stepped forward slowly and held out his arm, covered in goat skin. Isaac slowly ran his old, bent fingers along the hairy covering.

"Hmm," he said. "The voice... is the voice of Jacob, but the arms are the arms of Esau."

There was a long silence. Isaac was still troubled, and he touched his son again.

"Are you really my son Esau?" he asked.

"I am," said Jacob with confidence.

"Then bring me the food you have prepared, and I will eat it, and then I will bless you."

So Jacob served his father.

"Come here," said Isaac. "Kiss your father." Jacob went up to him and kissed him. And when Isaac smelled Esau's clothes on him, he was finally convinced. He pronounced his blessing, "May God give you dew from heaven and the riches of the earth. Let people serve you, be lord over others and master of your brother!"

Jacob smiled at his triumph. But he quickly left his father's side to hide from Esau, who was already walking towards the tent, carrying the game he had hunted and prepared with his own hands.

"Father!" said Esau. "Here I am."

"What?" said Isaac, lifting himself up from his bed, seeing nothing but hearing the voice of his firstborn son, the voice he knew so well.

"Father," said Esau, "sit up and eat the food which I've brought. I've cooked it specially for you, just as you like it. Then give me your blessing."

"Who are you?" asked Isaac.

Esau smiled at his father's curious question. Perhaps he had been sleeping and was confused.

"It's Esau," he said, "your firstborn child!"

At this, Isaac trembled. He began to shake violently. "No, no..." he said.

"Father?"

"Who was it that came with the food and served it to me just now? Who came and knelt down and received my blessing?"

Immediately, Esau guessed and started to cry. He knelt beside his father.

"Father, Father," he pleaded, "bless me, bless me too!"

Isaac waved his hands, and shook his head, in terrible sorrow. "I have made him lord over you," said Isaac. "I have blessed him with all good things on earth. What can I do for you?"

"Have you only got one blessing? Bless me too!" Esau cried.

So Isaac blessed him and promised that one day Esau would be free of his brother Jacob's power.

ESAU'S ANGER

GENESIS 27, 28

From the day that Jacob tricked him and stole the blessing that should have been his, Esau held a grudge against his brother. He could not hide his terrible anger.

"As soon as my father is dead," he said, "I will kill Jacob."

Their mother, Rebekah, heard what he said and sent for Jacob secretly. "Your brother is comforting himself with the thought of murdering you," she whispered. "You must run away at once."

Fear gripped Jacob. "Where can I go? There is nowhere on earth I can escape from Esau's hatred!"

"Go to my brother, Laban, in Haran," said Rebekah. "It is

many days' journey and you can hide yourself there. Esau's rage will cool in time."

Jacob looked at his mother doubtfully, but she insisted. "One day, Esau will forget you ever did him this wrong. Then I'll send for you, I promise, and you can come back!"

Jacob stood there, gazing at Rebekah and wondering if he would ever see her again. She pushed him away softly. "Go," she said. "Go! Do you think I want to lose both my sons in one day?"

So Jacob turned away sadly and began to run. He ran as hard as he could. The dust streamed from his sandals as he fled into the desert.

Rebekah could not bear to look at the tiny, lonely figure, disappearing into the haze along the horizon. Jacob, the child she adored, had gone.

JACOB'S DREAM

GENESIS 28

Jacob ran until he was too exhausted to go any further. The sun set and the light faded in the sky. Night closed around him, and he lay down, taking a bare rock as his pillow.

The cold stone pressed against his face, but he was too weary to care. Now he was far from his brother Esau's anger; he was safe. But he was also far from home, from his dear mother and father. Jacob felt his life had come to an end. All alone under the open sky, he fell asleep there. As he slept, he had a dream.

He dreamed that the shapeless stone under his head was a huge step, the first step in a stairway that reached from earth to heaven. And up and down this endless stairway, angels were walking. Jacob gazed right up to the top, past the crowds of angels, to the very height of heaven. There he saw a brilliant light all around him and heard a voice: "I am the Lord, the God of Abraham and of Isaac, your father. The ground where you lie and the land all around it I will give to you and all your descendants. All the peoples on the earth will be blessed through you! Know this for certain, Jacob: I am with you. I will keep you safe wherever you go and bring you back to this land. I will never desert you, but I will bring to pass everything that I have promised to you."

When Jacob woke up, he looked around him in wonder. "The Lord was in this place," he thought, "but I never knew it."

He felt glad because he was not alone after all. But he also felt afraid. "What an awesome place this is!" he whispered, hardly daring to break the deep silence. "This is the house of God, and here is the gate of heaven!"

DOUBLE-CROSSED!

GENESIS 29

Jacob had tricked his brother and run away from home, fearing for his life. But God had spoken to him and promised to be with him, even in his darkest moments.

Now Jacob was heading for Haran, as his mother had advised. There he could stay with his relatives, but he did not know how to find them. He sat down beside a well and began talking to some local shepherds. They told him they were from Haran. They knew his uncle Laban too.

Just at that moment, a young woman, a shepherdess, came down to the well, leading her flock. The shepherds told Jacob that she was Laban's daughter Rachel.

Jacob ran down to haul the big stone away from the mouth of the well and began to draw water for his uncle's sheep. Rachel looked at him in astonishment – who was this generous man?

Jacob gazed at her. He could not speak for a moment because he was so overcome. He began to cry.

"Your father, Laban," he told her, "is my uncle."

Rachel looked at the stranger, stained with dust, exhausted, his clothes torn, tears rolling down his cheeks.

"You are my cousin?" she asked.

"Yes," he nodded. "Tell your father that the son of Rebekah has come to see him."

Rachel ran home to her father, Laban. He came rushing out to meet Jacob and kissed the young man. It was years since Laban had heard news of his beloved sister.

Jacob told Laban everything that had happened, including how he had cheated his brother, and Laban looked at him shrewdly. "So," he said, almost as if he were impressed by Jacob's deception of his brother, "you really are my flesh and blood!"

And he hugged him again and called for a feast for Jacob.

Jacob worked for his uncle for one month, but then Laban came to him. "You're working without pay," he said. "That can't be right for a nephew of mine! What do you want from me?"

Now Laban had two daughters – Leah, the elder, and Rachel. Leah had lovely eyes, but Rachel was truly beautiful and Jacob had fallen in love with her. "I'll work seven years for you," said Jacob, "in exchange for your younger daughter, Rachel."

Laban mused for a moment. "Agreed," he said. "Stay with me!"

Jacob was overjoyed. He worked hard for seven long years, but they seemed like only a few days to him because he loved Rachel so much.

The time came for the wedding. Laban held a marriage feast, and afterwards Jacob took his bride, still in her veil, into the darkness of his home. They made love that night, but in the morning, when the sun streamed through the window, Jacob looked at the woman lying beside him. It was Leah!

His uncle had tricked him. Just as Jacob had once pretended to be his older brother, Esau, so Leah had pretended to be her younger sister, with the help of her father, Laban.

Jacob was devastated. He went to Laban. "What have you done to me?" he shouted. "I worked all those seven years for you, and Rachel was my payment, and now you have deceived me."

"Nephew," said Laban calmly, "you have to understand our ways here. It really isn't possible for the younger daughter to get married before her older sister!"

Jacob stared at him. He could not believe that he had been so cleverly outwitted.

"I tell you what…" said Laban. "In a week's time you can marry Rachel as well if you promise to work for me for another seven years."

Jacob, who was deeply in love with Rachel, had no choice

but to accept. He took Rachel to be his second wife and then worked for Laban for another seven years.

A JOURNEY INTO FEAR

Jacob had arrived in Haran as a young man, a fugitive, on the run. He left with two wives, eleven sons and one daughter, and great wealth. Jacob had decided to return to his own family in the land of Canaan. Now he would rather face his brother Esau's anger than live in a strange land and quarrel with his uncle Laban. He knew Laban would try to stop him, so he left secretly while Laban was away.

When Laban realized what had happened, he was furious and pursued Jacob until he caught up with him in the land of Gilead. There the two rivals shouted and argued and paced around, throwing their hands in the air, threatening, blaming, accusing each other, until at last they sat down by the dying embers of the fire and made their peace.

Laban kissed his two daughters, Leah and Rachel, farewell. He kissed all his grandchildren and hugged the youngest, Joseph, who was Rachel's only child, and watched them leave for Canaan.

Now Jacob set out on the most frightening journey of his life. Night after night, year after year, he had dreamed of his brother's vengeance. He had imagined Esau swooping down from the mountains with screaming warriors; he had feared the terrible bloodshed and the furious battle. He knew he deserved his brother's hatred, and he had no excuse. After all, he had done Esau a great wrong. It was time to go home, and either he would make peace with Esau or he would die.

Jacob sent his servants ahead to Esau with this message: "Your servant Jacob has been living with Laban all these years and has become very rich. I am telling you this in the hope that I can win your approval."

The servants came back with the news that Esau was already on his way with four hundred men.

"I must be a fool," Jacob told himself. "Why did I think I could make peace with Esau? We're enemies, and we'll be fighting forever! Now my brother is hurrying towards me with an army of his followers!"

Then he fell down on his knees and prayed to God,

"O Lord God, I do not deserve your love at all, but you have blessed me. Please save me from Esau's murderous hatred! I am afraid that he will attack my family and kill my wives and children. Please save me!"

Jacob stood up slowly. He decided to send many gifts ahead to Esau, three different groups of servants, each leading camels and sheep and goats and oxen. Esau would come across each party in turn, and perhaps Jacob's generosity would change everything.

All his life, Jacob had been struggling and plotting his way through every difficulty. Even now, he wanted to make sure that everything worked out for him. Jacob found it hard to trust God completely.

THE WRESTLING MATCH

Genesis 32, 33

Night fell and Jacob was alone with his thoughts. He was
terrified. What would his brother, Esau, do to him? He shivered
in the darkness, but then something extraordinary and
mysterious happened. Something that changed Jacob forever.

In the darkness, a man came up to him. Jacob could not see
who it was. Suddenly, the man seized Jacob and began to fight
with him. Jacob defended himself. He twisted and fought and
struggled with all his might.

The two men fell to the ground, writhing and wrestling.
They battled for hours, until the sun began to peer over the
horizon and a ray of light shone on the stranger's face. Then
Jacob was filled with the deepest fear, because there was
something about this enemy – a brightness, something
different, a mysterious, wonderful power.

At that moment, the stranger struck Jacob on the hip and
put it out of joint. Jacob cried out and staggered back, but he
would not let go of the man and he would not admit defeat.
He held on to him, he fought, he carried on struggling, locked
in combat.

"Let me go now," said the stranger. "The day is breaking."

"No!" said Jacob. "Never! Not until you bless me!" He
sensed that his opponent was no ordinary human being.

"Tell me your name," said the man.

"Jacob," he replied.

"No," said the man softly, "you will not be Jacob any longer.
From now on you will be named Israel, because you have

struggled with God and with men, and you have won."

Jacob was wounded and limping, but still he would not let the man go. "Now you must tell me your name!" he replied.

"Why do you ask my name?" said the man, and the way he spoke made Jacob tremble with fear. Then the man blessed Jacob and turned from him, and in one moment, he was gone.

The light of dawn shone all around Jacob as he stood there unsteadily, feeling the pain in his hip. He was gazing into the light, but he could see no one at all. Only brightness.

"I have seen God face to face," he said, "and yet…" he looked around in astonishment, "I am still alive."

He named that place Peniel, which means "the face of God" in Hebrew.

As he looked up, he saw his brother, Esau, coming towards him with his four hundred followers. He went to warn his family and all his men, then walked forward slowly alone to meet Esau. He bowed down to the ground seven times, humbly, but Esau ran to meet him, seized his brother in his arms and wept for joy.

"My brother!" he cried. "My brother, Jacob!"

Jacob was overwhelmed. He, too, began to weep.

"Who are all these people?" asked Esau.

"They are my wives and my children and my servants," said Jacob. "The Lord has been very good to me."

Then Esau held him again and looked at him long and hard. He hugged him, and Jacob could hardly believe the great love that his brother had towards him.

"What were all those processions of goats and cattle I met on my way?" asked Esau.

"They are presents to you, my Lord," said Jacob, "because I wanted you to look kindly on me."

"Brother," said Esau gently, "I have enough. Keep what is yours."

But Jacob begged him to keep the gifts, and at last Esau agreed. So the two brothers were reconciled on that day – the day when Jacob met God face to face.

THE JEALOUS BROTHERS

GENESIS 37

On the way back to his homeland, Jacob's beloved wife, Rachel, died while giving birth to their younger son, Benjamin. Jacob was heartbroken, and the two sons he had by Rachel became very special to him. From then on, Joseph and little Benjamin were always at his side.

When Joseph was seventeen, Jacob had a special coat made for him. It had long sleeves and was richly decorated. Joseph's elder brothers were jealous. They hated Joseph because of his coat.

"Who does he think he is?" they asked. "A royal prince?"

One day, Joseph came to his elder brothers, breathless with excitement. "Listen to this dream I've had!" he said.

When they heard the dream, they hated him even more.

"We were binding these sheaves of corn in the field," said Joseph, "when suddenly my sheaf rose up high above all the others. Then your sheaves gathered around mine and bowed down to it, and then –"

"So you want to be king over us, do you?" The brothers

moved towards him angrily. "*You* want to lord it over *us*? *You!*"

They were beside themselves with fury, but Joseph took no notice. He was not boasting; he was simply telling them about a dream.

Some while later, Joseph had another dream. He found it impossible to keep silent and told his whole family this time, "I've had an amazing dream!"

The brothers sneered at him. "Dreamer! What story has he made up this time?"

But their father, Jacob, held out his hand. "Go on, my son. Tell us about this dream."

"I was standing in the fields," said Joseph simply, "when the sun, the moon and eleven stars in the sky…" He hesitated for a moment. He realized that the dream sounded strange.

"Yes," said Jacob curiously.

"The sun, the moon and eleven stars in the sky all began to bow down to me."

The meaning of the dream was clear to everyone.

Jacob was shocked. "Well, this is a fine dream to have!" He began to scold Joseph. "So your whole family's going to bow down to you, is that it?" Jacob shook his head.

The brothers did not dare show their hatred of Joseph in front of Jacob, but their rage grew darker. They waited until they could get their revenge on Joseph.

Meanwhile, Jacob remembered Joseph's dream and kept his thoughts to himself.

REVENGE!

GENESIS 37

Jacob had many flocks of sheep and many sons to look after
them. One day, Joseph's brothers went to graze their father's
flocks at Shechem, and Jacob called Joseph to him.

"My son," he said, "find out how your brothers are doing
and see if they have found good pasture for the sheep."

So Joseph went to Shechem. He saw his brothers camped in
the fields. He waved and ran towards them. His brothers
recognized him from a long way off. That long, splendid coat
was all too familiar. They hated the sign of their father's love for
Joseph, and, as the brightly woven cloth gleamed in the
sunlight, it was as if the coat set fire to their hatred. Even
before he arrived, they were burning with jealousy. They began
to plot his death.

"Here comes the dreamer!" they said to each other.

"Come on," said one, "let's kill him and throw him down
one of these dried-up wells!"

"Yes," said another, "we can say that he was eaten by wild
beasts. Then we'll see what comes of his dreams."

But Reuben, the eldest brother, was afraid.

"Wait!" he said. "Don't take his life. There must be no
bloodshed!"

"No, no, kill the dreamer, the liar!" shouted one of them, his
hand clutching a dagger.

"No!" shouted Reuben. The angry mob of brothers glared at
him. He was risking trouble.

"All right," said Reuben. "You can put him down this

dried-up well, but don't lay a finger on him!"

Reuben was hoping to come back quietly and rescue Joseph, so he walked away without a backward glance. He went off to tend the sheep.

As soon as Reuben had left, the brothers seized Joseph, stripped him of his robe and threw him down the dry well. Joseph shouted and begged them to haul him out. They could hear his shouts, rising from the darkness of the old well, echoing around and around, but they just sat down to eat their meal.

While they were eating, some merchants from Gilead came by. They were heading for Egypt, and their camels were laden with spices and perfumes.

"Why kill Joseph?" said Judah. "We can get rid of him without shedding any blood. Let's sell him as a slave!"

They all agreed. So they pulled Joseph out of the well and sold him to the traders for twenty silver shekels.

Later Reuben returned and shouted down the well, but there was no answer. He let down a rope, but no hand grasped it.

"Joseph, Joseph!" he shouted. Suddenly he realized that the boy was gone. He rushed to find his brothers. "What have you done? What are we going to say to our father?"

The brothers decided to take Joseph's coat, dip it in animal blood and show it to Jacob. When they handed the torn and bloodied cloth to the old man, he was horrified.

"Some wild animal has captured him and torn him to pieces!" they said. Everyone gathered around Jacob, and all his household tried to console him, but he pushed them away. Jacob would not be comforted, saying, "Now I will live in sorrow until I die."

JOSEPH THE SLAVE

GENESIS 39

Far away in Egypt, Joseph was taken to the marketplace where slaves were sold. A man named Potiphar, who was captain of the guard, came along that day and saw Joseph standing there, quiet and dignified, amid all the noise and excitement of the trading. Something about the young man's look, his clear eyes, his strong face and his powerful figure, set him apart from all the other slaves.

"I'll take that one," said Potiphar.

"Forty shekels," said the trader.

"Thirty," said Potiphar.

"Thirty-five," said the trader. The deal was done. Joseph said nothing. One day he had been the dearly loved son with anything he wanted. Now he had lost everything. His beautiful coat was like a mirage disappearing in the noonday sun.

"On!" shouted Potiphar.

Men went before him shouting, "Make way!" He was an important man. Joseph said nothing and walked after his new master with great calm.

Potiphar was soon impressed by the young slave's character. Joseph was different from all his other slaves and servants. God was with Joseph and made him successful in everything that he did. Potiphar soon realized that he had much more than a slave – he had a brilliant manager who could be trusted with everything.

POTIPHAR'S WIFE

GENESIS 39

Potiphar left Joseph in charge of his household and had little to do with the running of his own estate. He ate and drank, visited his friends and left all the work to Joseph.

Now Joseph was very handsome. He was tall and strong, and Potiphar's wife had been eyeing him for some time. She would stare at him or deliberately brush past him in the hallway. But Joseph took no notice. He carried on with his work.

One hot day, she was standing in the doorway to her bedroom as Joseph passed.

"Joseph," she said softly, "you're always so busy. Too busy. You need a rest…"

Joseph looked away from her.

"Joseph, I'm talking to you."

"My mistress should not talk to me," said Joseph.

"You're a fine, intelligent man," she said. "Surely you realize that my husband doesn't care what happens here now. He's left everything up to you."

"Not everything," said Joseph.

"Come on," she laughed. "Do I have to command you as my slave? Come into my bedroom and sleep with me!"

"No!" said Joseph.

She was shocked by his tone. He had never spoken so strongly.

"Never!" he said. "My master Potiphar has entrusted me with everything except you, his wife. How can I betray him and do this terrible thing? It would be a sin against God!"

From that moment, Potiphar's wife would not leave Joseph

alone. She tried day after day to tempt him, but although she used all her charm and every persuasion, Joseph refused. He would not even be alone in the house with her.

One day, by chance, Joseph went into the house, not realizing that all the other servants had left. Potiphar's wife saw him. She crept out of the shadows and grabbed his cloak. "Come and sleep with me, Joseph!"

Joseph ran away. He left the cloak in her hand and fled out of the house, out into the fields.

Potiphar's wife was angry and hurt that she had been rejected, so she called all the servants together and said, "This Hebrew slave has been making a fool of us! You see! He was in my bedroom." The servants could hardly believe it. "Joseph was here," she cried. "I screamed for help and he ran away, leaving his cloak behind."

When Potiphar came home that night, she showed him the cloak and told him the same story. "This is how your precious slave has treated your own wife," she said.

The blood drained from Potiphar's face. Was this possible? Could Joseph have done such a wicked thing?

In spite of everything Potiphar knew about Joseph, he believed his wife's lies. Burning with anger, he had Joseph hauled away to prison.

THE DREAM-TELLER

GENESIS 40

When Joseph was flung into prison, it looked as though he was finished. But even there God was with him and helped him in all he did. The prison guard soon discovered that this Hebrew slave was a good manager and could be trusted. He began to give him jobs to do, and before long, Joseph was almost running the prison.

Later, two men were jailed because they had offended Pharaoh, the great ruler of all Egypt. One was the chief cup-bearer to the court, and the other was the chief baker. Both men were anxious and upset and longed to win the approval of their royal master once more.

One night, they each had a dream, and in the morning they woke up even more worried.

"Why are you looking so sad today?" asked Joseph.

The cup-bearer spoke first, "We've both been troubled by dreams, but we don't know what they mean."

"Has no one told you that dreams are God's business?" They looked at Joseph a little perplexed, but something made them listen very carefully to him.

"God," said Joseph, "is the only one who can interpret dreams. He will show me the meaning of your dreams."

"Well," said the cup-bearer, "let me tell you my dream first...

"I saw a vine and on it were three branches. It budded and then blossomed all at once, and suddenly there were clusters of grapes. I had Pharaoh's cup in my hand and I took the grapes and squeezed them into the cup. I then handed the cup to Pharaoh."

"Here's what it means," said Joseph. "The three branches are three days. Within three days, Pharaoh will set you free from prison. You will return to your job as cup-bearer, and once again you will place the cup in his hand."

The cup-bearer gazed at Joseph in astonishment and then smiled slowly.

"Three days…?" If Joseph was right, he could scarcely believe his luck. "Freedom in three days! If this comes true –"

"When it comes true," said Joseph quietly, "remember me. Mention my case to Pharaoh. I have done nothing wrong. I was captured and sold into slavery. Now I am in prison, although I am completely innocent."

"What about my dream?" said the baker. "Tell me about my dream! On my head were three baskets of bread. And in the top basket were lots of pastries, the kind I make for Pharaoh. Suddenly, lots of birds were swooping down and eating them."

"After three days," said Joseph sadly, "you will be taken from the prison and hanged, and the birds will feed on you."

Both these dreams came true. One man was given his freedom, and the other man was executed. But the chief cup-bearer, who was restored to his job in the palace, did not remember Joseph.

PHARAOH'S NIGHTMARES

GENESIS 41

After Pharaoh's chief cup-bearer was released, it seemed as if the whole world had forgotten Joseph. He looked around at the other prisoners, many of them old and white-haired, who had wasted their whole lives in the deep darkness and loneliness of the prison, and Joseph feared for his future.

Far away in the land of Canaan, Jacob, his father, mourned his dead son. He had no idea that Joseph was enduring a living death in an Egyptian prison. Even after all these years, the loss of his precious son was still painfully fresh. He would wander into the fields alone, sobbing with grief at the very mention of his name.

As for Judah and the other brothers, they kept silent because of their terrible guilt. They had sold their brother into slavery, without caring if he lived or died. The brothers were in a different kind of prison, a cage of regret and sorrow which they had built for themselves. There was no escape from their crime, which haunted them every day.

But God had not forgotten Joseph. After two years, it so happened that Pharaoh himself had a dream, and God used this dream to change everything.

In Pharaoh's dream, he was standing by the River Nile, where he saw seven fat and healthy cows grazing happily in the lush grasses. Suddenly, seven horribly thin and wretched-looking cows staggered out of the water. They went up to the fat cows and ate them whole.

Pharaoh woke up with a start. It was a strange, menacing nightmare – what could it mean? He tossed and turned in his bed throughout the night, and then he fell asleep and dreamed again. This time, he saw seven ears of corn, full and ripe, growing on a single stalk. Then seven other ears of corn, thin and scorched by the east wind, sprang up. The thin ears leaned towards the healthy ears and swallowed them up in one single mouthful.

Pharaoh woke up sweating. There was some meaning to these nightmares, some secret message from the gods of Egypt, but who could tell him and how? He sent for all his magicians and his wise men and his advisers, every official who could help him.

"Tell me the meaning of my dreams," he demanded, but no one could help him.

"Tell me – one of you must know!" he pleaded. But there was not a single wise man in the court who could offer an interpretation.

Pharaoh rose and paced around his marble palace, furious and afraid. "There must be someone!" he shouted.

And that was when the chief cup-bearer remembered Joseph. In an instant, the memory of the Hebrew slave flashed into his mind, and the cup-bearer gasped. "My Royal Lord," he said, "I know a man who can interpret dreams! He is in your prison. A slave. I... have done him wrong, my Lord. I..." The cup-bearer stammered in shame at the memory of his broken promise. "I said I would speak of him to you. The chief baker and I, we both had dreams in prison. We told the young man about them, and he gave us the interpretation, and every single word he said came true."

"Fetch me this dream-teller!" commanded Pharaoh.

SET FREE!

GENESIS 41

The door of the prison burst open and light streamed in upon Joseph. He stared into the brightness, blinking, struggling to focus – the sunlight was painful after the darkness of the cell.

"Come on – out!" the guards urged him.

"Where are you taking me?" Joseph was suddenly afraid. Was it death now? Would his life end like the baker's, executed as a criminal?

"We're taking you for a bath," said the guard.

"A bath? What for?"

"And a shave."

"And new clothes." The guards pushed him. "Quickly! Pharaoh has commanded you to appear before him!"

Washed, shaved and clothed in fine robes, Joseph was led into the palace.

Pharaoh was still pacing around and scowling with worry.

"So," he said, "you are the dream-teller."

Joseph stood before him calmly and quietly, as if he had been in the palace all his life.

"I have had a dream," said Pharaoh, "and no one can interpret it. I hear that you have the power to interpret dreams?"

"I do not have that power," said Joseph.

A gasp went around the throne room. The chief cup-bearer sweated profusely and swallowed hard.

"You do not!" thundered Pharaoh.

"No, my Lord," said Joseph. "I do not have that power myself. But God will give Pharaoh the answer that he desires."

"God..." said Pharaoh. "Your God?"

"Tell me your dream," said Joseph. "And the God of the heavens and the earth will interpret it."

Pharaoh was amazed at the young man's confidence. So he told Joseph about the thin cows eating the fat cows and about the thin ears of corn gobbling up the fat ears, and he waited to hear what he would say.

"Your dreams mean exactly the same thing," said Joseph. "God has revealed the future to Pharaoh. The seven fat cows are seven years, as are the seven ripe ears of corn. These are the years of plenty in the land. There will be seven years of abundance, seven huge harvests, but then there will be seven years of terrible famine. Like the thin cows which ate the fat cows and the thin ears of corn which swallowed up the fat ears, these seven years of famine will consume everything. There will be nothing left..."

"Nothing...?"

"Nothing... unless My Royal Lord looks for a wise and discerning man and puts him in charge of the whole land of Egypt. He must appoint officers who will store up a fifth of every good year of harvest, and keep the grain under the protection of Pharaoh. Everything must be carefully organized and great barns filled with supplies, so when the famine comes, there will be plenty of food to share out among the people."

Pharaoh turned to his courtiers and said, "This man has spoken the truth. Where can we find a man who has the Spirit of God to carry out all these plans?" Even as he said this, Pharaoh knew that he was speaking of Joseph himself.

"God has revealed this truth to you," he said, "so you shall be in charge of my palace, and every single person in my kingdom will obey your orders. I will make you governor of Egypt. You will be second only to the throne of Pharaoh!"

Pharaoh took a signet ring and put it on Joseph's finger. He dressed him in the finest robes and put a gold chain around his neck. From that day, Joseph rode beside Pharaoh in the royal chariot, and men ran before him shouting, "Make way! Make way!"

Joseph spent the next seven years journeying throughout Egypt and organizing all the food supplies. He filled great storehouses in every city, piling up the grain from the seven years of plenty. There was so much grain, no one could measure it.

Then the seven years of good harvests came to an end, and a terrible famine struck the land. So Joseph, the governor of Egypt, opened up the storehouses and began to hand out the food.

SURPRISE VISITORS

GENESIS 42, 43

Far away, in the land of Canaan, there was also a famine. Joseph's father, Jacob, and all his family were facing starvation. So the old man called his sons to him. "I've heard there is food in Egypt. Go down there and buy some for us and save us from death!"

So the brothers went down to Egypt, all except Benjamin. Jacob would not let the young man out of his sight. Losing Joseph had made him fearful.

When the ten brothers arrived, they went to see the governor of Egypt. They had no idea that the governor was the brother they had sold into slavery as a young man.

"Who is it now?" Joseph asked a servant.

"Hebrews, my Lord – begging for food."

"Hebrews?" Joseph looked up curiously as the visitors entered.

One by one, his ten brothers came before him and bowed low to the ground. Not one of them recognized Joseph. All they saw was a ruler in magnificent robes, surrounded by servants.

Joseph stood up, pretending not to know them at all.

"Spies!" he shouted.

"No, sir," they pleaded with him. "We are honest men, come to buy grain –"

"You look like spies to me," said Joseph.

Reuben stepped forward, trembling a little. "My Lord Governor," he said, "we are simply one family of brothers.

There used to be twelve of us, but the youngest brother has stayed behind with our father, and the other brother… is no more."

"I will test whether you are speaking the truth," said Joseph, sitting down on the great seat of judgment with ostrich feathers and columns of gold.

"Fetch your youngest brother and bring him here! If you do this, I will spare your lives."

The brothers were horrified.

"One of you must go back to your father," said Joseph, "and the rest of you can stay in prison till he comes!"

Joseph had used an interpreter for this conversation, even though he could understand every word his brothers said. Now he listened as they turned to one another in consternation. "It's our punishment," they said. "Look what we did to Joseph all those years ago! We ignored his cries for help, and now this disaster has come upon us!"

When Joseph saw their anguish, he turned away and began to weep. Tears streamed down his face, but he wiped them away. He breathed deeply and turned back. He frowned at the brothers again. "Take that man as hostage," he commanded. And guards immediately took hold of Simeon. "The rest of you can go home. Fetch your brother and bring him back here." Then he sent the brothers on their way.

Joseph made sure that their bags were filled with grain and secretly arranged for all the money they had paid for the grain to be returned and hidden in their sacks.

That night, when the brothers made camp, they found the money and were terrified.

"What is happening?" said Reuben. "Why has God done this to us? Now they'll come after us and kill us like thieves!"

No one guessed that it was Joseph, their brother, who had given them everything for free.

They returned to their father, Jacob, fearfully, hardly daring to speak. Not only had they lost one more son – Simeon – but they had to persuade him to let go of Benjamin.

"No! Never!" said Jacob, weeping and storming from the room. "Never, I will never let Benjamin go. If Benjamin is lost, I will fall into my grave in terrible sorrow." And he lay down on the ground, weeping.

So the brothers did nothing for a long while, but eventually they ran out of grain again. They decided to return to Egypt, taking Benjamin with them.

"May the Lord God Almighty grant you mercy," said Jacob, "so that the governor of Egypt will return all my sons to me."

When the brothers arrived in Egypt, they were met by the chief steward. They hastily explained to him about the money in their sacks – they offered to pay it all back – but the steward, who had been instructed by Joseph, just smiled. "What money?" he said. "All my accounts are correct. I am not missing any money."

The brothers looked at each other, amazed. They handed over presents of spices and balm, honey, nuts and delicacies which they had brought from Jacob. Then they bowed low to the ground as Joseph walked into the hall and stood gazing across the line of his brothers.

"How is your old father?" asked Joseph.

Reuben looked up. "Our father, Jacob…?"

"How is he?" said Joseph, fighting back his tears.

"He is alive and well," said Reuben.

Joseph beckoned to them all to stand up. They stood, in awe of this governor of Egypt. He walked down the line until he came to Benjamin.

"Is this the youngest one you told me about?" he asked. They nodded.

"May God be good to you, my son," Joseph said, and then rushed out of the room. He ran to his own private chamber, where no one could hear him, fell down on his bed and burst into tears. Then he got up, washed his face, controlled himself as well as he could and returned.

"Let a banquet be served," he said. And to their amazement, the hungry brothers were seated at the governor's table, and Benjamin, sitting at the end of the table, was served five times as much as everyone else.

THE SILVER CUP

GENESIS 44, 45

That night, when everyone was feasting, Joseph ordered his steward to fill up each of the sacks belonging to his brothers with grain. Joseph also instructed the steward to return their money to them, hiding the silver in the grain. Then Joseph said to the steward, "Take my finest silver cup and hide it in the mouth of Benjamin's sack."

At dawn, the brothers loaded their donkeys and set out for Canaan, still not aware that the generous governor of Egypt was their own brother whom they had treated so badly. They had only gone a short way when the steward caught up with them. Acting on Joseph's orders, he said to them, "How can you treat my master like this? You have repaid his kindness with a wicked act!"

The brothers looked at him in shock and confusion. The

steward pointed at them angrily. "One of you has stolen the sacred silver cup, the most precious possession of the governor of Egypt."

They all denied it at once. "We would never do such a dreadful thing! Look how we offered to return our money to you when we arrived in Egypt. Why would we steal anything from your master's household?"

Reuben stepped forward. "If any one of us has done this, then he will die, and the rest of us will become your slaves!"

"Very well," said the steward, "let it be so!"

One by one, the brothers opened their sacks. The steward went through every single one until he came to Benjamin's sack. He put his hand into the grain and pulled out the silver chalice. Benjamin staggered backwards. He was overwhelmed with horror – how had this happened? He knew he was innocent. But the other brothers looked at him in silence, grief-stricken. They tore their clothes – a sign of their great sorrow – and followed the steward back to Egypt.

The steward ushered the brothers into the presence of the governor, and they fell to the ground before him.

"We offer ourselves as your slaves," said Judah, "every single one of us, as well as the one who has stolen the cup."

"No," replied Joseph firmly, "I do not want you as my slaves. You may all go free – except the guilty one." And Joseph pointed at Benjamin.

Then Judah begged Joseph not to take Benjamin. He told him about his father, Jacob, and how the old man loved Benjamin above all his sons, how he had lost one beloved son, Joseph, and how Benjamin was the last surviving son of Rachel.

Joseph looked on, deeply moved, as Judah – who had acted

so cruelly in the past – now pleaded and begged for the life of Benjamin. "My father will die if the young man is thrown into prison here. If we do not bring him back alive, it will break his heart with grief. Please, my Lord, take me as your slave instead of him. Take me – I will serve you forever! Please let the boy go."

Judah began to cry and, at this, Joseph could contain himself no longer. He shouted to all his servants, "Leave the chamber, leave us alone!" They all went, including the interpreter, and then Joseph broke down and cried so loudly, it was heard by everyone in the building.

The brothers looked at him, bewildered. One moment he had been so stern, and now the great governor of Egypt was weeping like a little child.

He lifted his head and spoke to them in their own language. "Don't you know me?" he asked.

They looked at him in astonishment. They shook their heads.

"I am Joseph," he said.

They were trembling with fear and did not know what to make of him.

"Joseph," he whispered softly. Then he said, "Is it true that my old father, Jacob, is still alive and well?"

Gradually, as if the scales of the years were falling from their eyes, they began to recognize him – their own brother in the royal costume of an Egyptian ruler.

"Look at me closely," said Joseph. "I am the brother you sold into slavery."

A deep dread fell on the brothers – if this were true, he would kill them all in revenge – but Joseph held out his arms. "Don't be distressed, and don't be angry with yourselves for what you have done. You intended to do me harm, but God turned it all to good

– look, he sent me to Egypt to save many lives, including yours. So it wasn't you who sent me to Egypt, it was God himself. Tell my father, Jacob, that God has made me governor of all Egypt. Tell him to come down immediately with his flocks and all his people, tell him to bring his children and his grandchildren and all his possessions. You must all come and live in Egypt with me, so you will be rescued from the famine that is still to come."

Still they didn't move. Not one of them dared to move or breathe, it was too incredible. They just stared, but the tears were running down Joseph's face as he held out his hands.

"Benjamin – you can see that it's me!" said Joseph, and he went up to Benjamin and hugged him. Both men started crying for joy together. Soon all the brothers were crying and embracing Joseph.

A HAPPY REUNION

GENESIS 45–50

The brothers returned to Canaan with many gifts and extra wagons from Egypt to bring back all their belongings. Full of joy, they told their father, Jacob, "Your son Joseph is alive. He has become governor of all Egypt."

Jacob was shocked. For a long time, he was stunned into silence.

"Joseph," he said. Surely Joseph was dead. Long dead. He looked at them as if they were tormenting him with the idea. "My boy Joseph…?" He shook his head. It was impossible. He did not trust them.

"It's true," said Benjamin.

"Joseph is alive?" asked Jacob in disbelief.

"Come and see the wagons he has sent to bring you and all your possessions to Egypt," said Reuben.

Jacob walked outside and saw the procession of carts, and he opened the gifts from Joseph, and the old man began to tremble. "It's true," he said. "It's true. He's alive, and I will see him before I die."

So Jacob and all his household went down to Egypt. When Joseph saw his father, Jacob, he ran to him and clung to him for a long time. The old man kept shaking his head and trying to speak, but no words would come. Then he held Joseph in front of him and stared at him as if it were all a dream.

"It's you," he said at last. "It's you." And Jacob wept.

There was no parting them. They stayed together for many hours. They walked together and talked about all that had happened over the many years of pain and sadness.

"Now I am ready to die in peace," said Jacob, "because I have seen for myself that you are alive."

Joseph gave homes to all his brothers, and lands for their flocks, with the permission of Pharaoh. They all lived there, in the land of Goshen, and survived the famine years which Joseph had foretold.

Jacob made Joseph promise that when he died, he would bury him in the land of Canaan, in the place where God had promised that he would make Jacob's descendants into a great nation. Then he blessed Joseph's sons and Joseph and all his brothers, and soon afterwards he died. Joseph kept his promise, and he took his father's body back to Canaan, where he buried him with great sorrow.

Joseph himself lived in Egypt until he was one hundred and

ten years old. Then he gathered his family around him and told them that their descendants would one day have trouble in Egypt, but God would come to their aid, as he had come to Joseph's when he was in deep distress.

"When all the descendants of Jacob – the children of Israel – leave Egypt," he said, "you must take my bones with you and bury them alongside my forefathers, Jacob, Isaac and Abraham, in the land that God has given to us."

Joseph had been through many ups and downs in his life. He had known happiness as a child, terrible disasters and tragedy as a young man, and peace and good fortune as he grew older. Through all these times, good or bad, God had been with him.

THE BABY IN THE BULRUSHES

Exodus 1, 2

Many years after Joseph's family settled in Egypt, a new pharaoh came to the throne. When he saw the vast number of Israelites, the descendants of Jacob who were living in his kingdom, he grew afraid of war.

"Look at these Israelites," he said. "One day they will rise up against me, join with my enemies and escape from Egypt!"

So he forced the people into slavery and put cruel taskmasters over them. The Israelite men were made to drag huge stones for the building of cities and make bricks out of mud, while the slave-drivers whipped them into obedience. They suffered terribly, but Pharaoh was not satisfied.

First he asked the Israelite midwives to kill all the boy children at birth, but they refused. Then he ordered his own soldiers to seize every newborn baby boy and hurl it into the River Nile.

In the middle of this great terror, one woman gave birth to a beautiful boy and immediately hid him from the prowling soldiers. When he was three months old, she could no longer hide him safely, so she took a basket of reeds and coated it with tar to make it waterproof. Then she wrapped up her baby tightly and put him in the basket. She set him afloat among the reeds and bulrushes by the river bank.

The little basket bobbed around for a long time, while the boy's sister, Miriam, watched from a distance. She was amazed to see an Egyptian princess, Pharaoh's daughter, wading into the Nile to bathe. Her maidservants were standing on the bank when the princess saw the mysterious basket.

"Fetch it here," she called, and one of her servants waded into the river and pulled it onto the bank. The princess sat down beside the basket, opened the cover and immediately found the crying child. "Oh," she said, "this must be one of the little Israelite babies!" And she picked him out and cradled him and held him close against her face.

When Miriam saw the royal princess holding her baby brother so tenderly, she guessed that the princess wanted to keep the baby for herself. So she walked towards her timidly and said, "Shall I fetch an Israelite nurse for my Lady, so she can look after the baby for you?"

"Oh yes!" said the princess, delighted. So Miriam went and fetched her own mother.

"Take this baby and nurse him for me," said the princess. And she agreed to pay the woman to care for him.

The princess named the baby Moses, which sounds like "drawn out" in Hebrew, because she had saved him from the river. So the boy's mother looked after him until he was old enough to go to the palace. Then Moses lived with the princess as her own son.

MURDER!

Exodus 2

Moses grew up as a royal prince of Egypt, with all the fine clothes and wealth and education of the greatest in the land. He dressed and spoke like an Egyptian, but he never forgot that deep down he was an Israelite. Indeed, he could never forget, because all around him he saw how the Israelites suffered. Everywhere he looked, he saw men crushed under their burdens, women slaving to make bricks in the fierce glare of the sun, children in rags, old people whose backs were scarred with whiplashes.

As he grew older, it became more and more difficult to live two lives: one as an Egyptian prince and the other – a secret life – as an Israelite grieving for his lost family. One day, his two lives came crashing together in a single moment. He was out walking alone when he saw an Egyptian taskmaster viciously beating one of the Israelite slaves. Moses tried to stop him, but the Egyptian took no notice. He went on savagely attacking the poor man who lay groaning in the sand.

"Stop!" Moses grabbed his hand, but the taskmaster sneered, "Why should I take orders from you?" At that, Moses flew into a rage. He knocked the Egyptian taskmaster to the ground, and before he knew what he was doing, he had killed him.

The Israelite slave had already run away, and Moses looked all around him fearfully. He could see no one – only the desert and the sun sinking on the horizon, and at his feet the dead Egyptian. In a frenzy, he dug away the sand and made a grave. He rolled the body into it, piled up the sand, smoothed it out, trod it down and then walked away, hoping and believing that no one had witnessed his crime.

The next day, Moses saw two Israelites fighting, and he stepped boldly up to the man who had started the quarrel.

"Why are you hitting a fellow Israelite?" he asked. Moses felt that all Israelites should be brothers, but the young man looked at him knowingly.

"Who made you a judge over us?" he asked. "Are you thinking of killing me, just like you killed that Egyptian yesterday?"

Suddenly, Moses was afraid because they knew his secret.

Pharaoh soon heard what Moses had done. Immediately he ordered soldiers to capture Moses and bring him back for execution, but he escaped.

He ran away from Egypt, from all his wealth and fine clothes and the luxury of living in a royal palace. He went away from all the Israelite people, far away from his own family, and wandered many miles into the merciless desert.

THE BURNING BUSH

EXODUS 2–4

Moses was on the run. He had killed a man, and now Pharaoh wanted to kill him. From Egypt he had journeyed far into the land of Midian. It was a desolate place.

As Moses was sitting by a well, he met the seven daughters of Jethro who had come to fetch water for their flocks. Some local shepherds were pushing them away from the well, but Moses defended the girls and drew their water for them.

Their father, Jethro, was the priest of Midian, and from that day, Moses was welcomed into Jethro's family. Now he lived in the desert, helping to guard the flocks in the wild and lonely hills, and there he married Zipporah, one of Jethro's daughters.

Forty years passed, but God had not forgotten the plight of the Israelites, slaves in Egypt, nor had he forgotten Moses and his harsh and lonely life in the desert of Sinai.

One day, Moses climbed Mount Sinai, also known as Mount Horeb. He was searching for a stray sheep when he saw a bush on fire. He thought nothing of it for a moment – it was a common sight on the hillsides in the blazing heat of the sun – but then he stopped. The bush was burning furiously, a ball of flame, but no branches fell off, no leaves turned to ash. The fire was so bright it almost blinded him, and he shielded his eyes. He took a step forward, then a voice called out, "Moses, Moses!"

He looked around. He could see no one. Fear gripped him.

"Take off your sandals because you are standing on holy ground," the voice said.

Moses shook off his sandals and stood there in terror, although he wanted to run away and hide.

"I am the God of your ancestors, the God of Abraham, Isaac and Jacob. I have seen the misery of my people in Egypt, and I am sending you to Pharaoh to rescue them!" said the voice. "I have chosen you to lead them to the land I have promised to my people, a land flowing with milk and honey."

Moses hid his eyes. He did not know what to do or say.

Why was God appearing to him, Moses the failure, Moses the murderer? How could he go to Pharaoh? And why would his fellow Israelites believe him in the first place?

"What if the Israelites ask your name?" Moses asked. "Who shall I say is sending me?"

The bush erupted in flame, searing the sky, and Moses stumbled back.

"I AM WHO I AM. Say that I AM has sent you!"

Moses bowed low to the ground, trembling, hardly daring to ask another question. At last, he looked up. "What if they don't believe me – why should they listen to me?"

So God commanded Moses to throw his staff onto the ground. Immediately it turned into a snake.

"Catch it by the tail," said God. Moses did so, and the snake suddenly stiffened into the staff of wood once again. God gave him other miracles to perform in front of the Israelites and Pharaoh, but Moses still hesitated.

"Please, Lord," he said, stammering, "I… I am not very good at speaking, I'm too slow and I won't know what to say!"

"Who makes a person's mouth?" said God, and the flames of the bush brightened and sparked in anger. "Who gives voices and words and sight to mankind?"

But Moses was still terrified. "Please send someone else," he pleaded.

"I am sending your brother, Aaron, to you," said God. "He is a good speaker. You can pass on my message through him to all the people!"

MOSES AND PHARAOH

Exodus 4–6

After Moses saw the burning bush on Mount Sinai, he set off at once for Egypt. In the desert he saw his long-lost brother, Aaron, approaching him from afar. He ran to him and told him about the marvel of the burning bush, the voice of God, the miraculous signs and God's promise to save the Israelite people.

Aaron in turn told Moses how he had never forgotten him, although many people in Egypt thought that he was dead. But now God had spoken to him too. He had been told to find his brother in the vast and lonely desert and bring him back to Egypt. They could not believe that they were standing face to face after so many years: two old men, two brothers, weeping and hugging each other.

"Is Miriam – ?" asked Moses.

"Yes, our sister's alive! She's been praying for your return every day."

The Israelite elders who remembered Moses gazed in astonishment as two men appeared through the dust along the desert track. Aaron's companion was a tall man with grey hair and clear eyes and a face lined by years of suffering and hardship.

"MOSES!"

They embraced him and questioned him. Some touched his cloak as if he were a dream.

"I am no dream," he said. "I have come in the name of the Lord God of Israel to set his people free."

So Moses and Aaron and the elders went to Pharaoh and

asked him to let the Israelite people go into the desert to worship their God. At that, Pharaoh flew into a rage.

"Your God means nothing to me! These people are my slaves!"

Then Pharaoh ordered his taskmasters, "Don't give the Israelites any straw to make their bricks. From today, they can find it for themselves. And tell those lazy good-for-nothings to make the same number of bricks. That will make them work harder, scrambling around looking for straw, so they won't have time for the lies of Moses and Aaron!"

Then the Israelites complained to Moses. "Look what you've done! You've ruined our lives now, Pharaoh will kill us with this crushing burden."

Moses walked alone in the night, troubled and desperate.

"Things have become far worse," he said to God. "I've come all this way, and nothing has happened but disaster!"

"I will deliver you from all your troubles," said God. "I will lift up my mighty hand against Pharaoh and save my people. Go to Pharaoh now and tell him what I'm going to do."

THE TEN PLAGUES

EXODUS 7–11

Moses took courage and marched into the royal palace, where the lamps were burning and the huge columns towered into the dark. He felt small, but he knew that the God of all the earth was with him, for God had promised that Pharaoh would see his mighty hand at work.

Now Moses and Aaron were once more ready to ask Pharaoh to free the Israelite slaves.

Aaron threw his staff down before Pharaoh, where it suddenly twisted and buckled and then slithered into the dark. Pharaoh stepped back in horror, but then his magicians – who were very cunning – performed a conjuring trick with their staffs, turning them into little snakes.

"Hah!" said Pharaoh. "The gods of Egypt can do better than the feeble God of the Israelites!" But then Aaron's staff swallowed all the other snakes in one mouthful, and he seized it by the tail and it became a stick once again.

But when they asked Pharaoh once more to free the Israelites, he refused to listen to them.

"I will never let your people go – never!" he shouted.

The next morning, Moses and Aaron went down to the River Nile, where Pharaoh was bathing. Moses began, "This is what the Lord God of Israel says: 'If you do not let my people go, I will turn the river into blood, the fish will die, and no one will be able to drink the water!'"

Pharaoh refused, and so Aaron stretched out his staff and the whole river turned instantly to blood. Then the magicians performed their own tricks with a few bowls of water. Pharaoh again walked away, waving his hands, saying, "Never – I will never let your people go!"

So God brought more plagues on the land of Egypt. The second was a plague of frogs, teeming out of the blood-red Nile, sliding into the houses of the Egyptians, into their beds and their ovens and their pots, jumping and slithering all over them. They cried out to Pharaoh, and for one moment he said to Moses, "I'll let your people go." But as soon as Moses brought the plague to an end, he changed his mind. He shouted, "No, never!"

So then came the gnats, like dust, clouds of insects rising, infesting everywhere, biting, swarming. The magicians could no longer copy the miracles – they could not produce a single gnat. "This is the work of their God," they said fearfully, but Pharaoh would not listen.

So God told Moses and Aaron to bring down another plague on Egypt, a plague of great flies that blackened the air and clustered on the houses of the Egyptians, on their food and livestock, everywhere except in the homes of the Israelites.

Pharaoh promised to let them go, but when Moses freed the land of this plague, Pharaoh changed his mind again. "No, never!" he shouted stubbornly.

Then came a plague on all the cattle and sheep of the Egyptians; then a plague of boils festering on all the Egyptians; then a plague of hailstones hurling from the sky. The great stones lashed the trees, stripped them bare and crushed the early crops to the ground. Seeing the devastation of his land, Pharaoh relented. "All right," he said, "I'll let you go! All the people can go!" But when Moses lifted up his hands to stop the hail, Pharaoh changed his mind yet again. "No," he said furiously, gritting his teeth, "no... never!"

So then came a plague of locusts, a vast army of rustling wings and biting jaws, which stripped all the remains of the crops that were left from the hail, until Pharaoh himself was nearly choked from the invasion of huge insects which filled the palace. "Moses, Aaron," he called, "forgive me, I have sinned. I will let your people go. This time I promise." So they brought that plague to an end, but once again Pharaoh's mind turned, his eyes grew dark and his fists clenched on the side of his throne. "No," he shouted, "never! Never!"

So Moses called down darkness, the ninth plague, a swirling

cloud of thick darkness for three days, until Pharaoh came to him in anger and despair. "Get out of my sight," he said. "If you ever come near me again, you will be killed!"

"Very well," said Moses, "you will never see me again, but because of your evil heart and your stubborn ways, the Lord, the God of Israel, will strike the firstborn son in every Egyptian household, from the firstborn of Pharaoh who sits on the throne to the firstborn son of the servant girl who grinds the corn. No one will escape, not even your cattle, but the Israelites will not be touched."

Moses and Aaron walked away in anger and in sorrow because they knew that the pharaoh would do nothing until death came to his own household.

THE PASSOVER

EXODUS 12

After Pharaoh refused to let the Israelites leave Egypt, God told Moses that when he sent the final plague, on that night the Israelites would leave Egypt forever.

God gave Moses instructions for a special meal, and Moses told the people everything they had to do: "It is on this night, the most important of all nights, that the Lord will give you freedom.

"Every family must take a lamb, the very best from the flock without any blemishes, and prepare it for a meal. Spread the blood on the lintel and doorposts of your houses, and then God will see this sign. He will pass over your houses when he comes to bring judgment, and you will be safe.

"You must be ready to leave at any moment. First, roast the lamb, then eat it with bitter herbs and unleavened bread. Keep your sandals on and your cloaks tucked into your belts, and have your staffs at the ready, because you will walk out of your houses and begin your great journey before dawn!"

The Israelites obeyed. They spread the blood of the lambs on the doorposts and the lintels of their houses.

At midnight, the judgment of God came upon the Egyptians, striking the firstborn as he had warned. But God passed over every house where he saw the blood, until he came to the houses and the farms and the palaces of the Egyptians.

That night, there was terrible grief and wailing as the Egyptian people felt the touch of death on their own homes, and as Pharaoh himself discovered his own firstborn son lying dead. Then Pharaoh knew that he had brought this destruction on his own land because of his pride and cruelty.

FREEDOM!

Exodus 12, 13

It was the middle of the night. Pharaoh sent for Moses and Aaron. "Take your people," he said. "Take them all, I beg you. Leave us forever! Go now and pray to your God for me!"

As Moses and Aaron led the people from their homes, the Egyptians came running to them, offering gifts of gold and silver, crying out, "If you stay one day longer, we will all die!"

The Egyptian people respected Moses and knew he was

God's leader. They knew how Pharaoh had kept the Israelites in desperate slavery, and how he had proudly refused to listen to their God, so now they begged them all to leave quickly before it was too late.

Some of the Israelites ran; some walked. Younger people helped older people; parents carried children. Families herded their cattle and their sheep. They all sang praises to God and cheered as they left behind the great building sites and the whips of their taskmasters and the huge piles of bricks. Tears fell as they thought of their years of slavery and torment.

They were free!

Moses walked ahead of them, alone, striding into the empty desert which had been his home for so many years. He would lead them safely, as he had led his flocks of sheep. He would lead them in the power of the Lord, the one who had called from the mysterious fire on Mount Sinai, "I AM WHO I AM." He would lead them to the land which God had promised to give them.

A MIRACULOUS CROSSING

EXODUS 14, 15

As soon as he realized that the Israelites had finally gone, Pharaoh flew into a rage.

"We should never have let them go, never!" He was already striding down the vast hall of the royal palace, calling into the night.

"I want my slaves – all my slaves – back at work, building my cities! We must fetch them back now!"

His generals obeyed. They summoned all their bravest men and set out at once with more than six hundred gleaming chariots, the finest and fastest in Egypt. Pharaoh himself rode at the head, whipping his horses and shouting his army onwards through the streaming dust and into the darkness.

The Israelites were camped near the Red Sea, a wide stretch of water also known as the Sea of Reeds. They looked up to see chariots appearing on the horizon. The shout went around: "The Egyptians! Egyptian horsemen! Pharaoh's army!"

The people surged towards Moses. "Now look!" they called in terror. "The Egyptian army is coming to destroy us!"

They were trapped: Egyptians on one side; water on the other. Moses looked at them calmly, completely untroubled by the wild panic which was spreading through the crowd.

"Don't be afraid. Stand still and see how God will save you! All these Egyptians that you see today, you will never see again. God will fight for you." They looked at him doubtfully, fearfully, but he raised his hand. "All you have to do is stay calm," he said.

Then God told Moses to stretch his arm out across the water. "The Israelites will walk over on dry land," God said, "but the Egyptians will follow them to their deaths."

It was dark when the Israelites heard a howling wind coming from the east. They saw Moses stretching out his hand across the great waters. Behind them were the Egyptians, ready to pursue them and take them back into slavery. The wind was roaring. Right in front of them the waters were rising, separating into two huge cascading walls.

"Go!" shouted Moses, and the Israelites walked across on dry land – every man, woman and child. They passed safely between the vast, dark, rumbling walls raised by the furious gale that was blowing.

It was nearly dawn when the Egyptians saw what had happened. Pharaoh urged his warriors onwards. "Come on! After them, capture them!" They rode madly and recklessly towards the great pathway and hurtled onwards into the mud.

Moses lifted up his hand once more. The Egyptian chariots floundered and sank, their wheels breaking loose. Slowly, terrifyingly, the great walls of water collapsed in thunder, a storm of waves returning, until the whole sea was level once again. Not one single Egyptian could be seen. Not one survived.

The Israelites gathered around Moses in the light of day and blessed God for saving them with his almighty power.

Moses and his sister, Miriam, sang songs, and all the people joined them in celebration:

Sing to the Lord,
for he is mighty.
He has rescued us
and he will reign forever.

FOOD FROM HEAVEN

EXODUS 15–17

Within three days, the Israelites' joy had vanished in the savage heat of the desert sun.

"We're dying of thirst!" they said. "We've escaped the Egyptians only to collapse and die in the sand."

Moses shook his head sadly. The Israelites had very short memories.

They camped by a waterhole, but the water tasted horrible. "The water is bitter in this place," Moses said to God. "No one can drink it, and they are blaming me."

God showed Moses a special piece of wood which he threw into the water to make it sweet. Thousands of people clustered around, and soon everyone had enough fresh water to drink. But within weeks, they were shouting and grumbling and accusing Moses again.

"There's no food here," they said. "The Lord should have killed us all in Egypt! Why bring us all this way to starve us to death?"

Still Moses kept his patience and walked silently into the distance. The people watched his lonely figure as he walked away from them. They knew he was going to talk to God alone.

After a long time, Moses returned and gave them this message: "'I have heard all your grumbling,' says the Lord. 'Tonight you will eat meat, and tomorrow I will rain down bread from heaven.'" Bread from heaven? What could he mean? But even as they were arguing and discussing this in the camp, a huge flock of quail landed in front of them. Every single family had meat to eat that night. Then in the morning, they awoke to find the ground covered with a strange white substance like frost.

They crept out of their tents, touched it with their fingers, tasted it and it was like wafers and honey.

"What is it?" asked everyone. "Manna!" said someone, which is "what is it?" in Hebrew.

"The Lord has sent us manna!"

"Manna, manna!" they shouted, laughing. They all ran out and began to gather the delicious white frost in baskets. Moses told them to gather just enough for each day. Some of the Israelites were greedy and tried to hoard piles of the manna, but it soon went bad.

"No," said Moses angrily, "just enough for each day, and then twice as much on the sixth day, so you can keep some for God's special day of rest, the Sabbath." So God sent manna to the Israelites every day for forty years, as long as they were in the desert.

But it wasn't many months before they were grumbling bitterly at Moses again. Near Mount Sinai they ran out of water, and once more they blamed Moses for leading them to their deaths.

"Why are you arguing with me again?" he asked in despair, walking off into the streaming sand which was whipped along by the wind. "Why do you test God's patience?"

When he was alone with God at last, Moses said, "What am I to do with these people? They're ready to stone me to death!"

So God showed him a rock and told him to strike it with his stick in front of all the people. When he did so, streams of water came flowing, tumbling out onto the dry sand, flooding towards them. Once again, God had provided water for everyone to drink.

FIRE AND THUNDER!

EXODUS 19

The Israelites made their way through the desert and came to the foot of a huge, dark mountain. They gazed at the steep crags which towered into the sky. Although they did not know it, this was the place where God himself had appeared to Moses in the burning bush – Mount Sinai, the holy mountain of God.

Moses stood there in awe, trembling at the memory of the roaring flames and the presence of God which had changed his life forever.

"I will let the people hear my voice for themselves," said God. "Then they will see my power and learn to trust you."

So Moses gathered all the people together in hundreds of thousands around the foot of the mountain. "No one must go near the mountain," said Moses. "No one must set foot on it or touch a single stone. No one! If you do, you will die."

The people stood there in fear, promising to obey every word.

Three days later, Mount Sinai was covered in smoke, and God descended in fire. Thunder rolled through the sky, a deafening roar, terrifying the people. Smoke billowed down and lightning cracked and flashed, piercing the thick darkness. There were huge tremors as the whole mountain shook violently and a sound echoed across the desert like the blast of a thousand trumpets.

Moses began to walk up the mountain. He called out to God, and God answered him with a crash of thunder. The Israelites cowered far below – they heard words like deep rumbles and like the splitting of an earthquake, but they understood nothing. They hid in terror as their leader vanished into the swirling darkness. Many of them thought that even Moses would die because of the majestic power and dreadful holiness of their God.

THE TEN COMMANDMENTS

Moses climbed up the mountain steadily, bravely, without stopping. He went alone through the blackness, the great barrier of cloud that boiled and steamed around the sheer cliffs. At last, he stepped out of the dark storm into a brightness so great and dazzling that he had to hide his eyes.

Moses had entered the presence of the Holy One; he stood in the eternal love and glory of God.

Far below, the Israelites knew nothing of this. All they had seen was Moses vanishing, swallowed by the night and the thundering tempest. They were afraid, and as days, then weeks passed, they began to wonder if they would ever see their leader again.

But God was speaking to Moses, and as he did so, he wrote his Ten Commandments onto two slabs of stone:

- I am God who rescued you from slavery in Egypt. You shall have no other gods but me.

- You shall not make any idols or bow down to any statue or image. You must worship me alone.

- You shall not misuse the name of the Lord your God.

- Remember to keep the Sabbath day holy. For six days you can work, but on the seventh, you and your household shall rest.

- Show respect to your father and mother, and in this way you will enjoy your life, living securely in the land which I will give you.

- You shall not commit murder.

- You shall not commit adultery.

- You shall not steal.

- You shall not tell lies.

- Do not set your heart on anything belonging to other people – their house, their money or their husband or wife.

For forty days and forty nights, Moses stayed on the mountain, listening carefully to everything God said. God gave Moses many other instructions about how his people were to live.

Then Moses prepared himself to come down the mountain, carrying the Ten Commandments on the two slabs of stone. These would show God's people a good and right way to live.

THE GOLDEN CALF

EXODUS 32

The Israelites were impatient. Moses, their leader, had been absent for too long talking to God on the top of Mount Sinai. Already they had forgotten the thunder and the lightning, and the power of God that had shaken the mountain while they had looked on in awe.

Now they gazed up to the heights, and the huge cliffs were silent. There was no cloud, only the sun beating down on the wild emptiness. Moses was nowhere to be seen.

Aaron, Moses' brother, kept looking, hoping, scanning the sharp line of rocks high above, but he could feel that the people were growing restless and dangerously unsettled.

"Where's Moses?" they said.

"What kind of leader vanishes into the mountains forever? He's dead!"

"No!" Aaron tried to calm them, but they jostled all around him.

"You're his brother – you lead us. Make us a god to follow."

Aaron was afraid, and his courage failed him. He called to the people, "All right! Give me all your gold. Take the earrings from your wives and daughters, and we'll make an idol to worship."

So Aaron made a huge golden calf for the people. They cheered and sang and danced in a frenzy around the image, shouting, "This is our god who brought us out of Egypt!"

At the top of the mountain, God was angry. He spoke to Moses: "My people have turned away from me. I will destroy them and begin the whole nation again with you!"

"No, Lord," Moses pleaded. "Don't let the Egyptians mock and say that you led your people out of Egypt and into freedom only to kill them!"

God listened to Moses and spared the Israelites. So Moses came down from the mountain, carrying the slabs of stone with the Ten Commandments. But when he saw the screaming and the dancing and heard the evil chanting, he was seized with a furious anger himself.

"NO!" he roared.

The people stopped and stared at the great figure standing high on the rocks.

"Moses!" they whispered in terror. "It's Moses, he's alive!"

They let go of their drums and tambourines and sank to their knees in sudden horror.

Moses raised the two slabs of stone high over his head, shouting, "NO! NO!" and then hurled them onto the rocks below, where they shattered into pieces.

Aaron tried to explain. "We thought you were dead... I... I... didn't know what to do. The people wanted a god to follow, so I took their gold and... and... this calf suddenly appeared!"

Moses did not believe Aaron's story at all. He gazed sternly at the people. "Melt the calf!" he shouted. "Now grind it into powder, mix it with water and drink it." The people were afraid of an even worse punishment, so they obeyed in silence.

GOD'S AGREEMENT

EXODUS 34

Once more, God told Moses to climb up Mount Sinai.

"No one else is to come near the holy mountain – you must come alone. Bring two slabs of stone with you, and I will write the commandments again." God was prepared to give his unfaithful people another chance.

So Moses climbed up again, wending his way slowly, higher and higher, until the cloud of God's holy presence descended. Brightness came all around him – dazzling light – and there God himself passed in front of Moses and called out from the cloud, "The Lord, the Lord, God of tender mercy and compassion!"

Moses knelt down in awe as the God of all heaven and earth

declared his own name and spoke to Moses of his everlasting love. "I will make an agreement with you," promised God. "It will be a covenant with my people. I will work wonders greater than the world has ever seen, and I will prepare a way to the land I have promised you. I will defeat your enemies. But my people must not be like those other nations who worship idols and false gods. My people must worship only me and obey all my commandments."

When Moses came back to the Israelites carrying the Ten Commandments again, they were afraid to come near him because his face was shining, radiant like the sun. And they hid their eyes from him because they knew he had been standing in the presence of God.

A PLACE FOR WORSHIP

EXODUS 35–40

The Israelites were on a journey – to the land God had promised them. On the way, they stopped to rest and to worship God. God had given Moses instructions to build a tent which could be used as a special meeting place to worship him.

The tent, also known as the tabernacle, was made of woven goats' hair and was lined with blue, purple and scarlet linen. Inside was a beautiful box – the ark of the covenant – carved of acacia wood, covered with gold and decorated with golden-winged cherubim. This was for carrying the Ten Commandments. There was also a golden lampstand with seven burning oil lamps, an altar for sacrifices, a table with twelve loaves of bread – one for each tribe of Israel – a huge bowl for cleansing and special anointing oil for the priests.

At the tabernacle, God's people would sense the presence of God's holiness like the fire on Mount Sinai. There they learned to obey his commandments and began to know his everlasting love.

Many of the Israelites had helped to make the tabernacle. They had given their finest possessions, brooches and ornaments, onyx stones and precious gems, rare spices and incense.

Some of the Israelites had woven the cloth for the tent, and God's Spirit had come upon the finest artists – Bezalel, Oholiab and other craftsmen – and they had created rich and wonderful works in wood and metal, with precious stones, to glorify God. They had carried out all the instructions which Moses had given them to the last detail.

When at last the tabernacle was completed, the ark of the covenant with its golden-winged cherubim resting on the lid was placed in the most important room, the Holy of Holies, the place of the fire of God's presence.

JOSHUA AND CALEB

NUMBERS 11, 13, 14

Life in the desert was tough. The people moved from one oasis to another. Sometimes they remembered with longing the fertile fields of Egypt – the melons and cucumbers, the leeks and onions, and all the other good things they had to eat. So they complained about food, they complained about water and they tested the patience of Moses and God.

But there was one man who was always loyal to Moses, who supported him and served him through all the years in the desert. His name was Joshua.

One day, on the edge of the River Jordan, Moses decided to send twelve spies, one from each tribe, to explore the land God had promised to give to his people – the land of Canaan. Moses chose Joshua, another brave young man named Caleb and ten others.

"See what the land is like," he said. "I want to know how strong the people are, how many cities they have, how high the walls are. Find out everything."

The twelve men went off to explore, and they stayed for many weeks. When they came back, they carried with them a huge bunch of grapes, so heavy that two men had to carry it. But ten of the spies were shaking with fear.

"Well?" said Moses. "Give us your report!"

All the people listened eagerly, wanting to learn about the beautiful land which God had promised to them.

"We saw giants," said the ten spies. "That land is full of huge, powerful warriors living in massive cities!"

Caleb interrupted bluntly, "It's a wonderful land full of rich pasture, a land flowing with milk and honey! We can conquer it easily." "No!" said the others. "It's too dangerous. There may be good pasture – that's true – but we'll be killed, every single one of us!"

When the people heard this, they became terrified, and then their terror turned to rage.

"It's your fault," they screamed at Moses. "If only we'd died in Egypt!"

"We were better off there," someone called out. And then

another shouted, "Let's choose a new leader to take us right back to Egypt!"

Moses was horrified, but Joshua stepped forward and shook his fist in the air.

"Cowards!" he shouted. "The land is good and God can give us the victory if he chooses, no one can defeat him!" Joshua walked up to the ten spies and all the rebels and said, "Don't turn away from the Lord; don't be afraid. Go forward!"

But the Israelites would not listen, and they threatened to stone Joshua and Caleb to death.

Because of this, God's judgment finally fell on the Israelites. "Not one of you who left Egypt," said God, "will enter the Promised Land. You will all die here in the desert after wandering around for forty years. Only Joshua and Caleb, my faithful servants, will be allowed to cross the River Jordan and take possession of the land!"

MOSES SEES THE PROMISED LAND

NUMBERS 20, DEUTERONOMY 31, 34

For many years, God's people lived in the desert, moving from place to place, stopping to find water for themselves and their animals. The people were always dissatisfied. Moses was patient with God's people, but one day they were complaining about water again. God told Moses and Aaron to gather all the tribes of Israel before a great rock. He said to Moses, "Take your staff and stand before the rock; then command it to produce water."

But Moses could not control his own anger, and instead of

delivering a quiet command as God had said, he stood there with Aaron and shouted out, "You rebellious people! Have we got to create water out of this rock for you?" Then he furiously banged his staff twice against the rock.

Sure enough, the water flowed into the desert as it had done once before, and everyone had enough to drink. But God was grieved because Moses had not trusted him or obeyed him fully. God said, "You did not show respect for my word before all the people, and so I will not allow you to lead them into the Promised Land yourself."

Moses accepted God's judgment humbly. In time, everyone who had left Egypt died, and only those born in the desert survived – except Caleb, Joshua and Moses.

Moses took Joshua and presented him to the people.

"Be strong, be very brave!" he said to him. "Never be afraid, because the Lord is with you. He will never leave you; he will never forsake you." All the people heard what Moses said to their new leader. Then Moses gave his blessing to all the tribes of Israel.

The people watched Moses turn and walk into the hills as he often had done before. They watched him walking, upright and strong, his cloak blowing in the wind. They watched him until he was a tiny figure, a speck climbing on the ridge far, far away.

Moses reached the highest mountain, and from there God showed him the whole land of Canaan.

"This is the land I promised to Abraham, Isaac and Jacob," said God. "I will let you see everything with your own eyes, even though you cannot cross over the Jordan."

Moses was one hundred and twenty years old when he died, but he was still strong, and his eyes were as clear as ever.

God himself buried Moses, his servant, in that lonely place in the highest hills looking over the Promised Land.

ISRAEL'S NEW LEADER

God said to Joshua, "Moses, my servant, is dead. It is time for you to lead my people."

Joshua looked at the River Jordan, flowing through the valley, and beyond it to the great cities of the war-like tribes of Canaan. He looked back to the mountains where Moses, his master and teacher, had disappeared into the haze. Could he be as wise and strong and courageous as Moses?

"I will be with you, just as I was with Moses." The voice came to him, quietly, insistently. "Be strong, be courageous, and obey all the laws I gave to Moses. Don't be afraid!"

Joshua looked at the Israelites camped beside the river. He looked at their fires in the twilight and heard the laughter and the chatter of people longing to find their true home, the Promised Land. The whole nation needed him now.

"I will give you every place where you set your foot," said God. "The whole land which I promised to Moses will be yours. I will be with you wherever you go!"

Joshua stood there alone, praying, believing, gathering all his strength and all his courage, while God's words echoed in his mind and deep in his heart, "I will be with you!"

RAHAB AND THE SPIES

JOSHUA 2

Joshua was ready to lead God's people into the Promised Land. But first, he sent in secret for two of his bravest men.

"I want you to spy out the land of Canaan," he said. "You must cross the Jordan and find out everything you can."

Forty years earlier, Joshua had been a spy himself. He knew how dangerous it was. "Are you ready for anything?" he asked. The two men nodded. "I want a report on Jericho."

Jericho was the biggest city in Canaan. It stood like a great fortress in the desert, blocking the way into the Promised Land.

The men plunged through the dark river in silence and made their way stealthily into the city. They hid among mules and baggage and piles of crates until they found their way into the home of a woman named Rahab. Her house was built into the city walls. The two men thought they were safe, but someone had seen them. Word came to the king of Jericho: "There are spies in the city, Israelites, come to prepare for battle!"

So the king sent messengers to Rahab. "Bring out your visitors!"

Meanwhile, Rahab had hidden the men on her roof, under piles of drying flax. "I did have two strangers here," she said, "but I have no idea where they were from. They left before nightfall. Why don't you chase after them?"

As soon as the king's men had gone, Rahab went quietly up to the roof. She sat by the bundles of flax and whispered to the two men hiding underneath, "Everyone is afraid of the Israelites! We know that God has given the whole land to you,

and that is why the whole of Jericho is quaking with fear!
We've heard how your God helped you cross the Red Sea, so
when you conquer Jericho, remember me and my family!
Please spare our lives!"

"You save us, and we'll save you!" said the spies. "Tell no
one about us and help us to escape."

So Rahab let the men down from her window with a rope,
slowly and carefully in the darkness of night.

"Hang a scarlet cord from this window when you see the
Israelite army at the gates of Jericho," they told her. "Make sure
all your family are in the house, and you will be saved."

The men dropped softly into the deep, cool sand and then
crawled slowly out of sight. By morning, they were hiding in
the hills, and three days later, they made it back to Joshua.

They gave him their report. "The Lord has given the whole
land to us. All of Jericho is terrified of the people of Israel!"

THE BATTLE OF JERICHO

JOSHUA 3, 5, 6

At long last, the time had come for God's people, the Israelites,
to enter the Promised Land.

God spoke to Joshua, their leader. "When the people see the
wonderful things I am going to do through you," he said, "they
will know that you are my servant."

Joshua did everything that God told him to do. First he told
the priests to carry the ark of the covenant right up to the
banks of the River Jordan, and as soon as their feet touched the

water, the river stopped flowing and dry land appeared. Then all the people walked over in safety.

Only Joshua and Caleb had crossed the Red Sea with Moses. Now the younger Israelites saw that the power of God was with their leader.

They watched him in awe and amazement as he walked on alone ahead of them.

As Joshua neared Jericho, he met a man with a drawn sword. The blade flashed in the sunlight, dazzling Joshua, who shielded his eyes.

"Are you on our side, or on the side of our enemies?" Joshua asked.

"No! I am here as commander of the army of the Lord," said the man.

Then Joshua fell down in fear. "What message do you bring your servant?" he asked.

"Take off your sandals," said the commander, "because you are standing on holy ground." Joshua obeyed. He listened humbly to every word sent from God. "I have delivered Jericho into your power – its king, its soldiers and all its people. This is what you must do. Take your armed men and march once around the city."

He pointed at Jericho with its massive stone walls. It looked impossible to destroy.

"Let seven priests go with your men, carrying rams' horn trumpets and taking the ark of the covenant with them. March around the city like this, each day for six days. Then on the seventh day, march around the city seven times. At the final trumpet blast, let all the Israelites shout at the top of their voices!"

Joshua looked up meekly at the radiant figure in the shimmering heat. "Do that," the commander said softly, "and the walls of Jericho will come crashing down in ruins."

Joshua was alone. Before him was the great city, with soldiers pacing the walls. Behind him were his own armies and thousands of people waiting for his instructions. Would the people believe him? Would they follow this incredible plan and trust that Joshua had been given his instructions by God?

Joshua gave the extraordinary command to the people, and they obeyed him without question. They knew he was their chosen leader and had been in the presence of God.

The citizens of Jericho watched from the walls with a mixture of curiosity and bewilderment as the procession marched around at dawn on the first day. It was strange and troubling. No one invaded, no one unsheathed a sword or fired an arrow. The Israelites just marched and blew their trumpets.

On the second day, they marched again, and on the third, and the fourth, and the fifth, and the sixth.

At last, on the seventh day, Joshua gathered all the Israelite people.

"Today, Jericho is yours," he shouted. "But you must rescue Rahab and all her family. They are hiding in the house with the scarlet cord – they must be saved, because Rahab gave shelter to our spies."

The Israelites watched as their procession of soldiers and priests went around and around. The people of Jericho watched too, confused and angry. Some mocked, some hid, some prayed to their gods, as the whole city waited in fear.

The final trumpet blast sounded, an ear-splitting scream of sound, and suddenly the whole crowd of Israelites – thousands upon thousands – roared into the desert air, shouting the praises of the God of Israel. The walls of Jericho cracked, the foundations buckled, towers came tumbling, scattering stones, hurling dust into the sky. The great barricade of stone, hundreds of years old, collapsed with a furious thundering boom.

So the Israelites poured into the city, while Rahab and her family – showered with dust – were led to safety by the two spies, just as they had promised.

GOD'S LEADER

JOSHUA 7–9

There were other tribes living in the Promised Land, and Joshua won many great victories. Through his daring and courage, and his faithfulness to God, the land which Moses had seen from a long way off was conquered. Under Joshua's leadership, the Israelites lived in safety.

Other tribes in Canaan were in great fear of Joshua and his victorious army – so much so that one local tribe, the Gibeonites, came up with a clever plan to fool them. They did not want to be killed by the conquering Israelites.

This tribe sent a band of men to Joshua, dressed in old clothes and wearing patched sandals. The men led donkeys laden with dusty old sacks and wineskins. They pretended that they had come from far away.

"We've heard of your great exploits," they said. "Our people have sent us a long way to meet you, because your God is powerful. Please sign a treaty and make peace with us."

Joshua and the other Israelite leaders were a little suspicious. "What if you're a local tribe and you're trying to trick us?"

"Look at our worn-out wineskins, our tattered clothes!" they said. "We're exhausted from our long journey!"

Foolishly, Joshua and the Israelites did not pray to God and ask him what to do. So Joshua signed a peace treaty with the strangers, and the Israelite leaders swore an oath before God to keep it.

A few days later, the Israelites discovered that they had been cheated by a nearby tribe, and they were very angry. But Joshua said, "We have sworn an oath. We must keep our word to them whatever they have done."

Then Joshua said to the Gibeonites, "Because you have cheated your way into peace with us, you will have to be our servants and work hard for us."

The Gibeonites agreed. Because of the Israelites' success in battle, they were glad for peace on any terms. So Joshua kept his word, and the crafty Gibeonites escaped death.

FOLLOWING GOD

JOSHUA 23, 24

Before he died, Joshua gathered all the leaders of the Israelites together.

There were twelve tribes descended from Jacob's sons, and Joshua shared out the land between them with great fairness.

He said to the leaders, "If you obey God in everything, he will give you victory. All the remaining land will become yours, and no one will be able to defeat you. But if you turn to other gods, bowing down to idols, then you will lose everything."

"We will serve only the Lord God!" they said.

Then Joshua called all the people together in one place and gave them the same warning. "Look what the Lord has done for you," he said. "Serve him faithfully – have nothing to do with the gods of the people of Canaan, idols of stone and wood! Worship the true God and follow his commandments."

All the people nodded and agreed, but Joshua stared at them hard. He knew how weak they were, how easy it was to give up following God.

"Perhaps you don't want to serve him?" he asked. "Perhaps it's too hard for you?"

"No, it isn't," they said. "We will follow the Lord!"

"You must choose," said Joshua, "whether to follow the Lord or to go after other gods, but as for me and my family, we will serve the Lord!" "So will we!" chorused all the people, but Joshua still looked at them sternly. "You know that the Lord will not share your love and your obedience with any other god. And if you turn away from him, he will bring disaster upon you!"

"We won't turn away," the people shouted. "No, we will serve him faithfully forever!"

"Very well," said Joshua. "You are witnesses then – this is your agreement with the Lord your God. Keep to it!"

Soon after this, Joshua died at the age of one hundred and ten years. Throughout his leadership, he had faithfully served God, and the people had followed his example. Now God's people were settled in the land God had given them. The future lay in their hands, a bright future, if only they could remain loyal to God.

THE JUDGES

After the time of Joshua, with the passing of the years, children grew up who did not remember him. Sadly, the Israelites began to forget all their promises to serve God. They began to marry into foreign tribes and worship idols. They broke the commandments and laws which God had given to Moses and which Joshua had taught them.

Many of the Israelites forgot that God had called them to be a special people, serving only him. So a time came when they were weakened and often defeated by their enemies. Kings and warlords of the other tribes who lived in Canaan raided their villages and farms, and sometimes they became like slaves in the land they had once conquered.

But despite their failures and their sins, God still loved his people, and from time to time he sent the Israelites brave leaders, "judges" as they were sometimes known. These men and women helped the Israelites to give up their disobedient ways and turn back to God.

There was a time when their enemies, the Moabites, joined forces with the Amalekites and the Ammonites and captured Jericho. For eighteen long years, the Israelites were forced to bring precious gifts and money as tribute to Eglon, the king of the Moabites.

The Israelites cried out in desperation, "O Lord God, send us a deliverer! Save us from our enemies!" So God gave special courage and cunning to one man, Ehud, who found an unusual way to save his people.

Ehud was chosen to take the tribute to King Eglon, carts of gold, spices, fine linen and the best of the harvest. He arrived at the palace with his Israelite companions. When they had presented the lavish offering, Ehud sent all his men home. He turned to the king and said, "I have a secret message for you."

King Eglon was curious. He commanded everyone to leave. Then he took Ehud quickly into his private rooms.

"Well," he said, "go on – tell me your secret message."

"It's an important message," whispered Ehud, and with his left hand he reached over to a hidden sword on his right thigh. The king, not realizing that Ehud was left-handed, suspected nothing. Suddenly, Ehud drew the sword and shouted, "A message from the Lord God!" and plunged the blade into the fat belly of the king.

Then Ehud locked the doors of the king's private rooms and escaped through a back room. King Eglon's servants were sure their master had locked his own doors, so it was a long time before they dared to break in. But when they did so, they found the king dead on the floor.

And so Ehud gathered all the Israelites together and said, "The Lord has delivered the enemy into your hands!" That day, they fought a great battle against the Moabites. Because of Ehud's daring, they were free once again, and he became their chosen leader.

Ehud was one of the first of many judges.

TWO BRAVE WOMEN

JUDGES 4, 5

Another time, when the Israelite people were in great trouble again, God sent a wise and courageous woman named Deborah to their rescue. She sorted out every argument and problem and became famous as the best judge in Israel.

Deborah watched as Jabin, the king of the Canaanites, invaded their land with his huge army. She saw how his general, Sisera, boasted of his nine hundred iron chariots and all his warriors. None of the Israelites was brave enough to fight against them, so she prayed to God for wisdom and formed a battle plan with great daring.

Deborah sent a message to Barak, one of the Israelite leaders and a great soldier, saying, "The Lord God commands you, 'March to Mount Tabor with ten thousand soldiers! For I will lure Sisera with all his chariots and troops into the Kishon river and give them into your power!'"

But Barak did not have the courage to follow Deborah's advice. He wanted to follow her in person: "I will only go into battle if you lead the way."

"All right," said Deborah. "But because you have asked me to do this, the glory of this victory will not go to you. God will deliver Sisera into the hands of a woman."

So Barak set off up Mount Tabor with ten thousand soldiers. They were ready to do battle with Sisera, who soon followed with all his men and his chariots.

That day, Barak and Deborah won a great battle. All

Sisera's men were killed, and their chariots were mired in the mud of the river.

Only Sisera escaped. He fled on foot, finally running into the tent of a woman named Jael.

"Please hide me here," he begged. "Don't tell anyone there's a man staying in your tent." Jael gave him food and milk and blankets, and eventually he fell asleep, exhausted. But Jael was no friend of Sisera. As soon as she saw that he was fast asleep, she took a large tent peg and a hammer and drove the peg through his head. Sisera was dead.

Deborah's prophecy had come true. A woman had won the victory for the people of Israel.

AN UNLIKELY HERO

JUDGES 6

Time and again, the Israelites slipped back into idol worship; they built altars to Baal, the Canaanite god of the harvest, and prayed for good luck. They put up sacred poles to the mother-goddess, Asherah, and made offerings to rain and sun gods. They did not remember what God had done for them or try to follow him any longer.

So God allowed the tribes of Midian to invade the plains of Jezreel. There were so many Midianites, and their tents were so numerous that they seemed like a plague of locusts, and like locusts, they ate everything in sight. They ravaged the crops of the Israelites, stealing what they could and burning the rest, until the Israelites were forced to hide in caves in the hills.

One day, a young Israelite man named Gideon was threshing corn secretly because he was so afraid of the Midianites. He was hiding in a winepress when he heard a voice near him. Immediately he cowered in the darkness. He was sure it was another robbery – there had been so many – but the voice was speaking to him, very distinctly. "The Lord God is with you, O valiant warrior!"

Gideon peered out of the winepress, puzzled by this greeting and by the stranger who stood, mysterious and alone, like a visitor from a distant land. He couldn't quite see the stranger's face against the dazzling sun, but he climbed out of the winepress and replied, "Excuse me, sir, but if the Lord God is with us, why are these terrible things happening? Where are all the wonderful miracles which our ancestors told us about, when they crossed the Red Sea and found food in the desert?" Gideon shook his head and continued, "God has deserted us and we have been thrown into the hands of the Midianites!"

"You yourself will rescue Israel from the power of Midian," said the angel, for that was what he was.

"Me?" said Gideon, half-laughing, half-afraid.

"The Lord God himself is sending you," replied the angel.

"But... but... forgive me, sir, but my clan is the weakest in the tribe of Manasseh and I am the least important person in my whole family and –"

"I shall be with you!" said the angel of God. "You will crush the forces of Midian as if they were a single man."

Then Gideon became afraid, because now the stranger was speaking as if he were God himself!

"My Lord," he stammered, "please prove to me that it is really you... give me a sign." He hurried off, saying, "Wait here. I'll come back with an offering for you."

Then Gideon returned with bread and meat and put it upon a rock. The angel touched the offering with the tip of his staff and at once fire came out of the rock and burned everything up. Then the angel vanished.

Gideon was overwhelmed with fear, but he heard a voice saying, "Be at peace, don't be afraid." So there he built an altar and named it The Lord Is Peace.

At the command of God, Gideon destroyed the altar to Baal which belonged to his own family and built a new altar. Then he called together his family and tribe to prepare for war against the Midianites.

GOD'S VICTORY

JUDGES 6–8

The Israelites wondered where Gideon's new courage had come from, but before the great battle against the Midianites he was still very fearful.

Secretly, he asked God for another sign. "If you really are saving Israel through me," Gideon said, "then let me put down a goat skin on the ground tonight. If there is dew on the goat skin tomorrow morning, but none on the grass all around, I will know you are with me." So Gideon put down the goat skin, and in the morning it was soaking wet and the ground was bone dry.

"Forgive me, O Lord God," he said. "Please just give me *one* more sign! Do it the other way around and then I'll be absolutely sure." So he put the goat skin down again, and in the morning the opposite had happened – the goat skin was bone dry and the grass was soaking wet.

Now Gideon was ready to face the enemy, so he gathered a huge army of thirty-two thousand men. But God had not finished with Gideon yet.

"You have too many men," said God. "I do not want the Israelites to boast of *their* great victory. I will win the battle for you."

God told Gideon to allow anyone who was afraid of the battle to return home. So twenty-two thousand men left, leaving ten thousand.

"There are still too many," said God. Gideon was astonished, because the Midianite camp seemed to stretch forever towards the horizon, and the Amalekites and tribes from the east had joined them. Ten thousand men would hardly be enough, but God said, "Make the men drink at the river. Anyone who stands up and laps the water out of his hands like a dog can stay, but send home all the rest who kneel down to drink." When Gideon had finished separating the men, he was left with only three hundred.

God knew that Gideon was secretly very afraid, so he told him to creep down to the Midianite camp that night and listen. Hiding outside a tent in the dark, Gideon overheard two men talking. One said, "I dreamed that a little loaf of barley rolled downhill and flattened one of our tents!"

The other said, "This is a message that Gideon will defeat us all with his army!"

It was the final sign from God. Now Gideon was full of courage and confidence, and he said to all his men, "On your feet at once! The Lord has given the enemy into our power!"

Immediately he sent his men all around the valley, each one

holding a trumpet and an empty jar with a torch burning inside.

They surrounded the camp, and at Gideon's signal, they all blew their trumpets together and smashed their jars and shouted, "The sword of the Lord and of Gideon!"

The din of the breaking pottery, the trumpets and shouts, and the sudden flare of the torchlights in the darkness made the Midianites wake up with a start, terrified that they were being invaded by thousands of warriors. In their panic and confusion they turned on each other, killing their own men and fleeing in terror.

The victory was so great, and Gideon's pursuit of all the enemies of the Israelites was so successful, that the people came to him and begged him to become their king.

"I will not rule over you," said Gideon, "nor will my son. The Lord God is your king!"

From being a frightened young man, Gideon had become a great leader of his people because he had trusted in the power of God.

THE BIRTH OF SAMSON

JUDGES 13

Long after Gideon's victory came a time when no one listened to God and evil spread through the land. The Philistines conquered the Israelites and ruled over them for forty years.

During that time, an angel of the Lord appeared to the wife of an Israelite man named Manoah, a good man who served God.

The angel told her that, although she was infertile and had no children, she would give birth to a son, who would begin to save God's people from their enemies, the Philistines. The angel gave her many instructions about how the boy was to be brought up. He was to live by very special rules. Then the angel vanished as mysteriously as he had come.

The woman ran to her husband, trembling and afraid.

"What's happened?" he said.

"A man…" she said, but she did not know how to describe him. "An angel has come… He was so majestic, so bright!"

Now Manoah was afraid. "What is this? What did he say?"

"He said I was going to have a baby, and the child must be dedicated to God. He must follow the rules of the Nazarites and never cut his hair or take any strong drink. He must serve God all his life!"

Later, the angel appeared to Manoah as well and repeated God's promise about the boy. Manoah and his wife were filled with fear and excitement.

Before long, Manoah's wife gave birth to a boy, and they named him Samson. As the child grew up, God kept his promise and prepared Samson to serve him.

A DANGEROUS GAME

JUDGES 14, 15

Even before he was born, God told Samson's parents that he would start to defeat the Philistines. They brought him up according to the rules of the Nazarites; one of the rules was that he should never cut his hair. Some of the leaders of Israel had wisdom, and some had great cunning, but Samson was given the gift of strength. No man had ever been stronger, and when the Spirit of God came upon him, Samson could not be defeated.

But Samson had a great weakness; he often fell in love with the wrong women, Philistine women who wanted to betray him and his people.

On one occasion, Samson fell in love with a Philistine girl from Timnah and decided to marry her. His parents begged him to marry an Israelite, but he insisted on visiting the Philistine girl. On his way to Timnah, a young lion leaped out of the rocks, roaring and snarling, ready to kill him. Samson grabbed the beast in his bare hands as if it were a young goat and ripped it to pieces, leaving the carcass by the roadside. A few days later, he returned that way and noticed that a swarm of bees had made a nest inside the lion's carcass. He put his hand in, took out some honeycomb and ate it.

This gave him the idea for a riddle, and at his wedding he challenged thirty Philistine warriors to solve it. "If you can give me the answer within seven days, then I will reward you richly." They agreed, so he set the riddle before them:

"Out of the eater came something to eat;
Out of the strong came something sweet."

After four days, the men were enraged with frustration. They couldn't work it out at all, so they went to Samson's bride and said, "Have you invited us to your wedding to rob us? Persuade your husband to tell you the secret, or we'll burn you and your father's family to death!" She was terrified, and night after night she sobbed and clung to Samson, begging him to unlock the

130

riddle. At last he gave in, and she immediately went to tell the young men.

Triumphantly, they said to Samson, "What is sweeter than honey; what is stronger than a lion?"

Samson knew then that he had been betrayed. In his fury, he went off and killed thirty Philistine warriors in the city of Ashkelon, took their robes and handed them to the men of Timnah.

When his wife's family refused to let him see her again, he took his revenge by capturing three hundred foxes and tying burning torches to their tails. The creatures ran through the orchards and vineyards of the Philistines and destroyed them with fire.

Samson's own people from Judah sent thousands of warriors to arrest him and take him to the Philistines as a hostage because they were terrified of a war with their masters. They tied Samson up with strong new ropes, but he merely snapped them like pieces of string and flung them aside. That day, he took the jawbone of a donkey and killed a thousand Philistine men. For the next twenty years, Samson was the leader of the Israelites.

SAMSON AND DELILAH

JUDGES 16

Samson's strength was known throughout the land. The Israelites knew that God had given Samson his power and that he had been brought up to serve God. As a sign of his dedication, he had never cut his hair. But Samson fell in love with another Philistine woman, Delilah. He was so besotted with her that his enemies, the Philistines, realized that he would do anything for her.

They sent their leaders to Delilah, offering her a fabulous reward if she could discover the secret of Samson's amazing strength.

That night, she lay beside him, laughing softly, teasing him. "You're so handsome," she said, "so incredibly strong, you must have a secret. You must have some hidden power!"

"What is that to you?" said Samson.

"You're everything to me," murmured Delilah. "All I want to know is your little secret."

"Very well," he said at last. "If you tied me up with seven new bowstrings, I would lose my strength and become like an ordinary man."

Delilah crept away, smiling to herself, and told the Philistine warriors who were hiding in her house. While he was asleep, Delilah tied Samson up with seven new bowstrings. But when she woke him, he just snapped the strings and flung them away.

"You're making fun of me," she said. "You're lying to me because you don't love me." So Samson told her to tie him up with strong new ropes, but he broke those too. Then he teased her again, promising that if she wove his hair into a loom, all his strength would melt away. But when he awoke later, he simply pulled his hair free from the loom and stood there as powerful and as frightening as ever. The Philistine soldiers, waiting nearby to attack Samson, were left cowering in terror.

Delilah became angry and sorrowful by turns: she accused Samson of hating her, she wept, she hugged him and stroked him, then ran away from him in tears until he could stand her nagging and pleading no longer.

"All right," he shouted. "I'll tell you – but only you – my deepest secret, the truth about my power!"

She sat down, stroking his long hair lovingly as he confessed that all his strength lay in those dark locks, that if his head were shaved, he would immediately become weak. For by doing this, the vow his parents made to God before he was born would be broken. Delilah soothed him to sleep with promises of love, tenderly stroking his forehead; then she called a man to cut away every lock of hair until it lay deep and thick around her feet. At once, she called the Philistine soldiers, who took hold of Samson. When he woke up, Samson did not realize that his strength had gone, that the Spirit of God had left him. He flailed his arms at them, tried to push them away and kill them, but they had him in their power.

The Philistines blinded Samson. Then they took him in triumph to their capital city of Gaza, where they chained him and set him to work grinding grain in the prison.

FREEDOM IN DEATH

JUDGES 16

Blind and weak, Samson served out his last days hauling a massive mill wheel in the dungeons of Gaza prison. In the darkness there, the endless darkness of his mind, he longed to know God's power once again and bitterly regretted all that he had done. Delilah had tricked him into betraying the God of Israel, the true God.

Outside, he could hear the chants of the Philistine crowds: "Into our hands, the god Dagon has delivered Samson our enemy!"

But God had not abandoned him forever. One day, the Philistine rulers were having a festival, and they called for Samson to entertain them. "Let the strong man come and bring us some merriment!" they shouted.

A boy led Samson by the hand, down the prison corridors, out into the sunshine, across to he great temple where three thousand people had gathered on the roof to jeer at Samson.

No one remembered that the secret of his strength lay in his uncut hair and his vow to serve God. No one noticed that his hair had begun to grow again.

"Guide my hands to the two great pillars," said Samson to the boy, "so I can lean on them." The crowds were shouting down at him, laughing and spitting. Then Samson prayed out loud to God, "O Lord, I beg you, remember me one more time; give me back my strength so I can take vengeance on these Philistines!"

Then he grabbed the pillars with both hands, braced his arms against them and heaved and pushed the massive columns until they cracked apart, and the whole temple collapsed in ruins.

So it was that Samson, the blinded hero of Israel, killed more Philistines on that single day than in his whole lifetime.

RUTH AND NAOMI

In the days when the judges ruled Israel, there was a famine.
The harvest was so bad that a man named Elimelech left the
town of Bethlehem in search of food. He settled in the plains of
Moab with his wife, Naomi, and their two sons.

They were just starting their new life when Elimelech died
suddenly. Naomi was grief-stricken, but her two sons
comforted her. Soon, the sons married Moabite girls, Orpah
and Ruth, and Naomi began to look forward to grandchildren.
But there were no children, and then tragedy struck again.
Both her sons fell sick and died, so Naomi was left alone in a
foreign country, desperately poor and broken-hearted.

Orpah and Ruth loved their mother-in-law dearly and tried
to console her, but Naomi just shook her head. She felt that
God had dealt with her very harshly, and she would weep and
sit alone and stare into the distance.

"There is nothing for me here," Naomi said. "I must return
to my own people in Bethlehem."

The two young women followed her down the road, but she
stopped and said, "Go back, daughters! You must find new
husbands – perhaps the Lord will show kindness to you for all
that you have done for me." Then she turned away and
walked on, but Orpah and Ruth burst out crying and ran after
her. "No, no," she pleaded with them. "Go home! I'm too old
to marry again and have sons for you!"

So Orpah kissed Naomi gently and turned back towards
Moab. But Ruth clung to her.

"Your sister-in-law is going back to her people and her gods," said Naomi. "Go back with her."

"Never!" said Ruth, and she looked at Naomi, her eyes full of tears. "Never! I will never leave you! Where you go, I will go, and where you live, I will live. Your people will be my people and your God will be my God. Nothing but death shall ever separate me from you."

Naomi looked at Ruth, astonished at her great love and her loyalty. She shook her head, knowing that she had nothing but poverty and sadness to offer her. But Ruth continued to walk beside her.

When Naomi saw that Ruth was determined to go with her, she stopped protesting. So the two women walked on to Bethlehem.

RUTH IN BETHLEHEM

RUTH 1, 2

When Naomi and Ruth arrived in Bethlehem, the people said, "Can this be Naomi who left with her husband and two sons?" They could not believe that the poor, frail woman full of grief was the same person. And they were surprised to see her daughter-in-law, Ruth, with her. Why had she left the land of Moab to come here?

Naomi and Ruth settled in Naomi's old house. It was covered in dust and weeds and half-ruined, but Ruth cleaned it up and made it as comfortable as possible.

The barley harvest was just beginning. In those days, the

poor people of Israel had the right to follow the harvesters and pick up any grain that fell on the ground, so Ruth went out to the fields. That evening, they would be able to make bread with the grain she had gleaned.

Ruth found a field and gleaned all day. Later on, the owner of the field, a man named Boaz, noticed her.

"Who's that young woman?" he asked. She was different from all the other gleaners, dark and beautiful, although dressed very poorly. Boaz could see that she was a stranger.

"It's the young woman from Moab," the gleaners said, "the daughter-in-law of Naomi."

"Naomi?" Boaz was curious. He was related to Naomi by marriage, and he had heard of the wonderful love which Ruth had shown to her widowed mother-in-law.

Boaz said to Ruth, "You are very welcome to come each day to this field." And he told her that he knew how much she had done for Naomi. "May the Lord repay you for what you have done!" he said to Ruth. "May you be richly rewarded by the Lord God of Israel, under whose wings you have sought shelter!"

The way he spoke so tenderly to her made Ruth cry. She brushed her tears away. "O sir," she said, "you have given me so much comfort, speaking like that, although I am much less important than your own serving girls."

Boaz made sure that Ruth had plenty of grain, almost more than she could carry, and when she returned home, Naomi asked in amazement, "Where did you glean today? Blessed is the man who gave you all this!"

"I worked in the field of a man named Boaz," Ruth said.

"Do you know who he is?" said Naomi. "He is one of our closest relatives." Now it was Naomi's turn to cry for joy,

because God had guided Ruth to someone who could help
save them from their misfortune.

RUTH AND BOAZ

RUTH 3, 4

Naomi could see that Ruth was impressed by Boaz, and she
realized that Boaz was showing more and more kindness to
Ruth. One day, she said to Ruth, "It's time for you to find your
own home now."

"What do you mean?" asked Ruth. Naomi smiled and said,
"Just do what I say. Tonight, all the workers will sleep in the
open to guard the grain. Wash yourself, put on perfume and
your best clothes, and go secretly to the threshing floor. Wait
till Boaz comes away from the feasting and lies down to sleep
under the stars. Then, very quietly, settle down at his feet until
he wakes up."

It was a strange instruction, but Ruth obeyed Naomi without
question. She knew it had to do with an ancient custom, but
she did not know what would happen, or if Boaz would be
angry with her.

Sure enough, Boaz woke up in the middle of the night to
find a young woman lying at his feet.

"Who is it?" he said, alarmed.

"It's Ruth, my Lord."

"Ruth? But…"

"You are one of my closest relatives, sir," she said. "You have
the responsibility of looking after me and my family." Ruth, a

woman from Moab, wanted to live by the laws of the God of
Israel. These said that if a man died, his closest relative should
marry his widow so that the family line would not die out.

Boaz was amazed and deeply moved by her courage and her
love.

"You could have gone after any other man," he said to her,
"but because of your love for Naomi, you have come to me."

There was another close relative also, but Boaz went and
settled his right to take over all the property of Elimelech,
Naomi's dead husband, and so claim Ruth as his wife.

Ruth and Boaz were happily married, and the people rejoiced.
They prayed for God's blessing on Ruth, and before long she gave
birth to a son. The little boy was named Obed. He became the
father of Jesse, and Jesse became the father of the great king David.

A BABY FOR HANNAH

1 SAMUEL 1

In the time of the judges, people went to worship God at
Shiloh. Every year, a man named Elkanah went there to offer a
sacrifice to God with his two wives, Peninnah and Hannah.

And every year, Peninnah made fun of Hannah, taunting and
mocking her because she had no children. Hannah became
desperately sad. She cried and refused to eat.

"Why are you crying, Hannah?" her husband said, "Why
don't you eat? Isn't my love worth more to you than ten sons?"

It was true that Elkanah loved her very much, but nothing
would comfort Hannah. She struggled with her grief every day,

a grief that grew more painful when she visited Shiloh. There, in that holy place where people offered sacrifices to God, she wondered if he had forgotten all about her.

"You'll never have children!" Peninnah said. "Perhaps God doesn't care for you."

In those days, children were seen as a sign of God's blessing, so all the taunting made Hannah feel that God could not love her.

Then one day, as Hannah stood outside the temple at Shiloh weeping and praying, she cried out to God, "O Lord God Almighty, remember me! Please look down on your servant. Have mercy – look at my sorrow and my misery!"

She was praying silently and she was shaking and wandering around in anguish. She did not see the old high priest, Eli, looking at her disapprovingly, but carried on, "O Lord God, have pity on your servant! I beg you to give me a son, and if you do, I promise that I will give him back to you forever. He will serve you all the days of his life!"

Eli stood up. Who was this woman? She was staggering around and talking to herself, and she was clearly very drunk.

"Stop your drinking!" he said, "Get rid of your wine – this is a holy place."

"No, my Lord," she said, "I am not drunk. I am in great trouble and I am pouring out my heart to God!"

Suddenly, Eli realized he had made a mistake. "Then go in peace," he said gently. "Go in peace, woman, and may the Lord God of Israel answer your prayers."

From that moment, Hannah wiped away her tears, began to eat again and felt glad because she knew that God was listening to her prayers after all.

GOD CALLS SAMUEL

1 SAMUEL 1–3

God answered Hannah's desperate prayer, and before long she gave birth to a boy. She named him Samuel. She kept the promise she had made to God, and when Samuel was old enough, she took him to the temple at Shiloh to live with Eli.

The old high priest was amazed, but she said, "I am the woman who prayed here, and the Lord has graciously answered my prayers! So now I am giving Samuel back to the Lord forever." Before leaving Shiloh, Hannah gave thanks to God for Samuel's life. And when she went home, she prayed for him each day.

Every year, Hannah made Samuel a new little robe and brought gifts for Eli, and the old man prayed to God that Hannah would have more children, because of her faithfulness to God. In time, Hannah had three more sons and two daughters.

Samuel lived with Eli, the high priest, in the temple, serving him and helping the old man in everything he did. Eli's two sons lived with him at Shiloh, but they did not serve God in the right way. They were greedy and they stole the meat given for sacrifices. They did not listen to Eli.

One night, Samuel was lying down in the temple, where he always slept, when he heard a voice.

"Samuel! Samuel!"

Samuel got up and ran to Eli. "Here I am," he said, "you called me."

"I didn't call you," said Eli, "go back to bed."

Samuel went and lay down again.

"Samuel! Samuel!" the voice called again, so Samuel got up and ran to Eli.

"Here I am," he said.

"I didn't call you, my child. Go back to bed."

Samuel obeyed, but he knew he wasn't dreaming.

The next time the voice was even louder and closer. "Samuel! Samuel!" The boy got up and looked all around him. There was enough light from the temple lamp to see that no one else was in the room. He ran to Eli again.

"Here I am," he said. "You did call me!"

"No, no," said Eli. Then he realized that God himself was speaking to Samuel. "Go back, my child, and if you hear the voice again say, 'Speak, Lord, because your servant is listening.'"

Samuel went back to bed. The voice called again, a murmur in his ear: "Samuel! Samuel!"

"Speak, Lord," said the boy. "I am your servant and I am listening!"

Then God told Samuel that Eli's time as high priest and judge of Israel was coming to an end, because his sons had been disobedient and Eli had failed to control them.

The next morning, Eli came to Samuel. "What did the Lord say?" he asked. Samuel was scared to tell him, but Eli said, "You must tell me the whole truth. Everything!"

Reluctantly, the boy told him. The old man accepted God's judgment, saying, "The Lord knows what is right." He knew that God had chosen Samuel to lead Israel instead of his own wicked sons. Samuel would be the next judge, a priest and a prophet.

THE ARK IS CAPTURED

1 Samuel 4–6

Eli, the old high priest at Shiloh, was ninety-eight years old when he made a terrible mistake which led to his own death. For many years, the ark of the covenant had been in the temple at Shiloh. The ark was holy, a sacred box that held God's laws. It was a sign of God's presence with his chosen people.

Eli was a good man, but he was weak, blind and very old. The Israelites were constantly at war with the Philistines at that time, and Eli allowed the Israelites to take the ark away from the temple and into battle without the blessing of God. His two sons stood beside the ark, as if they were very holy men surrounded by the presence of God. The result of the battle was not what the Israelites expected: the Philistine armies defeated the Israelites, Eli's sons were killed, along with thousands of other Israelites, and the ark was captured.

A messenger took the news to Eli. The blind old man was sitting beside the temple gate. Hearing the messenger gasping for breath, Eli asked, "What is it? What's happened?"

"The battle... is lost..." The messenger stood there weeping. "Thirty thousand men lost! Your sons are dead and the ark of God has been taken!"

Eli was so shocked when he heard that the ark had been captured that he lost his balance, fell backwards and broke his neck.

Back at their city, the Philistines celebrated their great victory. They danced around the ark and placed it in front of their god

Dagon, thinking they had won power over Israel's God. But their joy soon turned to terror. The great idol of Dagon fell down into the dust in front of the ark. They put the statue back up, but the next day they found it smashed in pieces, the head and the arms of the huge stone statue snapped off like twigs.

The Philistines tried to keep the ark safely in one place after another, but in each place terrible plagues came upon them and hundreds of them died.

They were frightened and desperate to get rid of the ark, so they put it on the back of an ox-cart laden with peace offerings of gold. They were too scared to walk with the cart, so they left the oxen on their own to take the ark back to the Israelites, while they watched from a safe distance.

The Israelites rejoiced when they saw the ark returning mysteriously alone – they felt sure that God was with them once again.

ISRAEL ASKS FOR A KING

1 Samuel 8

Samuel was the last of the great judges of Israel. The people came to Samuel and said, "We want a king!"

"A king?" Samuel was shocked. God was the King of Israel. Why did they want a man to be king?

"Your sons are no good as judges – they are not wise or honest or fair, and we don't trust them. We want a great king, like other nations have, to lead us into battle!"

Samuel went away sorrowfully and prayed to God all

144

night. "The people have turned against me – all they do is shout for a king: 'Give us a king!'"

"They are not rejecting you," said God. "They are turning their backs on me, their true King, but if they want a king so badly, then let them have one!"

"But Lord," Samuel pleaded, "a king will lead them into disaster."

"You must warn them," said God. "Tell them exactly what it will be like."

So Samuel went to the people and told them, "A king will make slaves of your sons and daughters, he will take a tenth of your money and your possessions for himself, he'll demand the best of your cattle and your donkeys and your servants for himself! Is that what you want?"

"We know what we want," they said. "We want a king! A king who will lead us to great victories!"

Samuel sighed. He looked at their stubborn faces, then walked away to pray once more.

"Listen to them," said God, "and let them have their king."

GOD CHOOSES SAUL

1 Samuel 9, 10

Samuel did not want to face the difficult task of finding a king, but he knew he must obey God.

"I will send the man to you," said God. "He will come from the tribe of Benjamin, and you must anoint him as king."

Now there was a young man from the tribe of Benjamin named Saul. He was tall and handsome. One day, his father lost two donkeys, and Saul went with a servant to search for them. They searched for several days and journeyed many miles, without finding the donkeys, until they came to the place where Samuel lived.

"Let's ask the prophet of God where they are," said the servant. "He's a wise man."

When Samuel looked at Saul, he heard the word of God whispering, "This is the man!"

"Do not worry about your donkeys," said Samuel. "They have already been found. But you are the man that the whole of Israel is looking for!"

"Why me?" said Saul, very troubled. "I am from the smallest tribe in Israel and my father is only a poor farmer." Samuel smiled but said no more. Then he invited Saul to eat with him.

The next morning, Samuel took Saul aside in secret. "God has chosen you as king, to protect his people. His spirit will be with you!" Then he took out a flask of oil and poured it on Saul's head.

Despite all this, Saul was still worried. He was so afraid of being king that when Samuel gathered all the people together to choose their ruler, he ran off and hid.

Samuel addressed the crowds, then ordered them, "Separate into your tribes and clans and families."

The people did so, and gradually Samuel worked through every tribe until the tribe of Benjamin was chosen, and then Saul's family... and finally Saul himself.

But Saul was nowhere to be seen. The man, who was so tall he was head and shoulders above everybody else, had gone.

God told Samuel, "He's hiding over there." So Samuel brought him out.

"This is the man the Lord God has chosen!" he shouted.

And the people roared, "Long live the king!"

Saul stood there quietly, reluctantly. He knew it would be the most difficult thing of all to be king and to lead God's people.

A PROMISING START

1 Samuel 10, 11

Most of the people of Israel were delighted that Saul was their new king, and they brought him presents to celebrate the beginning of his reign. But not everyone was happy. "Who does he think he is?" some said. "Why does Saul have to be our king? He's not from an important family!"

Saul ignored them and with God's help very soon proved his right to be king. When the Israelite city of Jabesh was attacked by the Ammonite army, the Israelites were trapped inside the city. The leaders of the city begged for peace.

"Peace?" said the Ammonite leader. "You want peace? Then come out here and I'll blind every one of you in exchange for peace!"

It was a terrible bargain to strike, and the leaders of the city sent a message throughout Israel calling for help. The cruel Ammonite leader laughed because he thought the Israelites were weak and had no leader. But when Saul heard about his threats, he was extremely angry and sent out orders that every tribe should send him fighting men. If they disobeyed, they would be punished.

Before long, three hundred thousand Israelites and thirty thousand men from the tribe of Judah joined Saul and set out to relieve the city of Jabesh. The Ammonites were expecting the Israelites in the city to surrender, but Saul and his army took them by surprise early in the morning and destroyed them all.

The people of Jabesh ran out of their city, shouting for joy, and many of the Israelites demanded that the people who had questioned Saul's kingship should be put to death.

"No!" said Saul. "No one will be punished, because today God has rescued Israel!"

SAUL DISOBEYS GOD

1 Samuel 13, 15

Now Saul had great power and influence over his people. But soon things began to go very wrong, just as Samuel had predicted.

The first time was before another battle with the Philistines. Saul was supposed to wait for the prophet Samuel to arrive and offer sacrifices to God before going into battle. The army was growing restless and afraid, and because Samuel was late and the Philistines looked so powerful, many of the men began to run away and hide in rocks and caves.

Saul stared at the horizon, but all he could see were the chariots and horsemen of the Philistines. He grew impatient.

"Why should I wait for Samuel?" he said. "I don't need a priest now. I'm king and I can do everything." So he prepared the offering himself. Just as he was finishing, Samuel arrived.

"O Saul!" he said. "You foolish man! If only you had obeyed God, you and your descendants would have been kings forever."

"I was only asking for God's help in the battle," said Saul, but Samuel looked at him sorrowfully and in deep despair.

"The Lord God has already found another man to be king," he shook his head sadly at Saul, "a man after his own heart who will serve him!"

Saul went on to win many victories, but more and more he did things his own way, ignoring what Samuel told him about God's wishes.

After a while, Samuel rarely visited Saul, but the last time he came, it was to tell Saul that God had rejected him as king.

Saul had been told to wage war against the Amalekites, a wild and savage people who had been raiding and killing the Israelites from the earliest days. His orders from Samuel were that he was to take no prisoners and no plunder, to destroy everything. But Saul took the king of the Amalekites prisoner and brought back many of the best sheep and goats and cattle for himself.

Samuel came to him in anger. "Why have you done this? Why can I hear sheep bleating and cattle lowing?"

"Oh..." said Saul hastily, "those! Well, they're for the sacrifices. I've kept the best ones so I can offer them to God."

"Do you think God wants your burnt offerings?" asked Samuel, walking away from him for the last time. "No, he wants your obedience! He wants your heart!"

"Wait, please," said Saul desperately. "I know I've done wrong, but stay here and worship God with me... for the sake of appearances, just so the people can see I'm still God's chosen ruler!"

So Samuel stayed with Saul one last time, but then he left, sad and heavy-hearted, knowing that Saul's reign over Israel was doomed. Samuel never saw Saul again.

DAVID THE SHEPHERD BOY

1 SAMUEL 16

Samuel sat alone in the darkness of his home in Ramah. He had been weeping for many days. What would become of Israel now?

Once again, the voice of God came to him: "Samuel, how much longer will you go on mourning for Saul? I have rejected him as king, and you must go to Bethlehem."

"Bethlehem?" Samuel was surprised. It was a small village high in the hills, a place for shepherds and their sheep.

"Take a flask of oil and go to the household of Jesse. I have chosen a king from among his sons, and you must anoint him."

Samuel was worried that Saul might find out and be angry, but he obeyed at once. When he arrived in Bethlehem, Jesse was astonished and afraid. Why had the great prophet of Israel come into his humble home? Was some disaster about to happen?

"Don't be afraid," said Samuel, "I come in peace. Bring your sons to me."

Jesse had eight sons, and so he brought the eldest first. His name was Eliab and he was very strong, tall and handsome.

This must be the one! thought Samuel, but then he heard the word of the Lord softly whispering like the wind in his mind, "Do not be deceived by appearances! I am not impressed by height and good looks. No, I look deeply into the heart!"

So Samuel asked to see the second son, Abinadab, and he too was striking and powerful.

"Not this one," said God.

And so Jesse presented all his sons, one by one, but God did not choose any of them.

Samuel was troubled. "Have you any more sons?" he asked. "Well, yes," said Jesse, "there is the very youngest one, but he's out in the hills, looking after the sheep."

"Fetch him," said Samuel. "I will not eat with you until I have seen him."

So a message was sent to the boy. David came running down the hills, jumping over a stream, tumbling and laughing. He had no cares in the world and arrived with tousled hair, his cheeks glowing from the wind and the sun.

Samuel gazed at him and he heard God's voice: "He is the one!"

Samuel was filled with joy, and to the boy's amazement he took out the small flask of oil, poured it on his head and anointed David, the shepherd boy, as the future king of Israel.

DAVID AND GOLIATH

1 SAMUEL 17

Soon after Samuel had secretly anointed David to be the next king of Israel, the Philistines gathered an army to fight the Israelites. The two armies faced each other across a deep valley: King Saul and the Israelites on one side and the Philistines on the other.

The first morning, the Israelites stood on their side of the valley. Suddenly, they saw a huge warrior step out of the Philistine camp. He was a giant, towering above other men, wearing a bronze helmet, a massive breastplate of bronze and carrying a spear as long as a tree trunk.

His name was Goliath, and he struck terrible fear into the Israelites. He roared at them across the valley, shouting his challenge, "Choose one of your men to fight me! If he can kill me, we will become your slaves, but if I kill him first, then you will become our slaves and serve us forever!"

No man dared move, no one shifted a foot or a hand; they just stared. Even King Saul, who was the tallest man in Israel, looked small and weak against this fearful champion.

Goliath came striding down the valley, shaking his spear, mocking the Israelites and shouting his defiance: "I am one man against the whole army of Israel! Come on, pick your champion and let me fight him!"

Still no one moved, and no one stepped forward to volunteer. The Philistines jeered and laughed as Goliath returned to their camp.

Every day, for forty days, Goliath repeated his act. He strode down the valley, roaring his challenge, and stood there in his gleaming battle gear. No one spoke a word or moved. No one dared to make a sound.

Meanwhile, David was at home tending his sheep. His three eldest brothers had joined the battle line with King Saul. Their father, Jesse, began to worry about his sons, so he sent David with supplies of food and to find out what was happening to them.

When David arrived, he saw that the Israelite soldiers were living in terror. He saw Goliath marching down into the valley, shouting. And he saw how some of the Israelites were running away in terror.

David was shocked and angered by this sight.

"Who is this worthless Philistine who dares to mock God's people?" he asked.

When David's brother Eliab heard him talking like this, he was very angry. "Why did you come here? Go back and guard your little flock of sheep! You're too full of yourself."

"Is it a crime to open my mouth?" asked David, and he went on asking the other soldiers about Goliath until someone told King Saul about him. Saul sent for David.

When he saw the boy coming towards him, Saul was amazed. He looked so young and so utterly fearless.

"Why should anyone lose heart over this Philistine?" asked David. "I will go and fight him."

"You?" said Saul, "You're only a lad and this warrior has been fighting all his life!"

"Your Majesty," said David softly, "I have been fighting for many years too. With my own hands I have killed lions and bears who have attacked my sheep. Surely, the God who delivered me from the jaws of the lion and the claws of the bear can deliver me from the hands of the Philistine!"

"Go on then," said Saul, "and may God be with you."

Then Saul dressed David in his own breastplate and helmet, but the boy said, "I am not used to all this. Let me go as I am."

So David collected five smooth stones from a stream and put them in his shepherd's bag. He took his sling in his hand and walked down the valley towards Goliath.

When the giant saw that a challenger was at last coming down to meet him, he marched forward clutching his spear. But when he realized that it was only a boy, Goliath was furiously angry.

"You're treating me like a dog..." he roared to the Israelites, "throwing little sticks after me!" Then he cursed in the name of his Philistine god and shouted, "Come here, boy, and I will feed your flesh to the birds!"

"You are coming against me with a sword and a spear," shouted David, "but I am coming against you in the name of the Lord God of Israel. Today, he will hand you over to me because the victory is his – the Lord does not need spears and swords to save his people!"

As Goliath steadied his spear to take aim, David calmly loaded one smooth stone into his sling, swung it around his head and let it go. With deadly speed, the stone flew through the air and struck Goliath in the middle of his forehead.

The great Philistine champion fell to the ground, killed by a single stone.

David ran forward, took Goliath's sword from its sheath and cut off his head. When the Philistines saw that their champion was dead, they turned and ran off in fear, with the Israelite army pursuing them.

The Israelites won a great victory that day, and King Saul was leading them. But it was the shepherd boy David who was now the talk of Israel.

DAVID AND SAUL

1 Samuel 17, 18

After the victory, David was brought before King Saul, still carrying the head of Goliath.

Saul looked at him with admiration but also with suspicion. The boy was far too courageous and clever for his liking.

"Young man, you must tell me the name of your father," he said.

"I am the son of your servant Jesse of Bethlehem," answered David quietly.

"You must stay with your king now," said Saul.

David bowed humbly. He did not notice that Saul was fingering his spear nervously.

When Saul and his men returned home later, the streets were filled with women singing songs of victory: "Saul has killed his thousands and David his ten thousands!"

The chanting and the banging of the tambourines, and the women dancing and paying such attention to David, suddenly filled King Saul with rage.

"Why are they singing that?" he whispered to himself. "Why only thousands for me, but ten thousands for David? All the boy needs now is to steal my kingdom!"

Saul had no idea that God had already chosen David to become the next king, but he knew that he had to watch David very carefully.

From that time onwards, David helped the Israelite army to win many battles. All the time, Saul thanked him and praised him, but secretly he feared him. He would watch David passing and smile and finger his spear beside him.

BEST FRIENDS

1 SAMUEL 18

More than anything, King Saul hated the fact that his own son, Jonathan, was always talking to David, always laughing with him, hunting in the fields, feasting with him, sitting by his side in the cool of the evening. The two young men had become the best of friends.

They were closer than brothers and agreed to stay friends whatever happened. Jonathan gave David some of his own robes, his sword and his bow and arrows. No friends were ever more loyal.

Saul watched the friendship grow, and he saw how the people talked about David the whole time: "David the warrior, David the hero, David the giant-slayer, David... David...!"

No one talked of Saul any longer, and no one sang of Jonathan, who was a fine and brave warrior. Not only that, he was the prince, the next king! Why did he have to run after David as if David were the leader, the great champion of Israel?

Saul became jealous, despairing and angry as he sensed power slipping through his fingers, and so it was that he tried to kill David.

As a shepherd boy in the hills, David had sometimes made up songs. He could also play the harp beautifully and Saul would often ask him to play music. The cool notes, like a river running over stones, and David's voice singing so tenderly of God's faithful love, would soothe the king and sometimes calm his violent temper. Without the prophet Samuel to guide him, Saul flew into terrible rages, and people began to say that the king had an evil spirit, but David could play so gently and so movingly that Saul would soon calm down.

Yet, one evening, as he watched David playing, Saul clutched his spear. Suddenly, without warning, he hurled it at David's head. At that very moment, David turned away, and the spear slammed into the wall.

Saul was afraid because he could see that God had saved

David's life. God was with David now, just as he had once been with Saul.

ESCAPE!

1 SAMUEL 18, 19

Saul began to think of other ways to kill David. He knew that his own daughter Michal was in love with David, so he said to him, "If you kill one hundred Philistines, you can marry my daughter as a reward!"

Saul was sure that David would be killed in battle, but David succeeded, and Saul was forced to give his daughter in marriage.

Then Saul told his son Jonathan and his companions that he planned to kill David, but Jonathan warned David and told him to hide.

Jonathan went to his father and said, "Why do you want to kill an innocent man who has helped to save Israel? What has David done to you except good?"

When he saw his own son pleading for David's life, Saul was sorry and promised never to harm him again. "I swear by the Lord God of Israel that David will not be put to death!" he said.

Soon after that, David led the Israelites to another great victory, and jealousy seized Saul once again. As David was playing the harp, the king began to tremble with fury. He snatched up his spear and flung it so hard it smashed into the wall with a shower of splinters. Once again, David had turned his head slightly at just the right moment.

That night, Saul sent men to David's house to arrest him. Michal helped him escape through a window, and he ran towards the hills. Then Michal hid a wooden idol in his bed, dressed in a robe, with goats' hair on its head. She told the men, "He's ill, can't you see?"

So Saul's men went back to report this to Saul, but he told them, "Carry him to me in his bed and I'll kill him myself!" When the soldiers found that it was only a wooden statue and that David had vanished, Saul was furious.

David was forced to hide in the desert for a long time, knowing that Saul would do anything to kill him. In his loneliness and in his desperation, David would make up songs, just as he used to as a shepherd boy. Some of his most beautiful songs – now known as psalms – were written when he was in trouble.

DAVID SPARES SAUL

1 SAMUEL 23, 24

David was a wanted man. He was joined by many loyal followers, who lived with him in the desert, about six hundred fighting men in all.

Even though Saul wanted to kill him, David was always loyal to Saul. "No one must harm the king," he ordered. "He has been chosen by God!"

One day, Saul's son Jonathan journeyed into the desert to find his great friend. David wept for joy when he saw him. They hugged each other.

"Don't be afraid of my father," Jonathan said. "He will never be able to harm you, because one day you shall be king of Israel."

David was amazed. "How do you know this?"

"Everyone knows. Even my father knows!"

"What about you?" asked David softly.

Jonathan put his hands on David's shoulders and smiled.

"I will be your second-in-command!" he said.

Soon afterwards, Saul set out with three thousand men to capture David. Without knowing it, they camped very near David's secret hideout, and Saul walked alone into the very cave where they were hiding. Saul left his men in order to relieve himself, so David's warriors knew that he was unarmed.

"Kill him now!" they whispered. "You have the king in your power; take your chance!" David crept up behind Saul in the shadows so silently and stealthily that Saul did not notice, even when David cut a piece off his cloak.

When Saul left the cave and began to walk away, David called after him, "My Lord, the king!"

Saul turned in shock, immediately recognizing the voice.

David bowed right down to the ground.

"Why do you listen to evil men who say that I want to harm you? Now you can see I had the chance to kill you, but I let you go free." He waved the piece of cloth in the air.

"Is it you?" said Saul. "David, my son?" Then he began to cry. He reached out his hands to David.

"O David... my son... You have treated me so well and I have treated you very badly. The Lord God will reward you for this. It is true that one day you will be king."

David was astonished. Saul continued, in desperation,

"When I am dead, please spare my children and their children after them."

Seeing King Saul standing there alone, weeping, and in such deep sorrow, David promised to protect Saul's family. He watched him disappearing in the dusk, but he knew that Saul's feelings towards him would never change.

With tears in his eyes, Saul went back to his soldiers, and David and his men escaped into the hills. They never spoke to one another again.

SAUL AND THE MEDIUM

1 SAMUEL 28

When Samuel the prophet died, the people mourned him for many days, and they buried him in Ramah. This wise and holy man had not met with Saul for many years, although Saul had longed for Samuel's love and approval once more. Saul wanted to hear that God was on his side, but Samuel had not visited him.

Alone in his palace, Saul was in a nightmare of despair. Sometimes he hurled his spear into the walls, sometimes he raged and shouted, and sometimes he sat without speaking for days.

Then news came to him that a huge army of Philistines was gathering to destroy his whole kingdom.

"Fetch me prophets!" he shouted, but there were no prophets. "Fetch me priests," he insisted, but there were no priests who could reassure him or offer one ray of hope.

Saul went out to see the vast army of the Philistines spreading along the horizon, and terror filled his soul.

"Samuel…" he muttered. "If only I could speak to you once more, if only…"

"Samuel is dead, my Lord," said his servants, fearing that the king was losing his mind.

"I must speak to him!" shouted Saul. "Find me someone who can conjure up spirits!"

"A medium? But you have sent all the mediums and witches away from Israel. It is against God's holy law to meddle in magic or to try and speak to the dead!"

Saul blocked his ears. "A medium!" he shouted. And at last, someone whispered to him that there was still a medium living in the village of Endor.

Saul journeyed to Endor in disguise and found the woman. He asked her to call up a spirit for him.

"What are you asking?" she said, alarmed. "Don't you know that King Saul will kill me if I call on the spirits?"

"I will save you from King Saul."

"Very well," she said. "Whom shall I call for you?"

"The prophet Samuel."

"Samuel…"

The woman was preparing to trick Saul, pretending to call up the ghost of Samuel, but suddenly the real spirit of Samuel began to appear.

She screamed out in terror. "Now I know. You are King Saul of Israel!"

"Tell me what you see," shouted Saul, grabbing her arm.

"An old man, with a robe…"

"It is Samuel… it is him, the prophet!"

Samuel was angered at this final, terrible wickedness of Saul. "Why have you disturbed my peace, calling me up like this?"

"I am in great trouble," answered the king. "God doesn't

listen to me any longer, and the Philistines are waging war on me. You must tell me what to do."

"You already know that the Lord God has turned away from you and become your enemy because of your disobedience! He has chosen David to be king, and tomorrow the Lord will allow your armies to be defeated. You and your sons will be killed."

Samuel disappeared, and Saul was left alone to face the truth he had tried so hard to avoid. His kingdom and his life had come to an end.

DEATH IN BATTLE

1 SAMUEL 31, 2 SAMUEL 1

The very next day, the Philistine armies attacked the Israelites. They forced them to retreat, far up the slopes of Mount Gilboa, where thousands were killed in battle.

Saul and Jonathan fought bravely, wielding their swords and standing their ground to the last. First Jonathan was killed; then two of his brothers. Saul fought on, struggling and battling, until an arrow pierced his breastplate.

He leaned against a rock, bleeding, knowing he was dying. He turned to his shield-bearer and said, "Run me through with my sword, or the Philistines will come and kill me and gloat over me."

The young shield-bearer shook his head. He was terrified to lift a sword against his king. So Saul took his own sword and fell on it. Seeing that the king was dead, the shield-bearer took his sword and did the same.

When the news that Saul and Jonathan were dead reached David in the wilderness, he broke down weeping and no one could comfort him.

He mourned the king and his son for many days, and sang this lament in memory of these two great men:

How the mighty have fallen!
Saul and Jonathan –
lovely and gracious in life,
in death they could not be parted.
O Jonathan, my brother!
How I grieve for you.
My heart is breaking because of you.
Your love for me was wonderful,
even more wonderful than the love of women.
How the mighty have fallen!

DAVID THE KING

2 SAMUEL 5–7, PSALM 24

Although King Saul was dead, there was war between his followers and the people of Judah, who followed David, for more than seven years. Eventually, Saul's men, knowing that they would soon be defeated, came to David and said, "Rule over Israel as well as Judah! You are the king that God has chosen!"

David ruled over the whole kingdom of Israel and Judah for thirty-three years. The people loved him and obeyed him because he ruled with great justice and kindness.

The first thing he did as king was to capture the city of Jerusalem, a strong fortress set high on the rock. The Jebusites who lived there mocked him and said, "You'll never capture Jerusalem – even the weakest people could push you off the walls!" But David attacked Jerusalem from a direction they did not expect. There was a water tunnel from the city which went down through the rocks to a spring outside the walls. David sent soldiers up the tunnel and they took the city by surprise.

David made his home in the fortress there, and he extended Jerusalem, building up all the terraces until it became a great city – known as Zion, the City of David.

David wanted it to be God's city too, so he ordered his men to fetch the ark of the covenant and to carry it up to the heights of Jerusalem. He was so full of joy at the sight of the ark that he threw off his robe and danced wildly, singing and leaping and rejoicing. All the people followed him, shouting and cheering and blowing trumpets.

"Open up, you gates!" he shouted. "Swing wide open, you ancient doors, and let the King of glory come in!"

"Who is the King of glory?" chanted the people.

"The Lord strong and mighty!" shouted David.

And everyone called out together: "The Lord mighty in battle!"

"The Lord, the King of glory!"

David's wife Michal was ashamed to see her husband dancing wildly with all the people.

"The king has made a fool of himself today," she said.

"I don't care if I look foolish to you," said David. "What matters is the glory of God who has chosen me to be king!"

David was pleased that the ark of the covenant was in Jerusalem, but then he said, "Why should I live in a palace, and the ark have only a tent?" He began to think about building a great temple in Jerusalem, but God sent the prophet Nathan to talk to him.

"The Lord God says that your kingdom and the kings descended from you will last forever. The people will live in safety under your rule and your protection, but it is your son – your own flesh and blood – who will one day build a temple, a house for me."

When David heard Nathan's words, he was overwhelmed. He praised God and said, "O Sovereign Lord, how great you are! Although I am unworthy, you have chosen me, and you have chosen the people of Israel to be your own people forever and ever!"

DAVID'S KINDNESS

2 SAMUEL 9

Years after he became king, David had still not forgotten his friend Jonathan, and his promise to take care of Saul's family.

One day, he called his servants and said, "Is there anyone from the family of Saul that I can show kindness to, for Jonathan's sake?"

An old servant of Saul named Ziba was brought to him, and he told David, "Jonathan has a son..."

"A son still living?"

"Yes, my Lord, his name is Mephibosheth. He was injured when he was a baby, so he finds it difficult to walk."

Tears welled up in David's eyes.

"Jonathan's son..." he said. "Bring him to me at once!"

So Ziba fetched Mephibosheth. He was very frightened to come into David's presence and walked slowly and painfully up to the king, then bowed low to the ground.

"Mephibosheth?" said David.

"I am your servant," he replied.

David took his hand. "Don't be afraid. Don't ever be afraid of me! For the sake of your father, Jonathan, I will give back to you all the lands belonging to Saul, and you will eat at my table in the palace as if you were my own son!"

"How can you respect such a worthless person?" said Mephibosheth, shaking his head and bowing low before the king. But David lifted him up and looked at him, and all the love he had felt for Jonathan came flooding back to him once again.

From that day, Mephibosheth was included in David's household, and all the lands of Saul were restored to him and his family.

DAVID AND BATHSHEBA

2 SAMUEL 11

One spring evening, King David wandered onto the roof of his palace. The sun was sinking, and the king sat down, looking over the city of Jerusalem.

Most of the men were away fighting a battle, so all David could see was old men, sitting at the doors of their houses, and servant girls carrying water.

But then his eye caught sight of a woman alone, not many houses away from the palace, stepping into a bath.

David knew he should turn away, but he didn't. He found himself gazing at her because she was very beautiful.

"Who is that?" he asked his servant.

"It's Bathsheba, the wife of Uriah, the Hittite," he told him. "The man's away, serving in your army."

"Away?" said David, and he turned to look at the woman once more. Was there anyone more beautiful in the whole of Israel?

"Fetch her!" said David.

The servant obeyed, and Bathsheba was brought to the palace. No one dared to refuse the wishes of a great king, and Bathsheba gave herself to David. They made love together, while her husband Uriah was out in the desert serving bravely in David's army.

David knew he had done wrong, but he wanted to keep it a secret. However, soon after this, Bathsheba told him that she was pregnant. David paced around the palace gardens, wondering how he could avoid discovery.

I must get Uriah back, he thought. If I can persuade him to take some time away from the battle and go home to his wife, then he will sleep with her. He will believe that the baby is his, and no one will ever know what I have done.

So David sent a message to his general Joab, asking for Uriah to be sent back to Jerusalem. Uriah returned dutifully and went straight to the king's palace.

"Tell me how the battle is going," said David. "How are Joab and my soldiers doing?"

Uriah did not suspect anything, but he refused to go back to his own home. Instead, he slept on the steps of the palace.

"Go home," said David. "You've had a long journey. You deserve a rest!"

"How can I rest," said Uriah bravely, "when Joab and all the soldiers of Israel and Judah are camping in the open fields, facing the enemy? How can I go home and eat and drink and sleep with my wife? I will never do this."

The next night, David invited Uriah to a banquet and deliberately made him drunk. But still Uriah would not go home and fell asleep on a couch in the servants' quarters.

Finally, David sent Uriah back to the battlefield. Then David sent a message to his general Joab: "Put Uriah in a dangerous position on the front line; then leave him there to be killed!"

Joab obeyed, and Uriah was sent right up to the city walls of the enemy, where he was struck down by an arrow.

When Bathsheba heard the terrible news, she grieved for a long time, but David's plan seemed to work. After a while, the young widow became David's wife, and their baby was born. No one knew what David had done – except God.

DAVID IS FOUND OUT

2 SAMUEL 12

God was very angry that David had cheated and killed Uriah to cover up his adultery with Bathsheba, so he sent the prophet Nathan to the palace.

Nathan stood before King David and told him a story: "Once there were two men, one rich and one very poor. The rich man had huge flocks of sheep and herds of cattle, but the poor man had only one little lamb.

"The poor man fed his lamb by hand and loved it. It grew up with him and his children, it drank from his cup and it even slept in his arms. It was like his own daughter.

"Now, one day, a visitor came to the rich man's house. 'I'll prepare a meal,' said the rich man, but he did not choose an animal of his own. Instead, he went and snatched away the poor man's lamb, slaughtered it and served it up for supper!"

When he heard this, David was furiously angry. "What wicked man has done this?" he shouted. "He deserves to die, and he must pay for that lamb four times over!"

"*You* are that man!" said Nathan, looking straight into David's eyes. "Now listen to what God says to you: 'I gave you everything. I chose you to be king over Israel, giving you wives and lands and the whole kingdom. Wasn't this enough for you? But now, because you have shown such violence against Uriah, violence will never leave your family. There will be bloodshed and tragedy in your own home.'"

David wept. He said to Nathan, "I have sinned against God."

"God has forgiven you," said Nathan gently, but with great sorrow, because he knew that many sad things would happen to David's family.

David grew more and more ashamed of what he had done. He knew that God had forgiven him, but he wanted to make a new start in his life.

DAVID'S FAMILY

2 Samuel 13–15

David and Bathsheba's little boy died while he was still a baby, and they were broken-hearted, but God gave them another son after a while, whom they named Solomon. Nathan told them that this boy was greatly loved by God, and that one day Solomon would become king.

But while Solomon was only a little boy, David's other sons argued and fought. Absalom was tall, with long thick hair, and very handsome. He was determined to become king, and he spent his time scheming and plotting against his brothers, his half-brothers and even his father, David.

Nathan, the prophet, had warned David that, because of his disobedience to God, there would be sorrow and bloodshed in David's own family.

Absalom hated his half-brother Amnon, but one day he pretended to be nice to him, invited him to a party, made him drunk, then suddenly struck him down and killed him. Because of this, Absalom had to leave Jerusalem and for many years David would not talk to him. But David loved Absalom so much – and missed him – that at last, he allowed him back.

Even so, Absalom carried on scheming, and carefully made as many secret friends as he could. He was plotting to kill David and take over the throne of Israel. Indeed, David was getting older, and many people started to think that Absalom, who was young and good-looking and seemed like a great warrior, would make a better king.

One day, Absalom went to David and said, "Please let me go

and worship God in the town of Hebron – I made a promise to do that a long time ago."

"Very well," said David. "Go in peace to Hebron." He did not suspect what was in Absalom's mind, even though Absalom had asked to go to the capital of Judah, where David had first been made king. Peace was the last thing on Absalom's mind, for he sent a message to all his supporters: "When you hear the trumpets sound, shout 'Absalom is king in Hebron!'"

REBELLION!

2 SAMUEL 15, 17–19

Thousands of people joined Absalom's rebellion against his father, David.

When he heard that Absalom had proclaimed himself king in Judah, David fled from Jerusalem with his fighting men and his loyal followers and hid in the hills. Even David's wisest counsellor, Ahithophel, had gone over to Absalom's side, and it looked as if David's kingdom was doomed.

But David sent a spy, Hushai, into Absalom's camp, and he sent news to David of all Absalom's plans.

The following day, the two armies lined up against each other.

Even though Absalom wanted to kill David and take his place, David could not stop loving him. Before they went into battle, David said to his men, "If you capture my son Absalom, you are not to harm him. Do not lay a finger on him!"

All David's commanders agreed.

"No one is to touch my son, no one," David ordered.

There was a fierce battle, and twenty thousand people were killed. Absalom's army was utterly defeated, and so the young prince fled through a forest, riding his mule. Suddenly, Absalom's long thick hair was caught in some low branches, and he was left hanging in mid-air as the mule rode on.

One of David's men came to tell his general, Joab, and Joab shouted, "Why didn't you run him through?"

"How could I do that?" replied the man. "The king has commanded us to spare his son –"

"I'm not waiting around for you!" called Joab, as he ran towards the forest, where he stabbed Absalom through the heart.

When the news reached David that the battle had been won, all he asked was, "Is the young man Absalom safe?"

The soldiers looked at each other in silence. Then a messenger spoke up, "May all the king's enemies meet the same fate as that young man!"

David rushed out, sobbing. He went to his room over the gateway in Jerusalem and cried, "O Absalom! My son, my son Absalom! If only I had died instead of you, my son, my son…"

No one could comfort David, even on the day of victory, and he lay on the ground weeping. "My son, my son… O Absalom, my son!"

When Joab arrived, he was angry that David seemed to care about no one but his rebellious son who had caused such destruction.

"Hundreds of men have risked their lives for you!" said the general angrily. "Would you only be happy if we were all dead and Absalom was alive? You must appear before your army now and thank them, or by tomorrow morning they will all have deserted!"

David dried his eyes and did as Joab said, but he continued to grieve for his dear son Absalom.

THE PSALMS

David's life had both great joys and deep tragedies. He often found himself turning to God for strength. He wrote many poems and songs to express his feelings, his longings, his prayers and his praises, his tears and his troubles. These, and many songs and prayers written by other people, have been gathered together and are known as The Psalms.

FROM PSALM 8
THE WONDERS OF CREATION

O Lord, our Lord, your power and majesty
fill the whole earth!

Your glory is higher than the heavens,
even little children joyfully sing your praises.

When I look up at the sky you have formed
and see everything that you have made,
when I see the moon and stars
which you have placed in your heavens,
I wonder why you bother about us?
Why do you care about a child of Adam?

And yet you have made us the pinnacle of
  your creation,
you have lifted us up to the highest position
and put us in charge of the world,
  trusting us to look after it –
all sheep and cattle,
wild animals and birds of the air,
fish in the sea,
and every creature that swims
  through the ocean.

O Lord, our Lord, your power and majesty
  fill the whole earth!

PSALM 23
GOD'S LOVING CARE

The Lord is my shepherd, he gives me
  everything I need.
He lets me lie down safely in green meadows
and leads me beside peaceful streams.
He gives new strength to my soul.
He guides me in the way of goodness.

Even if I walk through nightmares and terrors,
down into the darkest valley of pain and death,
you are still there beside me;
your arms comfort me,
your shepherd's crook protects me.

You have prepared wonderful things for me,
a joyful feast, even though my enemies
surround me.
You anoint my head with oil;
my cup of happiness is so full, it is brimming over.

Goodness and mercy will follow me all the days
of my life.
I will make my home in the house of the Lord,
my God, forever and ever.

FROM PSALM 51
A PRAYER FOR FORGIVENESS

Have mercy, O God,
for your love never fails.
In your great tenderness wipe away my sins,
wash away my guilt
and make me clean once more,
for I have done wrong.

I cannot stop thinking about my sins;
they are always in my mind.
I have sinned against you, O God,
and have broken your laws.

Create in me a pure heart, O God,
and give new life and strength to my soul.
Do not banish me from your presence.
Do not take your holy spirit from me!

Give me the deepest joy of knowing you
and a heart ready and willing to serve you.

Then I will teach wrongdoers your ways;
I will help sinners to find their way back to you.

O God, save me, and I will sing of your goodness.
O Lord, open my lips, and I will praise you!

FROM PSALM 116
A MAN SAVED FROM DEATH PRAISES GOD

I am full of love for God
who listens to my cries for help.
Because he has listened to me
I will keep calling on him all my life.

I thought I was going to die,
and I was terrified.
But I called out to God,
"O Lord, save me!"

God is kind and full of goodness;
he is tender and loving.
He looks after his little ones;
he has rescued me from danger.

I will not worry; I will rest quietly
because God has been so good to me.

You, Lord, have kept me from death;
you dried my tears and saved me from defeat.

How can I repay the Lord for all his generosity?
O Lord, I will be your faithful servant forever.
I will offer you thanks
and always give you praise.

FROM PSALM 119
LIVING GOD'S WAY

Dear God,
how I love to do the things that please you;
I am thinking of them all the time.

I am wiser than all my teachers
because I study your commandments.
I have more insight than older people
because I obey your instructions.
I have kept my feet away from evil paths
so I can follow in your way.
I have not walked away from your wisdom,
because you have taught me yourself.
All your words taste delightful to me;
they are sweeter than honey!
Every word of yours is like a lamp,
lighting up the path in the darkness.

PSALM 131
TRUSTING IN GOD

I am not proud, O God.
I do not pretend to be stronger or cleverer than I am,
boasting of great things.
All I want is to be quiet and listen to you,
trusting you like a little child lying in its mother's arms.
O people of God, trust in the Lord
from this moment onwards, forever and ever!

FROM PSALM 139
GOD KNOWS ALL ABOUT ME

O Lord, you know all the secrets of my heart.
You know when I sit down and when I stand up;
you know everything I am thinking.
Before I open my mouth to speak,
you know every word I will say.

You are the one who formed me inside
my mother's womb.
I praise you for the wonderful and mysterious way
you made me
and for all your glorious works.
Before I was born, you knew all about my life.
I cannot begin to understand your thoughts;
like grains of sand they cannot be counted.
Whenever I wake up, you are still there.
You are always with me.

Uncover the secrets of my heart, O God,
and bring all my fears into the light.
Make sure I am not on the way to ruin,
but guide me on the road to eternity.

FROM PSALM 148
LET THE WHOLE WORLD PRAISE GOD!

Let everything in the sky praise God!
Praise him in the heights.
Let all the angels praise God!
And all the heavenly host.

Let the sun, moon and stars praise God!
Let everything in the world praise him
because he made everything that exists.
When he spoke he made the universe.

Let everything on earth praise him:
all sea creatures and monsters from
    the depths;
all types of weather – snow, hail, fog,
    lightning, storm winds;
all mountains and hills; all trees;
every animal – mammals, birds, reptiles and insects!

Let all the kings and rulers in the world
    praise God!
Men and women, old people, babies.
Let everyone praise the Lord.

For the Lord is mightier than all he has made,
and his glory is greater than anything in earth
or sky.
He strengthens his people and gives them courage
so that all his children, whom he loves, praise him.

PSALM 150
A SONG OF PRAISE

Hallelujah!

Praise God in his holy place,
praise him in the height of heaven.
Praise him for his mighty power,
praise him for his majestic greatness.
Praise him with a fanfare on the trumpet,
praise him with the harp and the lyre.
Praise him with tambourines and dancing,
praise him with strings and pipes.
Praise him with the sound of cymbals,
praise him with a resounding clash of cymbals.
Let every creature that breathes praise the Lord!

Hallelujah!

A WISE NEW RULER

When David knew that he was about to die, he chose his son Solomon to be king after him.

He was lying in his bed, very weak and old, but he whispered to his son, "Be strong! Be the man that God wants you to be."

Solomon knew that his father was not talking about being a great warrior, but about becoming a great servant of God.

"Follow God in everything," David said, "all his commandments, all his ways, then God will keep his promise to me: 'One of your descendants will always be on the throne of Israel as long as the house of David serves me faithfully.'"

David had ruled for forty years, and God had blessed him and brought great strength and wealth and peace to his kingdom. Now it was Solomon's turn to rule.

David died and was buried with great sadness and mourning.

Soon afterwards, the young King Solomon had a dream. He dreamed that God appeared to him and said, "Ask me for anything you want!"

In his dream, Solomon answered, "O Lord God, you showed great kindness to my father, and now I am in his place on the throne of Israel. Show your kindness to me, too, because I am like a little child. I do not know how to rule over this great people, so please give me the gift of wisdom. Help me to know the difference between right and wrong and how to govern your people wisely."

God was pleased that Solomon had asked for wisdom and

said, "Because you have not asked for riches, or for long life, or for victory over your enemies, I will give you what you have asked. You will have such wisdom in everything you do that you will become the wisest man on earth. No one, before or after you, will ever be as wise. And because you have asked for this, I will give you riches and respect and glory as well. No king will equal you, if you keep my laws!"

Then Solomon woke up, and he realized he had been dreaming. But the dream came true. He is remembered today, not only as a great king, but as someone who was a wise and understanding ruler.

THE TRUE MOTHER

1 KINGS 3

People journeyed from far and wide to seek the advice of King Solomon. One day, two women came to him with a very difficult problem.

The women were arguing bitterly over a baby. One said it was hers; the other said it was not. They both began to shout together, "The child is mine!"

Solomon raised his hand. "Tell me your story," he said.

The first woman began, "We both had babies when we were living in the same house. One night when we were alone, she rolled over in bed and killed her own child!"

"It's not true," interrupted the other.

"It is!" said the first, turning to the king. "This woman took my baby from my bed and put her own dead baby in his place. When I woke up, I found the dead baby but knew that it wasn't my son."

"This is *my* baby!" screamed the second woman, pointing to the living child.

No one in the court knew how to decide who was the true mother.

At last, there was silence. "Bring me a sword," said Solomon, and his servants brought him a great sword. "The only fair thing is to cut the baby in two, and you can each have half."

At this, the first woman burst out crying. "No, no, let the other woman take the child. Anything," she sobbed, "but don't kill him."

The second woman nodded to Solomon, "That's fair; let the baby belong to neither of us – cut him in half!"

"Give this baby to the first woman," said Solomon. "She is the real mother – she loved him and wanted him to live."

And so everyone in Israel knew that Solomon was a truly wise king.

GOD'S TEMPLE

1 KINGS 5–8

Solomon's greatest work was to build a temple to God in Jerusalem.

"My father was forced to spend his life fighting," he told the people, "but God has granted me peace. Now it is my task to build a temple to his glory."

For seven years, thousands of people worked on the temple,

and slowly it rose up on the highest place in Jerusalem. Outside it was built of huge blocks of stone, and inside the walls were made of fragrant cedar wood from Lebanon, carved with palm trees and flowers. Deep inside the temple was the sacred room known as the Holy of Holies. It was covered with pure gold, and there Solomon placed two huge winged creatures carved from olive wood – cherubim – to guard the place where the ark of God's covenant would rest. With their wings, the cherubim made an arch for the most sacred object in all Israel.

When the temple was finished, Solomon called all the elders and the leaders of the tribes of Israel together. Then with great singing and rejoicing, the priests took up the ark of the covenant and carried it into the Holy of Holies and placed it under the spreading wings of the cherubim, who cast their shadow over it.

As the priests left the Holy of Holies, the cloud of God's glory filled the room with such brightness that none of them dared to stay. All the priests praised God in silence from afar. Then Solomon offered thanks to God, and all the people rejoiced. They praised God with all their might because he had filled the temple with his glory

WISE WORDS FROM THE BOOK OF PROVERBS

Solomon was famous for his wisdom, and the sayings of Solomon and other wise people were gathered together into the Book of Proverbs.

If you want to be wise, respect and obey God.

1:7

Don't forget God's teaching, but always remember his commands. Then you will live for many years, and your life will be full of good things.

3:1, 2

Trust God with all your heart and don't rely on what you think you know. If you trust God in every part of your life, he will show you the way forward.

3:5, 6

Don't think you are wiser than you are; respect God and avoid evil. This is the way to a healthy life in body and in spirit.

3:7, 8

A kind answer soothes away anger, but an unkind response makes anger worse.

15:1

If you speak kindly to people, you bring life;
but lies and harmful words bring death.

15:4

Without fuel, a fire goes out; without gossip, disagreements melt away.

26:20

Don't go around with someone who gets angry all the time, for you may start to copy them and then you'll be in trouble too.

22:24, 25

Help people who are in need. Don't tell them to come back tomorrow if you can help them now.

3:27, 28

Pride always leads to arguments, but wise people will listen to advice.

13:10

Pride goes before a fall.

16:18

If you make friends with wise people, you will become wise. If you make friends with fools, you will become a fool.

13:20

A fool does not enjoy learning from others but loves the sound of his own voice.

18:2

SOLOMON'S FAME

1 KINGS 10

In a far-off land, the queen of Sheba had heard of Solomon's great wealth, his ivory throne inlaid with gold, his magnificent palace and his thousands of chariots and horses, and of his treasuries filled with gold and glittering gemstones. There was no one richer than King Solomon, and there was no one in the world who was wiser.

The queen of Sheba reigned over a powerful kingdom of her own, but she had found no one to answer her deepest questions. There was no one to open a door into the mysteries of heaven and earth, and so when she heard of Solomon's wisdom, she set out with hundreds of servants and lavish gifts – camels laden with spices, presents of rare jewels, shimmering golden bowls and sackfuls of treasure.

"I must test the wisdom of Solomon and his God for myself," she decided.

No one knows what was on her heart, what questions troubled her so deeply, but when she came to Jerusalem, she spent many days walking alone with Solomon in the fragrant gardens of the palace, questioning him, searching the depths of his mind.

At last, she said, "May the Lord, your God, be praised. He has set you upon the throne of Israel! Now I have seen your justice and your wisdom for myself. I did not know whether to believe all the reports from my servants, but they only told me the half of it. I am breathless with wonder! Your God has shown great love to his people in giving you such wisdom to rule them fairly."

Solomon sent the queen of Sheba home, laden with many gifts from his treasury, but his most precious gifts were the deepest thoughts of his heart.

A SAD ENDING

Even though he had been blessed by God with wisdom and riches and power, Solomon ended his life in failure.

He did not follow God faithfully like his father, David. Instead, he gathered together a huge harem of wives and slave women living in his palaces. Nothing would make him give up his harem, and he cared for many of the women, who had a great influence over him. Before long, he began to listen to their opinions, doing everything to please them rather than keep God's commands.

Among Solomon's wives were princesses and noble women from foreign lands who brought with them the worship of idols. "We have left everything to live with you," they told him. "Everything except our gods! Give us our own temples, altars and high places to worship!"

Solomon could not resist their flattery and their charm and wanted to please them. He was afraid to offend the rulers of their lands or break his trade agreements with them, so slowly, day by day, year by year, he added other gods, other temples and altars around Jerusalem.

Although he was very wise, the wisest man in the world, Solomon acted very foolishly and angered the God of Israel. He built altars for Ashtoreth, goddess of the Sidonians; a high place for Chemosh, the god of the Moabites; then a temple to Molech, the god of the Ammonites. And he allowed people to worship these pagan gods, who demanded dark and hateful deeds and cruel sacrifices.

Even though the God of Israel had made himself known when he appeared to Solomon, the king broke the covenant, his promise that God's people would worship God alone. Their reward had been that they would live in the Promised Land of Canaan which would be occupied by the original twelve tribes descended from Jacob.

God warned King Solomon that, after his death, part of that kingdom would be torn away from his family. "Because of my promise to David, your son will be king of Judah in Jerusalem, but ten tribes will rebel and form another kingdom, Israel."

Towards the end of Solomon's reign, Jeroboam, one of his officials, had many followers among the people.

One day, a prophet came to him when he was walking alone. Jeroboam was amazed to see Ahijah, the messenger of God, take off his cloak and suddenly tear it into twelve pieces.

"Here," he said to Jeroboam. "Take ten pieces! For this is what the Lord says: 'I am tearing the kingdom from Solomon and I will give you ten tribes. If you follow me and walk in my ways and obey my laws, then I will make your family as strong as David's, and you will be king over Israel!'"

When Solomon found out that Jeroboam was a threat to his kingdom, he tried to kill him, but Jeroboam fled to Egypt and bided his time.

So Solomon died – a great king who had ruled for forty years but in the end brought a deep shadow over the whole of Israel.

THE WORST ADVICE

1 KINGS 12

When Rehoboam, the son of Solomon, came to the throne, the tribes of Israel gathered together at Shechem to make him king.

The people, who in Solomon's reign had been worn down by hard work and high taxes, pleaded with the young prince to give them an easier time than his father had done.

"How should I answer the people?" Rehoboam asked his oldest advisers.

"Be kind," they replied. "Listen to their demands and they will serve you forever."

But Rehoboam was a rash and proud young man. Why should I give in? he thought. I'll make myself look like a fool. So he rejected the advice of the older men and turned to the young friends who had grown up with him.

"Talk harshly to them!" they advised. "Prove that you're powerful!"

Rehoboam smiled. He liked the idea. He wanted to strut around and order his people to obey him like a true king.

"Very good," he said.

His friends patted him on the back and said, "Tell those whining people, 'My little finger is thicker than my father's waist. If Solomon beat you with whips, I will lash you with scorpions!'"

Rehoboam was sure that he could force the people to respect him, but when they heard his harsh words, they were filled with anger and contempt.

"Everyone for himself," they shouted. "We'll have nothing to do with David's family!"

And so Rehoboam lost all the tribes of Israel except for Judah, who stayed loyal to him in Jerusalem, and the land was divided into two separate kingdoms with two rulers.

Meanwhile, in far-off Egypt, Jeroboam heard that the people were rebelling and knew that his moment had come. He returned home, and the rebel tribes crowned him king of Israel, just as the prophet had said.

THE DIVIDED KINGDOM

1 KINGS 12–15

When Jeroboam was crowned king, the prophet's words came back to him: "God says, 'If you follow me and obey my laws, you will be king of Israel.'" But Jeroboam quickly ignored the prophet's advice. He was more interested in protecting his new kingdom than in remembering to worship the God of Israel.

Jeroboam had a problem. He was king of Israel in the north; Rehoboam was king of Judah in the south. Jerusalem was now the capital of Judah. "If I let my people go up to the temple in Jerusalem," Jeroboam said to himself, "they will turn back to Rehoboam and kill me!"

So Jeroboam ordered two huge golden bulls to be made, and he set up shrines to them – one in the far north at Dan, and the other in the south at Bethel.

"Here are your gods!" he said to the Israelites. "Here are the

gods who rescued you from slavery in Egypt – worship them!"
And so the people turned away from the pure worship of God.

In Judah, Rehoboam was no better. He, too, allowed God's
people of Judah to worship false gods. He built shrines and set
up sacred stones and places where the people could take part
in many evil acts and worship idols, just as the original tribes
had done before God had settled the Israelites in the Promised
Land.

God's punishment came upon Rehoboam when Shishak, the
king of Egypt, attacked Jerusalem and stole the treasures from
the royal palace and God's temple.

In the northern kingdom, disaster came to Jeroboam's
family. One of his sons died and another, who became king
after his father, was killed and all his family with him. The line
of Jeroboam came to a terrible end.

Over many years, kings came and went in the two
kingdoms, and God was often ignored and disobeyed. Only a
handful of people, mainly prophets, were faithful to God and
brave enough to challenge their evil rulers.

AHAB AND JEZEBEL

I KINGS 16, 18

Ahab was worse than any king before him. He turned away
from the living God of Israel and made Baal his lord. In fact, he
behaved as if the sins of King Jeroboam were a light thing,
hardly mattering at all.

The Canaanites believed that Baal was the bringer of rain and the lord of the harvest. He was the most important of their many gods, and they had many idols of Baal in their cities. They asked their god to bless the land with rain and with his almighty power, chanting their prayers: "O Thunderer from Heaven, bring rain upon the earth!" or "O life-giving Lord! O Baal! O King of creation!"

Ahab was impressed and envious of this glittering world. He loved the huge idols in their dark, golden temples. He longed to have all this for himself. He dreamed of such immense power and began to wonder to himself, "Perhaps the god Baal will bless me in return for my worship? Perhaps, if I have a little help from the god of Tyre and Sidon as well as from the God of Israel, I can become the greatest king in the land!" And so he chose as his wife Jezebel, the daughter of the high priest of Baal in Sidon. Soon Jezebel began to wield her power over Ahab and his kingdom of Israel.

Ahab did everything that would please Jezebel. He built a magnificent temple of ivory, richly inlaid with gold, in the middle of the city of Samaria. He placed an altar inside the temple for the worship of Baal.

But Ahab's wickedness made God very angry because he was leading the people of Israel astray. Many of them followed the example of their king and followed Baal instead of the true God.

Before long, Jezebel began to hunt down people who were loyal to the God of Israel. She sent her soldiers after the prophets, God's special messengers, and had many of them killed.

But there was one man she did not find. He was the prophet Elijah.

ELIJAH THE PROPHET

I Kings 17

King Ahab was feasting in his palace when suddenly the curtains of the great hall were flung aside. There was a blast of air, the cold night wind invading the warmth. Ahab looked around, startled.

A man stood there. No one knew who he was. No one knew where he came from.

The man spoke: "The Lord God of Israel, the God whom I serve, says..." the wild-looking man stared hard into Ahab's eyes, "... there will be no dew nor rain in the years ahead except at my word!"

Then he was gone.

The man's name was Elijah. He was from Gilead beyond the River Jordan. Elijah was a prophet. He listened very carefully to everything that God had to say.

King Ahab was furious that his banquet had been interrupted by this strange prophet.

"Find him," he ordered his soldiers, "and bring him back to me!"

But God spoke again to Elijah: "Go and hide yourself in the Kerith ravine, east of the Jordan. Drink the water there, and I will send the ravens to feed you."

So Elijah hid by the brook at Kerith, and each morning and evening the ravens flew down carrying him bread and meat.

Meanwhile the drought God had promised came upon the land. At last, even the brook at Kerith dried up, and Elijah stared sorrowfully as the last drops of water vanished into the cracked earth.

A WIDOW AND HER SON

1 KINGS 17

Again God spoke to Elijah.

"Go to Zarephath," he said. It was a surprising command. Zarephath was a city in Sidon, beyond Israel, where the people had always followed Baal. But Elijah obeyed.

"You shall see a poor woman there, a widow gathering sticks," God told him. "I have told her to give you whatever food you need."

Sure enough, when Elijah came through the gates of the city, he saw the woman bending low and gathering sticks. He called to her and she looked up, astonished at the tall, wild stranger standing before her.

"Please bring me a little water to drink," he asked, "and fetch me some bread."

"O sir," she answered, "by the name of the living God, whom you worship, I have no bread... only a handful of flour and a little oil in a jug. This is all I have left because the terrible drought has ruined our harvest. Now I am gathering these sticks to make a fire and cook a last meal for my little boy and myself, before we die of hunger."

Elijah looked down at her and said, "Don't be afraid. First bake a small cake for me and then one for your son and yourself, because the Lord, the God of Israel, says: 'The jar of flour will not be used up, nor will the jug of oil run dry until I bring rain upon the earth!'"

So the woman ran to her home, and there she baked and cooked and poured out flour and mixed in the oil – once, twice, many times. It was true. The flour never failed; the oil never ran dry!

The God of Israel never failed in his promise. Day after day, the widow looked after Elijah, giving him an upper room to stay in. She fed him and fed herself and her little boy.

Then one day, the boy became ill. He was very unwell, and the mother was helpless. There was nothing she could do.

"What's the matter, my son?" she whispered, but the boy said nothing. He had stopped breathing.

Elijah ran down from his room when he heard her crying.

"Why have you come to me, man of God?" she sobbed. "You have brought down punishment on all my sins!"

"Give me the boy," said Elijah, and he took the child in his arms up to his room. Then he fell down upon his knees, and with tears he called out to God.

"O Lord, my God," he pleaded, "why have you allowed such a terrible thing to happen to this good woman? Lord, I beg you, give the boy life once more!"

Then Elijah stretched himself out upon the boy three times, and God heard his prayer.

Suddenly, the boy breathed. One breath. Then another; then he was breathing regularly and smiling and opening his eyes. He was climbing off the bed.

When the widow saw her little boy running to her, she clutched him and wept, turning to Elijah. "Now I know that you are a prophet who truly speaks the word of God."

THE GREAT CONTEST

Elijah had seen God answer his prayers and work great miracles through him while he was staying with the widow in Zarephath. Now he was ready to return to Israel. The famine was severe, and there had been no rain for three years. King Ahab was furious with Elijah. He sent out search parties for him, but Elijah found Ahab first.

When Ahab saw Elijah, all his plans to have the prophet arrested on sight and executed suddenly collapsed. He was afraid.

"It's you," he said, "the troublemaker."

"You are the troublemaker," roared Elijah. "You and all your family, because you have disobeyed God and followed Baal!"

Elijah walked up to the king and stared into his eyes. "Summon the people of Israel to Mount Carmel, and all the prophets of Baal, then we'll find out who is the true God of Israel!"

Ahab gathered the people together, along with the four hundred and fifty prophets of Baal, on Mount Carmel. Elijah stood high on the rocks and shouted to them, "How long will you people dither around between gods? Now make your choice. If the Lord is God, serve him, but if Baal is god, then serve him."

There was a deep silence.

"Well…?" said Elijah and waited. No one moved. Elijah began to stride up and down. "We'll have a contest! You build an altar for Baal, and I'll build one for the Lord God. We'll take two bulls and prepare them for sacrifice; we'll put wood on the altars."

He swung his arms up to heaven. "Call on the name of your god, and I will call on the name of my God, and the god who answers by fire, he is the true God!"

So the prophets of Baal prepared their sacrifice and then began to shout and call, wail and moan. But hours passed and nothing happened.

"Shout louder," Elijah mocked them. "Perhaps he's asleep or he's lost in thought, or maybe he's away on business!"

The prophets danced and wailed, cutting themselves with knives in a frenzy, "Baal, hear us! Baal, send down fire!" At last, they collapsed, exhausted.

Then Elijah built his altar, taking twelve stones, one for each tribe of Israel, and he ordered the people to dig a deep ditch all around the altar and to fetch water and soak the bull. There could be no trickery now, for nothing on earth could light the sacrifice.

Then Elijah prayed, "O Lord God of Israel, show that you are the true God and I am your servant. Answer me now, so that these people will know that you are the Lord and will turn their hearts back to you."

At once, fire streamed down from heaven, a cascade of flame sweeping over the altar, devouring the bull, the wood and the stones, and licking up every last drop of water from the ditch.

The people fell to their knees and cried out in sheer terror, "The Lord, he is the true God, the Lord, he is the only God!"

Then Elijah ordered, "Seize the false prophets of Baal and kill them!"

Not one of the prophets escaped, and when the judgment had been carried out, Elijah climbed up to the top of the mountain and prayed for rain.

At last, a tiny cloud appeared above the sea and grew bigger and swelled into a vast thunderstorm which exploded into rainfall – sweet drops of rain falling, hammering into the dry earth.

ELIJAH ON THE RUN

1 KINGS 19

When Queen Jezebel heard that her prophets had been killed by Elijah, she flew into a murderous rage. "Send this message to the *prophet*," she screamed. "'May the gods punish me if I do not destroy your life in the same way by this time tomorrow!'"

Suddenly, Elijah was very afraid. He turned and ran. He kept on running, fleeing for his life, until he was far from Samaria. Then he lay down in the middle of the desert beside a broom tree, and there he prayed that God would take his life.

"I have had enough," he whispered to God. "Let me die."

Elijah thought of all the rebellions and all the failures down through the centuries, how the people had disobeyed one leader after another. It seemed as though no one wanted to serve God in Israel except him. He was alone, despite all he had done, hunted by Jezebel, facing execution. How could he carry on?

Such thoughts swirled in his mind like the desert sand until sleep overwhelmed him. He lay there, exhausted by the heat and all the running, and the great contest on Mount Carmel which had drained all his strength. He slept for a great while.

Suddenly, he felt a touch on his shoulder, a soft gentle

tugging, and he awoke. "Get up and eat," whispered a voice on the wind, and he noticed a figure shimmering in the haze. Then it vanished. Elijah saw some bread, baked on hot stones, and beside it a jar of water. He ate and drank and then fell back into a deep sleep.

"Get up and eat," the voice came again. Elijah felt the touch on his shoulder and he stood up, astonished. "You must eat and drink because you have a long journey ahead of you," said the voice.

Elijah looked down and there again was bread and a jar of water. By the time he had finished eating and drinking, the angel had gone.

Strengthened in this way by God, Elijah began his journey of forty days and forty nights into the depths of the wilderness, until at last he came to the holy mountain of Sinai. It was in this lonely place that Moses had met God face to face, and God had written on the tablets of stone with fire. Now it was Elijah's turn to meet God and be changed forever.

THE STILL, SMALL VOICE

1 Kings 19

Elijah climbed the steep crags of Mount Sinai in the gathering twilight until at last he came to a cave. He crept inside and lay down for the night. Suddenly, he heard a voice in the darkness asking, "What are you doing here, Elijah?"

"I have been working so hard for the God of Israel," he replied. "I have given everything for him! The people of Israel have broken his covenant, smashed down his altars, killed his prophets, and now they are trying to kill me too."

"Go and stand on the mountain, for the Lord God is coming!" commanded the voice.

Immediately, there was a terrifying gale, splitting the rocks and hurling them into the air, but the Lord God was not in the hurricane. Then came an earthquake, thundering through the ground and shaking the huge crags, but the Lord God was not in the earthquake. Next came a fire, roaring through the air, crackling through the thorn bushes and blazing across the mountain ridge, but the Lord God was not in the fire.

Then Elijah heard a whisper, a gentle voice rising like a breath all around him. It was a still, small voice, drawing him to the mouth of the cave. He covered his face with his cloak, because he knew now that he was in the presence of God himself.

"Elijah..." The voice spoke to him as he wrapped himself and hid from the holiness of God. "Elijah, what are you doing here?"

Elijah poured out his sorrow and despair about how he had given his whole life to the God of Israel, and how he was fighting the battle alone.

"You are not the only person in Israel who loves and serves me," said God. "There are seven thousand Israelites who have not bowed their knees to Baal nor kissed his image. I have kept them safe, and I know them."

Elijah was humbled. He realized that he did not know everything, whereas God knew the secrets of every heart. Suddenly, he felt that he knew nothing of the past nor of the future.

"Go," whispered the voice that surrounded him, shaking his

soul more surely than the earthquake had rocked the mountains. "Go now and anoint Jehu as a new king over Israel and anoint Elisha, the son of Shaphat, to be a prophet to work with you and carry on your task."

ELISHA IS CHOSEN

1 KINGS 19

Elijah walked down slowly from the mountain. He thought about the stillness of God's power and holiness, and he knew now that the future did not lie in his control but in the hands of God. He no longer felt weary or a failure, and his fear of Jezebel had lifted like a nightmare vanishing in the bright sunlight of morning.

He journeyed for many days until he reached the River Jordan. There he saw a man ploughing with oxen. This young man was Elisha.

Elijah walked steadily towards him and then with one hand snatched off his own cloak and laid it like a blanket across the young man's shoulders.

At that moment, Elisha knew that he had been chosen by the prophet to serve him and to become the messenger of God.

"Let me go and kiss my mother and father farewell," he said.

"Go," whispered Elijah. He knew that it would cost Elisha everything to follow him, to leave all his land and possessions behind and trust only in the word of God.

Elisha took his own yoke of oxen and slaughtered them for a feast for all the people in the village. He used the wooden plough as firewood, burning it up as a sign that he would never turn back. Then he set out to follow Elijah.

NABOTH'S VINEYARD

1 KINGS 21

King Ahab continued to live his life as if Elijah would never trouble him again. He was glad that the prophet had disappeared so suddenly and mysteriously, and he hoped with all his heart that Elijah was dead.

Next to one of Ahab's palaces in Jezreel was a beautiful vineyard with huge clusters of grapes. Ahab thought it would make a fine vegetable garden, so he went to the owner, a man named Naboth, and begged him to sell it.

"How can I part with my family inheritance?" said Naboth. In those days, it was considered a very bad thing to sell the family property. "This belonged to my ancestors, and it will belong to my descendants!"

Ahab stormed away angrily. He rushed back to his chamber, threw himself upon his bed and turned his face to the wall. He lay there sulking for many hours until his wife, Jezebel, came and sat beside him.

"There now," she said soothingly, "what can have upset the king so much that he won't eat his food?"

"Naboth's vineyard," said Ahab, without turning. "He won't sell."

"A fine king you are, when you can't even get hold of a little vineyard..."

Ahab sat up slowly. He could see in Jezebel's steely eyes that she had a plan.

"Wash yourself, eat and drink," she murmured to him sweetly, "and I will get you the vineyard myself."

Then Jezebel sent letters in Ahab's name to the elders of Naboth's city, ordering them to put Naboth on trial. "Find two villains who will accuse him of cursing God and the king, then take him out and stone him," said the letter.

The elders were terrified of Jezebel and obeyed all her instructions. When the people heard the lies against Naboth, they rushed him outside the city and stoned him to death.

THE DEATH OF AHAB

1 KINGS 21, 22

As soon as he heard that Naboth was dead, Ahab took possession of the vineyard. He was looking forward to walking beneath the curling vines and listening to the sounds of the crickets on warm summer evenings.

Then God spoke to Elijah: "Go to Ahab, who is sitting in Naboth's vineyard, and pass my judgment on him for the murder he has committed."

Ahab stretched out his hand and plucked a ripe cluster of grapes, pressing them to his mouth. Everything seemed so still, so calm in his new vineyard, and he smiled to himself.

Suddenly, a figure stepped out from the shadows. Ahab dropped the grapes, leaping to his feet. He knew who it was, but there was nowhere to run.

"Have you found me, my enemy?" he said.

"I have found you," said Elijah, "because you have sold your soul to evil! Hear the word of the Lord: 'I will destroy you and your royal line forever. Just as the blood of Naboth was spilled, your blood will be spilled, and outside these city walls the wild dogs will tear the body of Jezebel to pieces.'"

Before Ahab could plead for mercy, Elijah had vanished into the darkness. Ahab felt very guilty and sorry for what he had done, and he fasted and tore his clothes. But it was too late to change his ways.

Three years later, disobeying God's command again, Ahab went into battle against the Syrians. He was a coward, and he decided to disguise himself as an ordinary soldier so that he would be safe. By chance, someone fired an arrow which pierced his breastplate. So it was that King Ahab's reign ended in bloodshed.

THE CHARIOT OF FIRE

2 KINGS 2

Elijah had brought God's judgment on Ahab and the prophets of Baal. He had stirred up the people of Israel with his call to turn away from idol worship and back to God. Now it was time for a new prophet to speak God's words and for Elijah's own life to come to an end.

The two prophets, Elijah and Elisha, walked silently through the fields around Gilgal. They both knew that this was their last day together – the day when Elijah would be taken up to heaven.

"Stay here," said Elijah. "God has told me to go to Bethel."

"As surely as the Lord God lives," replied Elisha, "I will never leave you!"

So they walked on together until they came to Bethel. This was the place where, many years before, Jacob had dreamed of angels climbing up a great staircase into heaven. Elijah stood alone, silent and deep in thought.

"Stay here, Elisha," he said quietly, "for God is sending me to Jericho."

But Elisha took hold of his master's arm. "As surely as the Lord God lives, and as you still live, I will never leave you!"

Seeing he was determined to follow, Elijah walked on to the city of Jericho, where Joshua had once met the shining commander of God's army before the battle of Jericho. He stood there in silence.

Elisha could see Elijah listening and watching with his whole being.

"Stay here, Elisha," he ordered, "because God is sending me to the River Jordan."

Elisha shook his head with tears in his eyes. "No, master. As the Lord God of Israel lives, and while you still live, I will never be parted from you!"

Elijah looked at his young servant with gentleness and with pride at his great determination.

"Very well," he nodded. So they walked on to where the River Jordan flowed through the desert. They stood at the very place where the people of Israel had entered the Promised Land.

Elijah waited there, gazing into the distance, and then, suddenly, he tore off his cloak, rolled it up and waved it over the river so that it hit the water. Immediately, the river divided into great walls of water surging to the right and the left as the two men walked over on dry land.

Elijah stopped on the other side and asked, "What would you like me to do for you before I am taken away from the earth?"

Elisha looked at him, remembering how the great prophet had called him away from his family farm. On that day, he had left his old life and his inheritance.

"May I be like your son," said Elisha, "but instead of leaving land or money to me, give me a spirit like yours. Ask God to give me a double blessing."

"You have asked a very hard thing," said Elijah. He knew that only God could grant such an extraordinary prayer. He put his hand on the young man's shoulder.

"Elisha... if you see me being taken from you, your request will be granted. If not, then it will not be so."

The two men walked on, talking quietly. Then, suddenly, fire streamed down from heaven, separating them, and a chariot of fire appeared with burning horsemen, and a great whirlwind of flame carried Elijah into the clouds.

Elisha fell back, calling out, "My father! My father! The horsemen and chariots of Israel!" But the gates of heaven opened and Elijah was gone.

Elisha stood staring into emptiness, tears streaming down his face because his master had left him forever. He tore his clothes apart in grief. Then, at his feet, he saw the cloak which had fallen from Elijah's shoulders. He picked it up slowly, wrapping his arms around it, and walked to the edge of the River Jordan. There he flung the cloak across the river and hit the water with it, shouting, "Where is the Lord, the God of Elijah?"

The waters divided before him, surging to the right and the left.

Elisha walked over on dry land. In front of him lay the whole of Israel, the cries of the people, their hopes and needs, Jezebel and her wickedness, but Elisha was not afraid. He put on Elijah's cloak and walked forward with courage because the power of the God of Elijah was with him.

THE MAN OF GOD

2 Kings 4

There was a wealthy woman in the village of Shunem who showed great kindness to Elisha. She agreed with her husband to build him a room in their house so that the prophet could stay there whenever he wanted. Elisha was very grateful for her hospitality, but she would take no payment.

One day, Elisha asked his servant Gehazi, "Surely we can do something for her?"

"She has no son," replied Gehazi, "and her husband is getting old."

"Call her," said Elisha.

The woman walked up the stairs to Elisha's upper room. She stood in the doorway, her head bowed respectfully. "Do not trouble yourself over me, my Lord," she said.

Elisha looked at her with compassion. "This time next year, you will be holding a son in your arms."

"No, no, my Lord," she replied, weeping. "Do not deceive me with such promises, man of God!" Then she turned to hide her distress, because Elisha had touched on the one thing she wanted most in the world.

"It will be so," he whispered as she rushed down the stairs.

Sure enough, she became pregnant and gave birth to a little boy exactly one year later. Every time Elisha came to visit, she would take the child to him proudly, and he would hold him in his arms and bless him.

Years later, the boy collapsed suddenly and died. Overcome with grief, the woman laid the child on Elisha's bed in the upper room, closed the door and set out for Mount Carmel, where Elisha was staying.

Elisha saw her coming and wondered why she was hurrying towards him. She clung to his feet weeping bitterly. "Didn't I say to you, 'Do not deceive me, do not raise my hopes'?".

Elisha hurried back to the woman's home, shut the door of his room and stretched himself across the child. He called on the power of God, and the boy's body slowly became warm.

Elisha lay across the child again, stretching out until his hands touched the boy's hands.

Suddenly, there was a sneeze. The boy sneezed again and again, seven times.

Elisha's servant called the boy's mother. She ran upstairs and found the child sitting on the bed.

As the woman watched Elisha leave that day, she knew that another great prophet had been sent to the land of Israel.

NAAMAN AND THE
LITTLE SERVANT GIRL

2 KINGS 5

Naaman was the commander-in-chief of the Syrian army, a very
courageous and powerful man. Under his leadership the Syrian
army had won many battles. He had everything – power,
wealth, a beautiful home – but he also had a terrible skin
disease which no one could cure.

One day, Naaman's wife was talking to her maidservants
about her husband's illness when a little servant girl said, "I
know a man who could cure him."

The servant girl had been captured as a slave by Naaman's
army and brought all the way to Syria from her home in Israel.

"If only my master could visit the prophet in Samaria!" she
said. She was talking about the prophet Elisha.

And so Naaman told the king, who arranged for him go to
Samaria. I'll have to take many gifts with me, Naaman
decided, so he set out for the house of Elisha with all his
servants and his camel train laden with gold and silver and
perfumed robes. It was a magnificent procession, and all the
people in the villages came to stare at the famous soldier
passing by. Naaman hid his skin disease under his beautiful
clothes.

At Elisha's house, Naaman and his procession stopped and
waited. Elisha's servant came out and said, "My master says,
'Go and wash yourself in the River Jordan seven times, and you
will be healed.'"

Naaman was angry. "Wash myself in that filthy stream?" he

shouted, and he turned around and began to head back to Syria.

He felt insulted. He had come to see the great prophet and had been spoken to only by his servant.

But Naaman's servants came up to him courageously and said, "My Lord... if the prophet had asked you to do something very difficult, wouldn't you have done it immediately? Surely you can do something as simple as this?"

Naaman knew they were right. He walked up to the edge of the river and took off his shoes. His feet sank into the mud. He cast off his cloak and all his fine robes and walked into the middle of the river.

He dipped down once below the water and rose up. He looked at himself and saw that he was still covered in the terrible white sores of the disease. The prophet had said to wash seven times, so he held his breath and dipped down again, and the muddy waters swirled around his head.

At last, he came up for the seventh time. He looked at his hands. The skin was clear and pure. He looked at his arms and his legs. They were perfect, like the skin of a little child. The disease had completely vanished.

Naaman's servants stared in astonishment as the great general emerged from the river and knelt down humbly and praised and thanked the God of Israel.

Naaman dressed himself and rode back immediately to Elisha. "Now I know," he said, "that there is no other God in all the world!"

Elisha looked at him kindly, but when Naaman tried to offer his gifts, the prophet refused, saying, "I am the servant of the Lord and I will not take anything from you."

Naaman begged him, but he would not take a single coin or piece of fine cloth.

When Naaman returned home, he was greeted with rejoicing. The little servant girl was happy because, although she was far from home and a slave, she had been able to tell her mistress in Syria about Elisha and the power of the God of Israel.

THE HEAVENLY ARMY

2 KINGS 6

The king of Syria was at war with Israel, but time after time when he sent his soldiers on a raid, the prophet Elisha would warn the king of Israel, "Don't go there," or, "Avoid that place because the Syrians have set up an ambush!"

Back in Syria, the king was puzzled. "Who is betraying me?" he demanded. "Which traitor is informing on my soldiers?"

"There are no traitors," his men replied. "It's the prophet Elisha. He whispers to the king of Israel every word you say, even in your own bedroom!"

"Find out where this man Elisha is and capture him at once!" commanded the king of Syria.

The Syrians discovered that Elisha was staying in Dothan, and so they sent an army to surround the city by night. In the morning, Elisha's servant woke up early and looked out of the window. As far as the eye could see, hordes of soldiers and a great many horses and chariots surrounded the city. "O my Lord, what are we going to do?" The young man was shaking with terror. "We'll all die!"

"Don't be afraid," answered Elisha. "There are more warriors on our side than on theirs." Then he prayed to God, "Lord, open his eyes so he can see."

God opened the servant's eyes, and suddenly he saw a huge army in the heavens: horses and chariots of fire circling the whole city in the air and a vast array of angels guarding Elisha.

The enemy began to advance. Elisha prayed again, "Lord, strike these soldiers with blindness," and soon the whole Syrian force was stumbling around as if in the dark.

Elisha went out to them and offered to guide them. "You've come to the wrong place; let me lead you onwards," he said. And he took them all the way to Samaria, the capital city of Israel. As soon as they were safely within the city walls, Elisha asked God to restore their sight, and the whole army found itself trapped and at the mercy of the king of Israel.

"Shall I kill them all?" asked the king.

"No," said Elisha. "Would you kill your own prisoners of war? Feed them and send them on their way."

So the king of Israel prepared his captives a great feast and sent them home. The Syrians went home, ashamed and fearful. That was the last time they ever tried to capture the prophet of God.

THE KING WHO TRUSTED GOD

2 CHRONICLES 20

The land that God had given to his people was still divided into two kingdoms – Israel and Judah – when Jehosophat became king of Judah. He was one of the few rulers who loved and trusted God.

One day, messengers came to his palace at Jerusalem and told him, "A huge army is coming against you from beyond the Dead Sea. There are Ammonites and Moabites – all those who are enemies of God and his people."

Jehosophat was alarmed and sent word through the whole land of Judah, "Come up to the temple in Jerusalem with me and ask God for help."

So all the people gathered together in the temple courtyard, and Jehosophat prayed to God, "O Lord God, you rule the whole world. No one is as powerful as you, and with your help we conquered the people of this land. Now we are weak and helpless before this great army, and we do not know what to do, but we look to you to save us."

Then a prophet named Jahaziel was filled with the Spirit of God and called out, "King Jehosophat and all the citizens of Judah! Listen to what God says: 'Do not be afraid or discouraged, because this is not your battle but mine – go to the ravine near the desert of Jeruel, take up your positions and see how I will deliver you!'"

So in the morning, King Jehosophat set out with his troops. He encouraged his people to have faith in God and to trust him for the outcome of the battle. Then he chose singers to lead the army, and they set off, praising God with all their hearts.

As they began to sing and their voices echoed in the mountains, God sent confusion among the enemies of God's people, and they rushed into their own ambushes. In this way the enemies of Judah destroyed each other.

King Jehosophat went back with his people to the temple in Jerusalem, and there they sang praises to God who had saved them and given peace to the kingdom of Judah.

JEHU THE AVENGER

2 Kings 9

In Israel, wicked King Ahab's son succeeded him. His name was Joram.

The prophet Elisha knew that God had told his master, Elijah, that one day a man named Jehu would become king of Israel and wipe out the line of King Ahab forever. Jehu was the commander of the Israelite army, serving under Joram, the son of Ahab.

One day, Elisha sent a messenger to Jehu in secret, saying, "This is what the Lord God of Israel says: 'I anoint you king over my people, the people of Israel. You must destroy all those left in Ahab's family as a punishment for their disobedience in killing my people.'"

Immediately, Jehu harnessed his chariot and rode furiously to the city of Jezreel. King Joram's watchman saw the chariot coming from afar. He ran down from the lookout tower, shouting, "There are troops approaching!"

"Who is it?" said Joram, struggling to his feet. His servants scanned the horizon.

"It looks like Jehu because he drives like a madman!" said the watchman.

"Harness my chariot at once," ordered King Joram. Then he rode out to meet his commander and asked him, "Do you come in peace, Jehu?"

"Peace?" said Jehu scornfully. "What kind of peace is there when Jezebel, your mother, is still alive with all her idols and sorcery?"

Joram wheeled his chariot around at once, shouting,

"Treason, treason!" But it was too late. Jehu's arrow pierced the king's shoulder blades and he fell dead into the sand.

Jehu rode on until he came into the city. There Jezebel, Joram's mother, was in her palace tower. Although her husband, Ahab, was dead, she still thought of herself as the powerful queen of Israel. She put eyeshadow on her eyes and powdered her face and arranged her hair. Then she leaned out of the window and looked down on Jehu with contempt.

She hated anyone who followed God and in her life had ordered the murder of many of God's people. She began to taunt Jehu, laughing at his ambition to rule Israel.

"How long will your kingdom last?" she sneered. "Seven days?"

"Who is on my side?" shouted Jehu. "Anyone up there?"

Three of Jezebel's servants looked out of the window.

"Throw the hag down!" he shouted, and they threw the old woman down onto the road where she was trampled to death under Jehu's horse. That was the end of Ahab and Jezebel's evil influence on Israel.

A NEW KIND OF PROPHET

2 KINGS 13, AMOS

Elisha, the man of God, died and was buried. The people mourned, because he had shown God's great power and had taught them about goodness and justice.

All the great deeds of Elijah and Elisha were remembered down the years, but even so the people of Israel and Judah continued to disobey God and turn away from his laws.

After Elisha, God sent other prophets who began to write down his messages on parchment scrolls. One of these was Amos, a humble farmer who herded sheep in the hills of Tekoa and tended a grove of fig trees. Although Amos lived in Judah, God chose him to speak his message to the people of Israel.

The capital of Israel, the great city of Samaria, was full of rich and powerful people who were making God very angry with their greed and their wickedness. They did not care about people who were poor, but made them sell their land or borrow money at high interest rates.

The merchants and the officials of the royal household and all the powerful people of Samaria were shocked when this rough and forthright farmer came striding through the streets of their city.

"You trample on all the poor people like dirt on the ground!" Amos shouted. "You are selling innocent people as slaves and the poor for the price of a pair of shoes! Do you think God is blind to your crimes? Don't you know that his judgment is coming upon the whole of Israel and that soon you will be slaves yourselves?"

God had shown Amos what would happen in the future: a terrible disaster would one day fall upon the land and God's people would be captured and taken away into exile. Although the people went to the temple to worship him, God knew that all they really cared about was themselves and their riches.

"This is what God says," the voice of Amos thundered outside the palace gates and at the door of the high priest:

"I don't care for all your songs, I will block my ears to the music of your harps. No! Let there be justice, rolling down like a river. Let there be kindness and goodness like an everlasting stream."

Amos did not get a good hearing. Instead the people were angry and did not change their ways. They did not become fairer and kinder to the poor, nor did they turn away from doing bad things.

Amos must have felt like a failure as he returned home to Judah, but one day, when God's people were taken into captivity by the king of Assyria and became slaves in a foreign land, they remembered everything he had said.

THE LOVING HUSBAND

HOSEA

Hosea, the prophet, was living in the far north of Israel at a time when God's people were being unfaithful. They did not worship God, but bowed down before Baal and the gods of Canaan.

God told Hosea, "Go and marry a woman who will prove unfaithful to you. She will leave you for other men and cause you terrible sorrow. You will speak of *my* pain from the depths of your heart when you prophesy against the unfaithful people of Israel."

Hosea obeyed God and married Gomer. He loved her very much, and they had two sons and a daughter, but soon she betrayed her husband and ran away, leaving Hosea heartbroken.

Even though Hosea had known that Gomer would be unfaithful, it did not make his pain any easier. He sobbed and raged at what she had done, and when he went to give the people God's message, the tears streamed down his face. "God

218

says: 'What am I to do with you, my people? Your love is like mist in the early morning; it vanishes so quickly into nothing! How soon you have betrayed me, how soon you have broken all your promises!'"

One day, God told Hosea, "Go and find your wife even though she is unfaithful. I want you to love her just as I love my people."

When Hosea found Gomer, she had become nothing more than a slave. Hosea paid a large sum of money to buy her back and took her to his own home. From that day, he looked after her with great tenderness. This was a way of showing what God was like: full of mercy to his unfaithful people. Then God spoke through Hosea to his people: "'Come back to me, my people. What you have done has destroyed you, but I will love you with all my heart. I will forgive all your unfaithfulness.'"

A VISION OF HOLINESS

ISAIAH 1, 6

Isaiah lived in the beautiful city of Jerusalem, high in the hills of Judah, where King David had once led the people in praise and worship of God. Jerusalem was God's holy city, but now all Isaiah could see was the wickedness and selfishness of God's chosen people.

"O heaven and earth, hear what God says," Isaiah proclaimed on the steps of the temple. "'The ox knows its owner and the donkey knows who will feed it, but my own people have forgotten me!'"

The people did not listen but carried on doing evil, robbing the poor, telling lies and living greedy and selfish lives.

Isaiah wished that King Uzziah would change things for the better and lead his people back to God. Uzziah was a good man, but one day he died, and Isaiah was suddenly frightened of the future.

As he stood alone in the temple, Isaiah saw a light burning all around the holy place, rising up to heaven. He had a vision of such brightness that he fell back, shielding his eyes. He saw God seated on a throne, a great and mighty king. There were heavenly beings, seraphim, made of fire with six wings – two to cover their faces, two to cover their bodies, and two for flying. As they flew through the air, the seraphim called out to each other in loud voices, "Holy, holy, holy is the Lord Almighty; his glory fills the whole earth!"

At the sound of their voices, the stones of the temple shook, and smoke swirled around. Isaiah cried out, "There is no hope for me. I am lost! I am a wrongdoer, speaking sinful words and living in a land of sinners, and I have seen the King, the Lord Almighty!"

Then one of the seraphim picked up a live coal from the burning altar with a pair of tongs and flew through the air to Isaiah. The angel touched his lips with the fiery coal. "Look," he whispered, "fire has touched your lips and made you clean. Your sin has been taken away."

Isaiah knelt there, and suddenly the voice of God called from heaven, "Who can I send to my people?"

Isaiah answered, "Here I am. Send me!"

God told Isaiah to take his message to the people – words of warning and judgment, but words of comfort too: "You must speak to them even though they will not listen."

"For how long?" the prophet asked.

"Until the land lies in ruins," said God. "But even then, there will still be hope for my people."

THE MESSAGE OF ISAIAH

ISAIAH 2, 3, 11

Isaiah, like many of the prophets, had a difficult task: God sent him to warn his people that if they did not turn away from their sins – and turn back to God – then disaster would befall them.

The city of Jerusalem is doomed!
Judah will fall,
for the people turn against God
in everything they do and say.
They ignore his commands and disobey
*   his laws.*
Disaster stares them in the face,
and they have brought it on themselves.

But Isaiah also brought a message of hope: God's judgment would not last forever. One day he would bring peace between nations, between individuals, and in the whole of creation.

In the last days,
*   people from all over the world will say,*
"Let's go to the mountain
*   where the temple stands,*
to the house of God.

He will teach us his ways,
so that we can learn to please him."

God's laws will come from Zion,
his teaching from Jerusalem.
He will judge the nations
and will settle disputes for many peoples.
They will turn their swords into ploughs
and their spears into pruning knives.
Nations will not take up arms against each other,
nor will they prepare for warfare again.

Wolves will live side by side with sheep,
and leopards with goats;
the calf and the lion will feed together peacefully,
and a little child will lead them.

There will be nothing harmful or destructive
on all my holy mountain,
for the whole world will be
    as full of the knowledge of the Lord
as the oceans are full of water!

THE END OF ISRAEL

2 KINGS 17

Although God sent many prophets to the kingdom of Israel, the people continued ignoring him. One king after another encouraged idol worship, setting up places to worship the goddess Asherah on the hilltops and making golden statues of Baal. There were shrines on every hill and under every spreading oak tree. Some kings even sacrificed their own sons and daughters, burning them on huge bonfires, and the people followed their example. The whole land turned away from God and disobeyed his laws. There were sorcerers, mediums and astrologers, leading the people away from God.

All this stirred the furious anger of the God of Israel until he had no more patience with his wayward people. So in the time of the last king, God allowed the land to be conquered by the Assyrian army.

Shalmaneser, the king of Assyria, surrounded Samaria, the capital city of Israel, and laid siege to it for three years with his massive army. Hoshea, the king, was captured and thrown into a deep dungeon in chains. Finally, the starving citizens of Samaria gave in and the city fell to the Assyrian conquerors. The people of Israel were taken away, hundreds of thousands of them, into captivity in the Assyrian empire. In this way, all the ten tribes of Israel vanished and were never seen again.

From the time when King Jeroboam had set up the two golden calves at Bethel and Dan as idols to worship, the people had turned away from God. Now God's terrible judgment had fallen on them, and the story of these tribes had come to a tragic end.

A FAITHFUL KING OF JUDAH

2 KINGS 18, 19

While the kingdom of Israel was destroyed, Hezekiah, the king of Judah, remained faithful to God. He managed to resist the might of the Assyrian army and save his kingdom from disaster.

Hezekiah set about smashing down the altars to pagan gods which his father, Ahaz, had set up, and he destroyed the idols in his land. He opened up God's temple in Jerusalem, which his father had nailed shut, so the people could worship in freedom once more.

He refused to pay tribute money to the king of Assyria and put his trust in God.

Soon Sennacherib, the new king of Assyria, was marching upon the kingdom of Judah. He had a formidable army. Everyone in Jerusalem was terrified because they had seen how the Assyrians had overrun the whole of the northern kingdom of Israel.

Hezekiah tore his clothes and put on sackcloth as a sign of his grief when he heard about this. He went up to the temple and prayed for help from God.

Then Sennacherib sent a letter to Hezekiah. It said, "Where are the gods of all the other people I have defeated? The gods of Gozan, Haran and Eden? How can your God deliver you from my mighty army?"

Hezekiah prayed, "O Lord God of Israel, high on your throne above the winged cherubim, hear me and deliver my people! The king of Assyria has destroyed gods of wood and stone, but you are the living God. Save your people and show all the kingdoms on earth who is the only true God."

Then Isaiah, the prophet, sent a message to Hezekiah: "This is what the Lord says to Sennacherib: 'You are despising the Holy One of Israel. I will put a hook through your nostrils and a muzzle on your lips and drag you back to Assyria!'"

That night, God's judgment struck the Assyrian camp, and one hundred and eighty-five thousand men died. Sennacherib was forced to return to Nineveh. Soon afterwards he was praying at the altar of his god when his sons crept up behind him and murdered him.

Hezekiah had put his faith in God, not in his army, and because of this the kingdom of Judah was saved.

HIDDEN TREASURE

2 KINGS 21–25

After Hezekiah died, his son Manasseh became king. He soon destroyed all the good things his father had done, and once more the people in Judah turned away from God to worship idols. The temple in Jerusalem was filled with altars to foreign gods, and Manasseh even sacrificed his own son. He consulted witches and mediums instead of God's prophets, and he murdered anyone who spoke against him.

Manasseh's son, Amon, was no better, but the people rebelled against him and killed him. They proclaimed his little boy, Josiah, king. Josiah was only eight years old, but from the moment he came to the throne it was as if sunlight had pierced the great darkness over the land.

Josiah truly loved God and served him faithfully. He began to lead his people back to God, and the people willingly gave him money to help repair the broken-down temple. Carpenters, masons, builders and priests all worked together, rebuilding the walls.

One day, Hilkiah, the high priest, rushed out into the courtyard. He was clutching a huge scroll covered in dust.

"Look!" he shouted. "I've found this, hidden away in the temple."

The king's secretary, Shaphan, came running up to him as Hilkiah blew off clouds of dust.

Hilkiah unrolled it slowly.

"It's God's book… the book of the Law," he said.

Immediately, Shaphan carried the ancient scroll to King Josiah and began to read to him.

As soon as Josiah heard the words, he, too, realized that this was the great book of the Law which had been lost for many years. He tore his robes in despair, saying, "God must be very angry with us for forgetting his words and disobeying all his laws and commandments. Gather all the people together and let them hear what it says."

So all the people of Judah came together, and Josiah himself read from the holy book.

"We must promise to obey God's laws once again and to follow him faithfully."

All the people promised to obey God. Then Josiah ordered them to smash down every idol and every altar to false gods that remained in the land, and he expelled all the sorcerers and mediums.

But even though he could change the way his people behaved for a time, Josiah could not bring their hearts back to

God. The kings of Judah who came after him led the people astray once again until the time came for God's judgment to fall finally, and terribly, on Jerusalem itself.

THE RELUCTANT PROPHET

JEREMIAH 1–40, 52

Jeremiah lived in the time of King Josiah. When he was a young man, God spoke to him.

"I am too young to be a prophet," said Jeremiah, "and this job is too difficult for me."

"You were chosen long before you were born," God told him. "I appointed you, and I am with you forever. I will give you courage, and I will tell you what to say."

Even though he was only young, Jeremiah felt the pain and sorrow that God felt when he saw how the people lived, turning away from him.

But Jeremiah felt God's love too, so the reluctant prophet called out to the people of Jerusalem. "Hear what God says: 'Change your lives, and I may let you stay in Jerusalem. But if you continue to steal from widows, ruin the lives of orphans, hate foreigners, live greedily and act violently, then I will throw you out of my sight! Don't fool yourselves by thinking you're safe in God's temple!'"

No wonder the people of Jerusalem hated Jeremiah and refused to listen to him. They didn't want to hear bad news. All they wanted to do was silence Jeremiah by throwing him into prison or killing him.

Sometimes God told Jeremiah to speak to his people in

pictures. Perhaps these at least would help them understand. One day, the prophet said, "Just as a potter creates a pot and destroys it when it is faulty, so God will destroy his disobedient people." But still the people did not listen.

Jeremiah cried out to God, "Why have you given me such an impossible task? Why have you chosen me to be your messenger when no one listens? Yet your word still burns in my heart and my whole body is on fire with your commands."

Jeremiah had no choice but to carry on. Five kings of Judah came and went, but Josiah was the only one who listened; all the others refused to pay attention. Meanwhile, the empire of Babylon swallowed up the Assyrians, and so Jeremiah warned the people of Judah, "The Babylonians are coming, and they will bring God's judgment with them. You cannot resist them."

"Traitor!" the people shouted. "Do you want us to give in to King Nebuchadnezzar and the Babylonians?"

Jeremiah was thrown into prison more than once, and his scroll of prophecies was burned. But whatever people did or said, he kept on speaking God's words to everyone he met. God gave him extraordinary courage.

The day came when the Babylonians invaded Jerusalem and carried off the young King Jehoiachin and many nobles and courtiers. They put King Zedekiah on the throne instead, because they knew he would do everything they told him. But still the people refused to listen to Jeremiah. Instead they listened to false prophets, who said, "This exile will only last a little while – in two years everyone will be back home!"

"You're wrong!" said Jeremiah. "It will be seventy years before God's judgment is over; then he will show his love once again."

"Love?" The people and the priests thought Jeremiah was

mad, talking of God's love and mercy when he was predicting a great disaster.

"This is what God says," Jeremiah cried out, pleading with tears. "'I have plans to help you, plans to give you hope and a new future. In the midst of your pain and sorrow you will seek me once again with your whole heart, and I will lead you back to the land of Judah.'"

King Zedekiah grew furiously angry. He had Jeremiah thrown into jail as a warning, but soon released him. Then Jeremiah's enemies threw him down a huge empty well where he sank deep into the mud. When Zedekiah heard what had happened, he felt guilty and allowed his servants to rescue Jeremiah. But still he did not listen to Jeremiah's warnings.

Soon, King Nebuchadnezzar of Babylon marched on Jerusalem with a huge army. Zedekiah was captured, blinded and taken away to far-off Babylon, along with huge numbers of prisoners. Before long, just as Jeremiah had prophesied, the whole city of Jerusalem was broken down and destroyed by fire.

God's judgment had fallen on the people who had refused to listen. But there were some prisoners who loved God and continued to worship him with all their hearts. Now it was time for them to show great courage and prove that Jeremiah was right. God had plans to protect his people and, one day, to save them from their enemies.

DANIEL AND HIS FRIENDS

DANIEL 1, 2

Far away in Babylon, a number of young noblemen, captives from Jerusalem, attracted the attention of King Nebuchadnezzar.

"I want these young men to be trained in the royal household," ordered the king. "Put them on a special diet and prepare them for service."

One of them was named Daniel, and he had three friends, Shadrach, Meshach and Abednego. When Ashpenaz, the chief official in the court, came to them with the king's instructions, all four of them were greatly concerned.

"You must drink this wine and eat this food from the royal table – you must have the very best if you are to serve the great king of Babylon," said Ashpenaz.

"No," said Daniel. "We worship the God of our fathers, and therefore we cannot eat the royal food! We cannot eat anything which has been offered to the gods of Babylon."

Ashpenaz was worried. He liked Daniel and he could see that they were all good men. "But what if the king sees you all getting thinner? He'll cut off my head!"

"No," Daniel assured him. "Don't be afraid. Just give us ten days on vegetables and water, and see how we look."

"Vegetables and water? You really mean this?"

"Ten days," said Daniel.

After ten days on vegetables and water, the four men looked stronger and healthier than all the other captives who had eaten from the royal table, so they were allowed to continue with their diet. As time passed, they became famous in the court for their wisdom and learning.

Daniel had the gift of interpreting dreams and, on more than one occasion, helped King Nebuchadnezzar when all his other wise men had failed him. But the royal diet was only the first test of the exiles' trust in God.

THE FIERY FURNACE

DANIEL 3

King Nebuchadnezzar of Babylon made a huge statue of gold. It was enormous – the biggest statue in the world.

"Everyone will worship my god," he commanded, "and they will know that I am the mightiest king on earth."

His herald shouted to the crowds, "Hear the king's command: 'All peoples of the earth will bow down to the image and worship it. When you hear the sound of the horn and the flute and pipes and drums, then fall down on your faces before the golden idol.' This is the command of King Nebuchadnezzar! If anyone does not fall down and worship at once, they will be thrown into a burning fiery furnace."

Everyone obeyed – everyone in the kingdom except Shadrach, Meshach and Abednego, exiles in the land.

"We will never bow down to the golden image," they said. "We worship the Lord, the God of Israel."

When Nebuchadnezzar heard of this, he flew into a furious rage. "Bring these traitors to me!" When he saw the three young men coming towards him, quietly and so confidently, he was amazed. "Is it true that you will not bow down and worship my gods? I will give you one last chance. Pray before the golden image! If you do not…" his face twisted into a snarl and his eyes blazed with hatred, "… then you will be hurled into the burning fiery furnace. What god can save you?"

"Our God can save us," answered Shadrach, Meshach and Abednego, "and we do not need to defend ourselves before you, King Nebuchadnezzar! God can rescue us from the burning fiery furnace if he chooses! And even if not, we will never worship your gods or bow down to the golden image."

"Heat the furnace seven times hotter," shouted Nebuchadnezzar, "and hurl them to their deaths!"

Nebuchadnezzar watched with a cruel smile as the three young men, bound hand and foot, disappeared into the roaring fire.

But then the king stood up in amazement.

"What is it?" his advisers asked.

"I see four men!"

"Four, my Lord?"

"Didn't I throw in three men just now? So who is the fourth, walking in the middle of the furnace?"

Sure enough, Shadrach, Meshach and Abednego were walking around unharmed, and with them was a figure who shone more radiantly than the brightest fire on earth.

Immediately, Nebuchadnezzar called the three men out of the fire. "Servants of the Most High God," he shouted, "come out!"

The three men came out, and all the people saw that not a hair on their heads had been harmed. They did not even smell of smoke.

"Praise to the God of Shadrach, Meshach and Abednego, who sent his angel and rescued his servants!" said Nebuchadnezzar.

"They trusted in him and disobeyed me. They were ready to give up their own lives for their God!"

So Nebuchadnezzar ordered everyone in the land to pay homage to the God of Shadrach, Meshach and Abednego, and he appointed them to the most important positions in the whole kingdom of Babylon.

BELSHAZZAR'S FEAST

DANIEL 5

The years passed and a new king ruled over Babylon. His name was Belshazzar, and he was a proud and reckless man who brought his own kingdom to ruin. His reign came to an end very suddenly in one night.

Belshazzar was feasting with a thousand of his noblemen, drinking wine, laughing, jeering and gloating over the great conquests of Babylon. He waved his hands and shouted, "Bring me all the gold and silver vessels from the temple in Jerusalem – all the sacred vessels stored in my royal treasury!"

His servants fetched the beautiful golden cups and bowls that the Babylonians had looted when they destroyed Jerusalem. Belshazzar clumsily and drunkenly poured wine into one of them. "Here we are!" he called. "Let's drink a toast to all the gods of Babylon!" But as they were drinking, a mysterious hand appeared high on the palace wall. From its finger appeared strange words: MENE MENE TEKEL PARSIN.

"If any man can read this message," said Belshazzar,

trembling and shaking, "I will give him great rewards. He will be a governor of my kingdom!"

None of the magicians or fortune-tellers or sorcerers could read a word. Then the queen reminded Belshazzar, "In the time of Nebuchadnezzar there was a man named Daniel who had the spirit of great wisdom and could unlock all mysteries. Send for him!"

Daniel walked slowly into the banqueting hall, gazing in despair at the sacred cups and bowls from Jerusalem lying all around the room.

"I will give you great rewards if you can interpret the message," said the king.

"Keep your rewards!" said Daniel. "But I will give you the meaning of these words from the Lord of heaven! Since you have drunk out of the cups from his temple, praising idols and mocking the true God who has given you life and breath, here is what he says. *Mene:* God has counted the days of your kingdom and brought it to an end; *Tekel:* you have been weighed in the scales and found wanting; *Parsin:* your kingdom has been divided and handed over to the Medes and the Persians."

That very night, Belshazzar was murdered, and his kingdom was taken over by Darius the Mede.

THROWN TO THE LIONS!

DANIEL 6

Daniel served under King Darius and became his friend and most trusted adviser.

All the other advisers in the kingdom grew more and more jealous of him, and when they heard that Darius was going to make Daniel the most important man in the kingdom, they plotted against his life. They knew that, although he was part of the government, he was not a Mede, but a Jew. He was faithful in keeping God's laws and in his worship.

"Your Majesty," they said, "you are such a great and wise ruler; please pass a law to make all the people worship only you for thirty days."

King Darius was surprised and flattered at this suggestion. His advisers bowed low to the ground, saying, "Let anyone who worships any other god be thrown into the lions' den!"

So Darius took his royal seal, wrote out the law in his own handwriting and sealed it in front of them. Daniel's enemies were thrilled at their success, bowing low and smiling with triumph.

"Remember, O King," they said, "the law of the Medes and Persians can never be changed!"

When Daniel heard of the new law, he went straight to his home and began to pray to God. Three times a day, he went to his upper room where the windows opened towards Jerusalem. There he knelt and prayed, just as he had always done.

Soon, the word came to King Darius: "Daniel is disobeying the royal law! He refuses to worship the king, but prays to his own God."

Then Darius grew pale. He buried his face in his hands, deeply distressed, because he trusted and respected Daniel.

"Remember that the laws of the Medes and Persians cannot be changed," said the advisers slyly.

"Yes, I remember!" shouted the king and stormed away from them, desperately thinking of a way to rescue his friend Daniel.

But it was impossible. He had passed the law himself and could not change it, and so he was forced to have Daniel arrested and thrown into the lions' den.

"Daniel!" he called. "May your God, whom you worship so faithfully, rescue you now!"

A stone was rolled against the huge pit and sealed with the royal seal, and Darius walked away slowly and sorrowfully. He could not eat or sleep that night, and at the first light of dawn he rushed from the palace all the way to the lions' den. He stood at the entrance and listened. He could hear nothing. He leaned against it in despair. He called out, "Daniel, Daniel, servant of the living God, has your God been able to rescue you from the lions?"

Then he heard a voice echoing in the darkness. "O King, live forever!"

"Daniel... is it you... are you alive?"

"I am alive, Your Majesty. There is no mark or scratch on me at all because my God has sent his angel to shut the mouths of the lions!"

"Roll the stone away," the king commanded his soldiers, and he saw Daniel sitting down, surrounded by the lions who lay in a circle, sleeping peacefully around him. The soldiers hauled him into the daylight.

Then the king ordered the evil advisers to be hurled into the lions' den, where the lions leaped up at them and killed them before they even touched the floor.

"Now I will issue a decree," said King Darius, "a law that must be obeyed. Let everyone in my kingdom worship the God of Daniel, who saved his servant from the lions' mouths. He is the living God!"

QUEEN ESTHER

Xerxes was the ruler of the great Persian empire and a very powerful king. He lived in a huge palace and had everything he wanted.

To celebrate the third year of his reign, he threw a lavish banquet serving the finest wine and wonderful food.

While the king and his guests feasted, Queen Vashti, his wife, held her own banquet for the women of the palace. On the seventh day, King Xerxes was merry from all the drinking, and he stumbled to his feet.

"Bring me the queen," he ordered his servants. "Let her parade her beauty before all my guests!"

But Queen Vashti would have none of this. She sent a message: "Tell King Xerxes that Queen Vashti refuses his invitation."

When Xerxes heard this, he struck his fist on the table and asked his advisers, "What shall be done when the queen disobeys the king of the Medes and the Persians, whose word is law?"

"Banish her from the royal presence forever," they replied, "and let it be known that the king is seeking a new wife to take her place – one who will obey him and be an example to all the women in Persia!"

So the king issued a decree, and a great many virgins were chosen and taken into his harem so he could select a new queen.

A young woman named Esther lived in Susa. The fame of

Esther's beauty reached the ears of the king's servants, and she was taken into the harem. Before long, she was raised to the highest position among the women.

Esther's family was descended from the captives taken by King Nebuchadnezzar from Jerusalem, and she lived alone with her cousin Mordecai, who had adopted her when her parents had died.

"Tell no one that you are a Jew," he advised her. "Be careful! I will walk by the palace gates every day and find out how you are."

After twelve months of beauty treatments, Esther was ready to be presented to the king.

Immediately, Xerxes fell in love with her, preferring her to all the other women in the harem, and he proclaimed her queen of the Persian empire.

A TEST OF COURAGE

Esther 2–9

Each day, as he had promised, Mordecai went to the gates of King Xerxes' palace to see how his cousin Esther was doing now that she had become queen of Persia.

At this time, King Xerxes appointed a proud nobleman named Haman to the highest office in the land. All the officials bowed low to the ground every time Haman passed by, but one day he noticed that Mordecai would not bow.

"Who is that man?" he said to the doorkeepers.

"Mordecai, my Lord Haman."

"Why does he insult me?"

"He is a Jew, my Lord, and the Jews may only worship their God."

From that moment, Haman took a violent dislike to Mordecai and all the Jewish people. He began to poison the mind of King Xerxes against the Jews and persuaded him to issue a royal decree to murder them and seize their property.

Mordecai sent Esther a copy of the decree. "You must go into the king's presence and beg for mercy for your people!" he said.

Esther was overcome with grief when she read the order to destroy the Jewish people, but she knew how dangerous it was for her to approach the king.

No one could enter the king's presence without being summoned – anyone who broke this law would be sentenced to death.

Mordecai told her, "If you keep silent now, help will come from somewhere else, but you and all your father's family will die. Besides, maybe you have come to the royal throne for such a time as this."

"I will go in to the king," replied Esther, "and if I die, so be it – I will die."

After three days of prayer and fasting, Esther put on her finest robes and walked into the inner courtyard. She stood near the doorway to the king's hall, very still. The king looked up and saw Esther standing there alone. Her exquisite beauty touched his heart and he let her approach him. She knelt before him.

"What is it, my queen?" he said. "Anything you desire is yours. I will give you anything you ask, even half of my kingdom!"

"If it pleases the king," she answered, "come with Haman

tonight to a banquet I am preparing for you."

When Haman heard that he had been invited to a banquet alone with the king and the queen, he was so happy – but almost immediately his happiness was destroyed by the sight of Mordecai, refusing to bow down to him.

So Haman ordered his servants to go and build some huge gallows, towering into the sky. After the banquet, he would ask the king to have Mordecai publicly hanged for his disrespect.

That night, at the banquet, the king asked Esther for her request. "Grant me my life," she said.

"Your life?"

"My life and the life of all my people!"

"What do you mean – what is this?"

"My Lord," said Esther, "an order has been made to destroy the lives and the homes of all my people."

"Where is the enemy who has thought of this?" asked the king.

"There," shouted Esther, "beside you! The enemy is this vile man, Haman!"

The king ordered Haman to be taken away and hanged. Haman was executed on the very gallows that he had prepared for Mordecai.

From that day, the Jewish people were saved, and the king gave them the right to defend themselves against all their enemies. Mordecai was raised to the highest position in the kingdom, next to the king, and Esther was recognized as a woman of the greatest courage, as well as beauty.

The Jewish people declared a special feast named Purim, so that the deliverance of the Jews from death would be remembered forever.

THE JOYFUL RETURN

EZRA 1–6, PSALM 126

Ever since they had been taken captive by Nebuchadnezzar, God's people had longed to return to Jerusalem, the city of God.

Each day, they turned three times to Jerusalem to pray. Each day, they wept over the destruction of the holy city. They dreamed of their temple, once so beautiful, now broken and shattered and strangled by weeds. They longed to go home and to rebuild their city and to worship God once more in his holy place.

Many years passed, and it sometimes seemed that God was silent, but all the time God was at work, preparing for the day when his people would return.

The first extraordinary thing to happen was the decree of King Cyrus of Persia. He announced, "The Lord God of heaven has told me to build him a temple in Jerusalem!"

The great king, who believed in many other gods, was sure that the God of Israel had spoken to him clearly. He gave permission for a large number of Jewish families to set out for Judah and begin the work of rebuilding Jerusalem and the temple.

The men, women and children who returned from exile sang psalms of praise to God:

When God brought back the captives
  to Jerusalem,
it was like living in a dream;
We laughed with wonder
  and we sang for joy.

All the other people said,
"Look what good things their God
  has done for them!"
The Lord God has done great things for us
  and we are overflowing with joy.

REBUILDING JERUSALEM

NEHEMIAH 1–7

God's people returned from Babylon full of enthusiasm to rebuild the temple. But it was not an easy task; there were many people living around Jerusalem who tried to stop the work. And so what had started in the time of King Cyrus went on into the time of King Xerxes, and by the time of his son Artaxerxes the struggle was proving too great.

Word of this reached Nehemiah. He was the cup-bearer to King Artaxerxes of Persia, and he received a message that the walls of Jerusalem were broken down again, and the gates had been burned by fire.

When Nehemiah heard this, he wept bitterly. He prayed and fasted for many days and nothing could comfort him, even though he was prosperous and successful and highly respected in the court of the king of Persia.

Nehemiah's heart was in Jerusalem, and all he could think about was its shattered walls and the ruin of his homeland. He poured out his tears and prayers to God. He confessed his sins and the sins of all his people that had led them into exile so many years ago. "Listen to the prayer of your servant," he begged, "and grant me success with the king today."

Nehemiah walked slowly into the presence of King Artaxerxes with his eyes cast down to the ground and an expression of great sadness. It was considered a serious crime to be miserable in front of the king and Nehemiah was taking a great risk, but the king was very concerned.

"Why are you so upset, Nehemiah? You are not ill, so I can see that this is some grief in your heart!"

Nehemiah bowed very low. "O King, live forever! How can I help being sad when the city where my ancestors are buried lies in ruins."

"What would you like me to do for you?" asked the king.

Everyone in the court was amazed. Nehemiah prayed again silently to God and said to the king, "Let me return to Jerusalem and rebuild the city."

Artaxerxes gave Nehemiah permission, sending him with letters of approval and promising him timber from the royal forests to make new beams for the gates of the city. And so Nehemiah set off on the long journey to Jerusalem.

When Nehemiah arrived, he persuaded the people who were living there to help in the great work. He showed them his letters from the king and said, "God is on our side!"

The people, who had been too afraid to do anything, were filled with hope and courage. Every family set to work building the walls around their homes, working night and day. Nehemiah and all the people who had come with him from Persia prayed and worked until the walls were built to half their height around the city.

Then Sanballat, the governor of Samaria, and Tobiah heard about this. They were very angry that the Jews were rebuilding the city, and they rode up on their horses, mocking and laughing.

"What kind of wall is this?" they sneered. "A fox could jump on it and knock it over!"

Nehemiah stood up to them, even though they accused him of trying to rebel against King Artaxerxes, and they began to spread lies that Nehemiah was going to proclaim himself king.

Nehemiah gave the people weapons and made sure that there were plenty of guards on the lookout for their enemies.

"Keep building," he said. "Sanballat and Tobiah think they can wear us down with mockery and threats!"

Nehemiah was a good leader. He encouraged the people every day, organized them cleverly, reminded them of God's power, worked extremely hard and prayed, "Strengthen my hands so we can complete this work."

God answered his prayer, for in two short months the walls were rebuilt and all the enemies of God's people were put to shame.

REBUILDING GOD'S PEOPLE

EZRA, NEHEMIAH 8–13

Rebuilding Jerusalem, with its temple, its great walls and gates and its many houses, seemed like the greatest miracle to the Jewish people. But Ezra, the priest, helped them to understand that stone, bricks and mortar were just the beginning.

It was Ezra who began the rebuilding of the Jewish nation. He came to Jerusalem in the time of Nehemiah, and he called all the people together – a huge crowd of men, women and children from all over Judah. He summoned them into the square in front of the Water Gate. Then Ezra stood on a high platform and called out, "Blessed be the name of the Lord!"

The people responded loudly, "Amen, amen."

Slowly, Ezra began to read the book of the Law, and as the people heard the words of Moses they began to weep. The old people started to cry because it made them remember what they had learned as children. Then the young people cried because for many of them it was the first time they had heard God's holy words.

Nehemiah and Ezra told the people, "Today is a day of celebration. Do not weep or be sad. Go home and eat the finest food and the sweetest drink. Give help to the poor and rejoice!"

Ezra taught the Jewish people all about their laws and their festivals and customs. He brought them back to their faith in God.

Then Ezra and Nehemiah banned all marriages with foreigners who followed other gods. They could see that, since the time of Solomon, this had caused the greatest problems to their people, who had so often been tempted into idol worship.

Because of the courage of Nehemiah and the powerful teaching of Ezra, both the city of Jerusalem and the Jewish people were rebuilt. The way was open for a new beginning.

JONAH

There was once a prophet named Jonah.

"Jonah," said God, "I have a very special task for you. I want you to go to Nineveh."

"Nineveh? The evil empire of Assyria?" asked Jonah in disbelief.

"Jonah, you must go and warn them because I have seen their wickedness."

Jonah walked out of his house. He did not want to go to Nineveh, the capital city of their greatest enemies. An Israelite prophet wandering the streets of Nineveh, warning of God's judgment? No, it was impossible!

So when Jonah got down to the port at Joppa, instead of journeying to Nineveh, he jumped on a ship going in completely the opposite direction – to Tarshish in southern Spain.

When the boat was out at sea, God sent a hurricane. The ship was hurled around in the huge waves, and the sailors screamed out in fear. They prayed to their gods, but the storm got worse. Then the captain discovered Jonah snoring in the bottom of the boat. "Wake up!" he said. "How can you sleep when we're about to drown? Pray to your God at once and beg him to save us!"

The sailors decided that the gods must be angry with someone, so they drew lots. Jonah was chosen.

"Who are you? Where do you come from?" they shouted against the roaring wind. "Tell us! What have you done?"

"I am a Jew, and I worship the God of heaven and earth, but I have disobeyed him!" said Jonah.

"What shall we do now?"

Jonah knew that he could not escape from God anywhere in the world. "There's only one thing to do," he said. "Throw me overboard!"

The sailors did not want to do this, but at last they had no choice. They hurled Jonah overboard.

Immediately, the wind died down and the sea became perfectly calm. The sailors were amazed. They gave thanks to Jonah's God, who had saved them from death.

Meanwhile, there was no sign of Jonah, no hand waving – only the vast emptiness of the ocean. But God had instructed a great fish to swallow Jonah whole, and for three days and three nights Jonah sat in the belly of the fish.

Then Jonah prayed to God, and God heard him. He made the fish spit Jonah out onto dry land, and the prophet found himself alone on the beach near the great city of Nineveh.

There was no escaping the word of God now. So Jonah marched through the massive gates, proclaiming, "In forty days, Nineveh will be destroyed, and every single person will be judged by God!"

The Assyrians were shocked at the sight of the wild, crazy man wandering through their streets, but they listened.

They listened very hard to what Jonah said, from the poorest to the richest in the land. The king put on sackcloth and ashes and said, "We must all turn away from our wickedness, and perhaps we can still be saved."

Jonah carried on preaching judgment and doom on the city until, on the fortieth day, he marched to the gates of

Nineveh and waited for fire to fall from heaven.

He watched the sun go down and thought, Now our enemies will learn their lesson. They'll see the power and judgment of God!

Darkness came and Jonah waited. He looked up at the bright stars, but none of them fell down. There was no comet, no volcano, only the sound of the birds singing as the dawn appeared. The people of Nineveh began to weep and hug each other because they had been saved.

Jonah flew into a rage with God. "Why do you think I ran away? I knew you would do this. I might as well die!"

"Jonah," said God softly, "do you have a right to be angry?"

Jonah did not reply but walked off into the desert and sat down in the blistering heat.

That night, God instructed a plant to grow over Jonah to give him shade, and in the morning Jonah was delighted with his shelter. But then God told a worm to eat the roots of the plant, and it quickly withered. The next day, Jonah sat miserably in the heat again as God sent a scorching east wind. "Let me die," Jonah said. "Finish me off like the plant."

"Jonah," said God softly again, "have you the right to be angry with me about the plant?"

"I have every right. I am so angry I could die!" shouted Jonah.

"You are concerned for that plant which grew up overnight and which cost you nothing. So why do I not have the right to care for all the thousands of people in Nineveh and all their animals? Is it wrong for me to show my love to them?"

Jonah sat there quietly, thoughtfully, and listened to the sound of the people and the children singing in the streets of Nineveh.

All this was to remind God's chosen people that God loved other nations too. He cared for all his creation.

THE PROMISED KING

ISAIAH 9, MICAH 5

When God's people settled once more in Jerusalem, some of them remembered that God had promised to send the Messiah, the anointed one, to the world. This was what the prophet Isaiah had foretold:

The people who walked in darkness
have seen a great light.
They lived in the land of shadows
but now the dawn has come.

A child has been born for us,
a son has been given to us,
and he shall be our ruler.
He will be named Wise Counsellor,
   Mighty God,
Eternal Father and Prince of Peace.
He will bring peace and security forever.
He will rule from David's throne,
reigning over his kingdom,
governing with honesty and justice
forever and ever.

The prophet Micah prophesied that the Messiah would come from Bethlehem, and that he would be like a shepherd leading his people:

But from you, Bethlehem,
one of the smallest towns in Judah,
will come a ruler over Israel,
one whose family descends from an
     ancient line of kings.

He will be like a shepherd.
Feeding and protecting his flock,
     using God's strength.
He will have the power of the name
     of the Lord God!
His people will be happy and safe,
and his greatness will be known
     throughout the earth,
and he will bring peace.

Jesus said, "I am the light of the world."

JOHN 8:12

THE NEW
TESTAMENT

ZECHARIAH'S PRAYER

Over four hundred years passed after God's people returned
from exile. All this time, they longed for a new freedom,
because they were ruled by other nations. First they were
conquered by the Greeks and then by the Romans. The people
wanted to be free from the great Roman empire and to be ruled
by their own king.

Long ago, the prophets had promised that a king like David
would come, to save his people. He would be the anointed
one, the Messiah. Some people hoped the Messiah would raise
an army and fight against the Romans. Others had almost
forgotten about the words of the prophets. But a few faithful
people prayed that, when the Messiah came, he would bring
justice and peace to the whole world as God had promised.

One of these faithful believers was the old priest, Zechariah.
He had been married for many years, but he and his wife,
Elizabeth, had a great sadness in their life. They were already
growing old, and despite their prayers they had no children. In
those days, having a baby was seen as a proof of God's
blessing, and although everyone knew that they were good
people, Zechariah and Elizabeth sometimes wondered if they
had done something wrong in their lives.

One day, Zechariah was in the temple in Jerusalem. It was
his turn to burn the incense on the altar. He was alone, while
the people who had come to worship prayed and waited
outside. Zechariah cast the incense on the fire, and suddenly,
as the smoke rose up to the ceiling, a shining figure appeared

to the right of the altar. Zechariah was terrified.

"Don't be afraid, Zechariah," said the figure. His voice, filling the huge dark chamber, was like the wind passing through a forest and shaking down the leaves.

Zechariah immediately knew that the figure was an angel from heaven. The voice came again: "God has heard your prayer! Your wife, Elizabeth, is going to have a son and you must name him John. He will bring great joy to you, and many will be blessed by his birth. Your son will be a great man of God, full of the Holy Spirit, and he will prepare the people of Israel for the coming of their Saviour."

"How can I be sure this will happen?" asked Zechariah. "I mean... I am old now and my wife is getting on and..."

The angel looked at him severely. "I am Gabriel, and I stand in the presence of God himself, who has sent me with this good news. Because you are doubting, you will be unable to speak another word until it all comes true!"

With that, he vanished, and Zechariah tried to call after him, but his tongue would not move. He tried to shout, but no sound came. He walked out onto the steps of the temple, and the people called to him, but he was silent.

Zechariah returned to his home in the hills of Judea and, just as the angel had promised, his wife, Elizabeth, soon found that she was expecting a child.

GABRIEL VISITS MARY

LUKE 1

Six months later, God sent the angel Gabriel to the town of Nazareth, high up in the hills of Galilee.

A girl named Mary was living there. She was engaged to Joseph, the carpenter, but they were not yet married.

Mary was alone in her home when she became aware of a figure standing in the doorway, blocking out the sun.

Startled, she looked up, trying to make out the stranger's face, but she could not see who it was against the sunlight.

"Greetings!" said a voice that filled the tiny room and seemed to echo through the whole house. "God has chosen you," said Gabriel. "The Lord God himself is with you!"

Now Mary was afraid. She was trembling, hardly knowing what to say, or what these words could mean.

"Don't be afraid, Mary," Gabriel said. "You are blessed by God!"

"Blessed…" she whispered, "by God…?"

"Yes," said the angel, "for you, Mary, will give birth to a son, and you are to name him Jesus, for he will be great and will be the Son of the Most High. God will give him the throne of his ancestor, King David, and he will reign over his people forever."

"How can this be?" said Mary, staring in her innocence at the angel. "I am a virgin and not yet married to Joseph."

"Mary," the angel replied, "the Holy Spirit will come upon you, the power of the Most High God will cover you, the brightness of his glory will overshadow you. This is why the holy one to be born will be known as the Son of God."

Gabriel turned and walked back to the door, where the sunlight flamed all around him. He stopped and said, "Even Elizabeth, your cousin, who is old, is going to have a child!"

Mary laughed in astonishment. But the angel simply said, "Nothing is impossible with God!"

"I am God's servant," Mary whispered, slowly kneeling down in obedience. There were tears of joy shining in her eyes. "Let everything happen to me just as you have said!"

When she lifted up her eyes again, the angel was gone, and the sunlight streamed into the house, filling the darkness with glory.

MARY VISITS ELIZABETH

LUKE 1

In Judea, Elizabeth, the wife of Zechariah, was preparing for the arrival of her baby. When her cousin Mary walked through the door, Elizabeth's baby leaped inside her, and Elizabeth was filled with God's Spirit, calling out, "You are the most blessed of all women! And your baby is also blessed. Why should this wonderful thing happen to me, that the mother of my Saviour has come into my home?"

Mary sat down beside her, and the women embraced tenderly. "As soon as I heard your greeting, my child danced in the womb," said Elizabeth with amazement. "You are truly happy, Mary, because you have believed what God has promised to you."

Then Mary sang this song of praise to God:

My soul sings of the greatness of the Lord
and my spirit rejoices in God my Saviour,
because he has remembered me, his servant.
From today, all generations will call me blessed,
for the Almighty has done wonderful things for me.
Holy is his name!
His faithful love will reach all people
who fear him throughout the ages.
He has shown his great power,
he has thrown out all those who are proud,
he has toppled rulers from their thrones
and lifted up ordinary, humble people.
He has filled the hungry with good things
and sent the rich away empty-handed.
He has helped his servant Israel,
keeping his promises from long ago,
to show mercy to Abraham and all his
descendants forever.

"HIS NAME IS JOHN!"

LUKE 1

Soon after Mary returned home to Nazareth, Elizabeth gave birth to a son.

The baby was prepared for the special day of circumcision, in the way of all Jewish boys, but when the priest was about to name him Zechariah after his father, Elizabeth cried out, "No! The boy's name is John!"

The guests were amazed. "No one in your family has ever been known as that; we'll have to ask his father!"

They went to Zechariah and asked him, "What do you want your son to be named?"

The old man signed that he needed a writing tablet and a stylus to carve the letters. He wrote, "His name is John." As he did so, he was suddenly given back his speech and praises came pouring out to God.

Everyone then said, "What kind of child will this be? God is surely with him!"

And John grew up and became strong, full of the Holy Spirit.

JOSEPH AND MARY

MATTHEW 1

Joseph was working in his carpenter's shop, beside his home in Nazareth. From his window, he could see a little cluster of houses and smoke rising from the fires. He often looked out, hoping that Mary would come to visit him with her parents; he dreamed of the day when she would enter his house alone and become his wife. Joseph loved her with all his heart.

One day, Mary stopped by his house, and he ran out to meet her. She was very quiet and still, and she said nothing for a long time.

"What is it, Mary?" he asked.

"I have something to tell you."

"Yes…?"

"A baby is going to be born."

At first, Joseph thought she was talking about somebody else, but gradually he realized that she was talking about her own baby.

Joseph looked at her in astonishment, shaking his head. He could not believe that Mary was expecting somebody else's baby, and he could hardly hear what she was saying. "God's baby... the Holy Spirit... an angel from heaven...!" The words all jumbled in his mind as he walked away tearfully.

That night, Joseph decided to call off his marriage to Mary. He would do it very quietly and without any fuss. He would protect her as much as he could, but he knew he could not go on. His pillow was wet with tears as he fell asleep, still thinking of her. But in the darkness of his dreams, a light appeared. All around him, beyond him, a great light was shining, and a voice spoke to him: "Joseph... Joseph, son of David, don't be afraid to take Mary as your wife! Everything she has told you is true. She will give birth to a son and you are to name him Jesus. He will save his people from their sins."

The next morning, Joseph ran down to Mary's house.

"Mary, Mary... an angel... I've seen an angel and... God has told me that..."

The whole story came tumbling out, breathlessly, as Joseph promised to marry her and care for the child.

Mary listened, standing there very still in the sunshine. She looked at Joseph and smiled, because she already knew that everything would be all right.

THE BIRTH OF JESUS

LUKE 2

Just before Jesus was born, the emperor Caesar Augustus ordered his officials to collect the names of every person living in the Roman empire.

There was a strict rule that each man had to register in the town his family came from, so that no one would be missed and avoid paying taxes.

So Joseph needed to travel to Bethlehem, more than seventy miles away. He was anxious about Mary because she was heavily pregnant, but they had to make the journey.

On their way, they passed through ravines and wild places, along desert tracks, up steep hills, until they reached the little town of Bethlehem, high on the hills beside Jerusalem.

It was nightfall and very cold. The streets were full of Roman soldiers and people from different places, men and women running to and fro shouting, chickens squawking, dogs scavenging in the rubbish. Joseph looked to the left and to the right, but every home was packed with people; every inn was overflowing with visitors. At last, they struggled into an old courtyard at the back of the last inn in Bethlehem.

"There's only the stable for the animals," said the innkeeper. "That's all the space I've got. You can sleep in the hay."

"My wife's expecting a baby!" Joseph called after him, but the man had already gone back to his guests who were shouting for food.

Mary smiled and said, "I'll be all right here in the hay. It's very comfortable." And as she lay down, she felt her first birth pangs.

Soon, in the middle of the night, the baby was born.

In the darkness of that cold stable, Mary took her firstborn son, wrapped him in cloths, and put him down to sleep in the manger.

SHEPHERDS AND ANGELS

LUKE 2

That night, there were shepherds out in the fields around Bethlehem, guarding their sheep. They were sitting beside their fire, keeping warm and watching the flames crackle and spit into the darkness. There was no danger, no wild beasts prowling or thieves breaking into the sheepfold; there was only the roar of the fire and the smoke curling up to the stars.

They were chatting softly, making jokes, telling stories, when suddenly a great light flashed from the sky. The shepherds leaped up, terrified. They wanted to run, but there was light all around them – above them, behind them. The whole sky was burning, and the earth was on fire with glory and wonder. An angel towered over them, and they fell to the ground in fear. "Don't be afraid! I've come bringing good news for you and for everyone in the world."

The shepherds looked up slowly, peering through their fingers as the angel continued: "Today in the town of David, a saviour has been born for you. He is Christ the Lord, and here is the sign that this is true: you will find a little baby wrapped in cloths and lying in a manger!"

At that moment, the bright figure was joined by a great company of angels from heaven, thousands of them filling the sky and singing: "Glory to God in the highest and peace on earth to all those he loves!"

Earth and heaven shook with sound, thundering music echoed in the hills and rang from every stone until at last the glory faded, and the singing drifted away like smoke into the night air.

The shepherds were alone. They scrambled up nervously. "We'd better go to Bethlehem and see all this for ourselves," they said.

And so they ran to Bethlehem and went from house to house, inn to inn, until they found the stable.

Inside, they gathered around, their scruffy faces staring from the darkness into the lamplight that shone over the little family – Mary sitting calmly, almost as if she expected them; Joseph standing up, wondering who it was at this time of night and the baby lying in the hay and gazing at them so clearly.

The shepherds told Mary and Joseph everything they had seen and heard, and Mary kept the wonderful words of the angel in her heart, like treasures, stored up forever.

GREAT REJOICING!

LUKE 2

Soon after Jesus was born, Mary and Joseph took him into the temple in Jerusalem for a special blessing. They were following the Jewish custom of giving thanks for the firstborn child and offering him back to God.

Now there was an old man named Simeon in the temple, who loved God with all his heart. He longed for the day when a saviour would be sent into the world, and God had told him, "You will not die until you have seen my chosen one."

As he was standing in the cool shadow of the marble columns, Simeon saw the little family climbing the steps towards the inner courtyard. Simeon watched as Mary stopped to rearrange the cloths around her baby, the sun shining down on her face. She could still hear the words of the angel: "Glory to God in the highest and peace on earth to all those he loves!" She held Jesus close to her, and at that moment the old man knew that God's promise had come true.

Flooding through his heart came the certainty that this was the Messiah – this little baby in his mother's arms was the chosen one sent by God to save the world. He hurried towards them as fast as he could. "Let me hold the little one," he called out. "Let me touch the holy child!"

Mary and Joseph looked at the old man, astonished. Tears were rolling down his face and onto his long grey beard. Calmly, Mary held out the baby to him, and Simeon folded Jesus in his arms.

"Lord," he prayed softly, "now let your servant die in peace, for I have seen with my own eyes the salvation you have promised – a light for all the people in the world, and the glorious hope for the people of Israel!"

WISE MEN VISIT JESUS

MATTHEW 2

After Jesus was born, Mary and Joseph stayed in Bethlehem. One day, they had a visit – mysterious strangers who had journeyed from distant lands in the east. The wise men had journeyed for months, following a magnificent, new star that had suddenly appeared in the sky.

They had followed this star all the way to Jerusalem, where they sent a message to the powerful King Herod: "Where is the one who has been born king of the Jews? We have seen his star and we have come to worship him!"

King Herod was deeply disturbed. "King of the Jews," he said darkly. He wanted no rivals.

"My Lord," one of his attendants said nervously, "these strangers from the East... they say they are looking for a newborn child."

"A child? Whose child?" Murderous jealousy was rising in the old king.

A priest stepped forward. "There are prophecies in the scriptures... the promise of a child who will be born to save Israel."

"Where will this... Messiah... be born?" demanded Herod.

All the priests, scribes and experts were called together, and they told Herod that one day the Messiah would be born in Bethlehem.

Herod called the wise men secretly and pretended to welcome them. "Search for the child in Bethlehem, and when you find him, tell me so I can go and worship him too."

So the wise men went on their way, and when they saw the star appearing over Bethlehem, they were overjoyed. They came to the house where Mary and Joseph were staying with Jesus. They offered their gifts of gold, frankincense and myrrh and knelt to worship the little child who had been sent by God to save the world. Then they left secretly because they had been warned in a dream not to return to Herod.

Soon, Herod sent soldiers to Bethlehem with orders to kill every boy child less than two years old. An angel appeared to Joseph in a dream and warned him, "Herod is searching for the child – to kill him! You must escape at once."

Mary and Joseph fled that night and went to live in Egypt until the old King Herod had died and there was no more danger.

Then they returned at last to their home in Nazareth, where Jesus spent his childhood years.

THE LOST BOY

LUKE 2

When Jesus was twelve years old, Mary and Joseph took him to Jerusalem for the great Passover feast. It was the most important festival in the whole year, and Jerusalem was crowded with visitors. On the way there, they journeyed with all their friends and relatives and hundreds of other people from Galilee. The city was a wonderful sight, decked with flowers. There was always singing and dancing at Passover, and many visitors stayed in tents up on the Mount of Olives, sitting by their fires long into the night, laughing and celebrating the day when God had set the Israelites free from slavery in Egypt.

When the festival was over, Mary and Joseph set off for home, happily surrounded by many friends, and at first they hardly noticed that Jesus was not with them.

"I wonder where he is," said Mary, a few hours later.

"Don't worry," Joseph replied, "he'll catch up before long. He'll be with his cousins further back. The boy's twelve, he can look after himself!"

But as the sun began to sink in the sky, Mary became very worried. So Mary and Joseph turned back to Jerusalem, pushing their way through the crowd, calling out for their son. He was nowhere to be seen. They reached Jerusalem as night was falling and searched in the huge gateways and the shadowy streets. But they could not find Jesus.

They hardly slept and, at dawn, began their desperate search once more. There were still thousands of people thronging every square and narrow street. They stared at the face of each passing child and looked fearfully at the Roman soldiers parading along their battlements. Had Jesus been captured, had something terrible happened? All they could do was search and pray.

On the third day, Mary and Joseph climbed wearily up the temple steps. There were so many people gathering in the great courtyards, the temple was the worst place of all to find anyone, especially a child.

Then Mary caught sight of a tiny figure in the distance – was it a boy? Was it her son?

She began to run. Joseph followed her as she came to a crowd of priests seated in the colonnades. Right in the middle of all the teachers and the lawyers, sitting very calmly, was Jesus.

Mary gasped. She was so amazed that she could not speak for a moment. Jesus was asking questions and discussing the scriptures with all the wisest teachers in Jerusalem. They were listening to him in astonishment, because the boy was speaking with such wisdom.

"O my son," she suddenly called out, "why have you treated us like this? Look how worried we've been!"

Jesus looked into her eyes and said quietly, "Why were you searching everywhere for me? Didn't you know that I would be in my Father's house?"

But Mary and Joseph did not understand what he meant. Then Jesus followed them obediently to Nazareth, and Mary continued to think deeply about what had happened, holding his words in her heart.

THE BAPTISM OF JESUS

MATTHEW 3, LUKE 3

Jesus grew into a strong young man, working with Joseph in the carpenter's shop.

His cousin John, the son of Elizabeth and Zechariah, had already left home. He lived in the desert, a wild figure, with long tangled hair, wearing rough clothes of camels' hair and eating insects and honey. Word went around the whole of Judea that there was a strange new prophet, a man who lived in the wilderness but spoke like an angel, who was telling everyone to be sorry for their sins and to come and wash themselves in the River Jordan. This sacred sign of going under the water and coming up again became known as Baptism.

Hundreds of people came to John – tax collectors, merchants, priests, even soldiers, shouting their questions at him, and John was always ready with a strong answer that went straight to the heart.

"Repent!" John called to the crowds. "Turn back from doing wrong, make a new start. Wash yourself clean in the river!" Many people stepped down with him into the river and were baptized to show that they wanted to begin a new life, serving God in everything they did.

"Who are you?" people asked him. "Do you think that you are God's chosen leader, the Messiah?"

"No," answered John. "No!" he shouted into the wind. "I am only a voice crying in the desert, 'Clear the way! Prepare a path for the Lord who is coming!'"

John knew the secret that Jesus was the chosen one from God, the true Messiah, and he told them, "There is a man coming after me who is far more powerful than I am. I am only baptizing with water, but he will baptize people with the Holy Spirit and with fire!"

"What does he mean?" People shook their heads. The wild prophet often said things that were hard to understand.

Soon after this, John saw Jesus walking towards him and called out, "Here is the Lamb of God, the one who will take away the sins of the whole world."

Again, the crowd did not know what he was talking about, but John knelt down on the river bank. "Why are you coming to me for baptism," he whispered to Jesus, "when you are the one to wash me clean from all my sins?"

"This is how it must be for now," Jesus answered. "I must show that I follow God in everything I do."

So John took Jesus down into the river and baptized him. Jesus went down, vanishing into the darkness with the waters swirling over his head, but as he rose into the light John heard a voice calling from heaven, "This is my beloved Son!"

A dove fluttered in the streaming sunlight, hovering over Jesus, while the voice thundered, "You are my Son, the one I love. You are my delight, and I am well pleased with you!"

The crowd saw nothing and heard only what sounded like thunder in the hills, but John knew that the Holy Spirit had come down upon Jesus in the form of a dove. The Messiah, the Saviour of the world, had come at last.

TEMPTED BY THE DEVIL

MATTHEW 4, LUKE 4

After his baptism, Jesus walked alone into the harsh desert, where the hot winds blew the sand into his face and the sun beat down on him. He wandered alone for many days, praying, thinking, kneeling in silence beneath the stars at night. For forty days and forty nights he ate nothing at all, fasting and praying, offering his whole life to God.

At the end of that time, he was gripped with hunger, and he heard a voice behind him, soft and persuasive, sweetly urging him, "If you are the Son of God, tell that stone in front of you to turn into a loaf of bread."

"No," he answered, knowing that it was God's enemy, the

devil, who was tempting him to use his great powers selfishly, "it is written in the scriptures, 'A man needs more than bread to live; he needs every word that is spoken by the living God!'"

The wind whistled all around him in the wild emptiness, and Jesus walked on alone. But the devil returned suddenly, showing him all the kingdoms of the world – the great cities, the emperors, the towering castles, the mighty armies. "All this power belongs to me," he whispered invitingly, "but you can have everything – I will make you the ruler of the world! – if only you will bow down before me."

Jesus turned away, calling out, "It is written in the scriptures, 'You must worship the Lord your God and serve no one else!'"

Again the devil left him, like a shadow fleeing before the brightness of the sun, but he had not finished his temptations yet. As Jesus lay alone in the merciless heat, hungry and exhausted, the devil returned and swept him up to the highest pinnacle of the temple in Jerusalem.

"Throw yourself down," he murmured, pleasantly. "Go on – prove that you're really the Son of God and let everyone see you coming down from the sky, for it is written in the scriptures, 'The angels will guard you – they will lift you up so you don't even hurt your foot on a stone!'"

Jesus wheeled around at the great enemy of humankind. "Be gone!" he ordered. "For it says in the scriptures, 'Do not put the Lord your God to the test!'"

So the devil was forced to leave him alone at last, and Jesus knelt quietly before his Father in heaven. The words from his baptism echoed in his mind: "You are my Son, the one I love. You are my delight, and I am well pleased with you!" He felt the love and tenderness of God wrapping all around him, protecting him.

Then Jesus returned to Galilee, full of the Holy Spirit, and he began to spread the good news of God's love for the world. People gathered around him and listened eagerly as he told them, "Ask and you will receive; seek and you will find; knock and the door will be opened to you!"

He explained how God listens to prayers and answers them. He taught the crowds that the kingdom of heaven starts on earth in very small ways. "It's like a tiny seed that blows away, no bigger than a speck of dust, but when it lands in the soil, it grows up into the biggest tree of all, and all the birds in the air come and make their nests in its branches."

Everywhere Jesus went, people followed him, wanting to hear more.

WATER INTO WINE

JOHN 2

One day, Jesus, his mother, Mary, and some of his followers were invited to a wedding in the little village of Cana, not far from Nazareth. It was a wonderful occasion with music and dancing. Flower petals were strewn over the bride and groom, filling the air with their perfume. There was laughter and feasting and people sang joyful songs in the firelight as daylight turned to dusk. The feast lasted several days. Everyone said that the groom had spared no expense and that this was the finest wedding celebration in Galilee.

But Mary overheard two servants whispering desperately.

"We've run out of wine!"

"Impossible!"

"There's nothing left – only water."

"We're only halfway through the wedding. What are we going to do?"

Mary knew that it would bring great disgrace on the bridegroom's family if the guests were forced to drink water instead of wine.

"Don't tell the bridegroom yet," she said. "Wait here."

The servants looked at her in amazement as she ran quickly up to Jesus. "They've run out of wine," she told him.

Jesus gazed at her for a long time. "Woman," he said at last, "why are you asking this from me?"

She said nothing, but looked at him quietly and humbly.

"You know that my time has not yet come," Jesus said.

Mary knew that he was speaking of another time, when God would show his glory and his power, but she felt sure that Jesus would listen to her and save the family from their distress. She waved the servants over. "Do whatever he tells you."

The servants were puzzled. What could anyone do? No one could go and buy wine at this time of night.

Jesus pointed to six huge water jars standing empty in the corner.

"Go and fill those jars with water."

There was something about his look that made it impossible to disobey. The servants filled each jar to the brim.

"Now," said Jesus, as if it were the most natural thing in the world, "draw some out and take it to the master of the feast."

Take him some water? they thought, but they did not dare to question him. They simply followed Jesus' strange instructions.

The master of the feast took the water from the servants, tasted it and smiled.

"Excellent vintage! The best I have ever drunk."

He hurried off, delighted, as the servants ran back to the six jars. Every single one of them was brimming with wine.

The master of the feast whispered to the bridegroom, "Usually people serve the best wine first and only serve up the cheap stuff when everyone's had a lot to drink and won't notice. You've kept the most expensive, the finest, until last!"

The bridegroom was astonished. Where had this wine come from?

This was the first miracle that Jesus ever performed, and his followers came to understand that it was a mysterious sign of God's love for the world.

TROUBLE IN NAZARETH

LUKE 4

Jesus began to teach in many synagogues throughout Galilee, and word of his miracles spread far and wide.

The only place where people did not accept him was his own village of Nazareth.

"He's just the carpenter's son," they gossiped to each other. "We know all about him."

"Jesus? A great prophet? We've seen him grow up, we know his father and mother, he's just like us!"

"What makes him so special?"

The people there were jealous of his fame and suspicious of all the stories about him.

One Sabbath day, Jesus was in Nazareth and went to the synagogue. The attendant handed him the scroll of the scriptures and Jesus turned to a passage from Isaiah.

He began to read, loudly and clearly:

The Spirit of the Lord is on me,
because he has chosen me
to bring good news to the poor
and to heal the broken-hearted,
to give sight to the blind,
to release all those who are suffering
and to proclaim the time of God's blessing.

Jesus handed the scroll back and sat down, and everyone in the synagogue stared at him. He had read the words of the prophet as if they were about himself. There was a stunned silence, and then Jesus said, "Today this prophecy has come true before your very eyes."

Some people were impressed because Jesus spoke so powerfully. They sensed he had great authority, but then they began to whisper to each other, arguing among themselves.

"It's only Joseph's son!"

"He speaks so well."

"Yes, but who does he think he is? Some kind of prophet?"

Jesus looked at them all sadly. "Are you looking for proof? Do you want me to perform miracles for you, like the ones you've heard about?"

They stared back at him uncertainly.

"No prophet is ever accepted in his own town," he said. Then he stood up slowly. "When there was a famine in the time of the prophet Elijah, there were many widows in Israel, but Elijah was sent over the border to Sidon, to a woman in Zarephath!"

The crowd in the synagogue looked at him angrily. What was he saying? That Nazareth was not good enough for him? He could only help people somewhere else?

"There were lots of people with leprosy in the time of the prophet Elisha, but the only one he healed was Naaman the Syrian!"

Suddenly, the anger that was boiling up in the crowd exploded into fury. They rushed from their seats and grabbed Jesus, and they hurled him from the synagogue.

"Too good for Nazareth, are you?" they shouted. "Condemning your own people!"

The crowd surged around him, pushing him forward, outside the town, up to the brow of the hill. They were ready to push him over to his death, but Jesus turned abruptly. He looked from one person to the next, as they all fell silent. Then he walked back through the crowd, which all at once felt strangely afraid of him, and he went on his way alone.

THE KINGDOM OF HEAVEN

MATTHEW 4, 6, 13, LUKE 12

Jesus made his home in Capernaum, a fishing town by the shores of Lake Galilee. He already had many friends there, including Andrew, a fisherman who had been a follower of John the Baptist. Now Andrew was following Jesus, and many people in Capernaum welcomed Jesus and listened eagerly to his stories or parables.

"The kingdom of heaven is like this," he told them. "A man

found some buried treasure in a field. Immediately, he went and sold everything he had, so that he could buy the field and keep the treasure."

Jesus was teaching about a special kind of treasure, far more important than gold or silver. He talked about giving up everything to follow God. Jesus had met many people who loved money and spent their whole lives trying to make more money. He said to them, "Don't build up treasure on earth, collecting piles of fine clothes which can be eaten by moths, or lots of possessions which can be stolen by thieves or rust away! Build your treasure up in heaven where it will last forever."

Even the wealthy merchants who came to sell their goods in the markets sometimes listened to him, although his teaching often troubled those who were rich. "Wherever your treasure is, your heart is there too!" said Jesus. For some people, that meant their heart was locked up in a box with gold coins. "Build up treasure in heaven, and then your heart will be in heaven."

He also told a story about a merchant who collected pearls. One day, the merchant saw the most beautiful pearl, a fabulous white jewel, bigger than any pearl in the world. Immediately, he went home and sold every single pearl he had, as well as his house, his possessions, everything he owned, so he could buy the single, glorious, exceptional pearl.

"That's like finding the kingdom of heaven," said Jesus. He wanted to show that there is nothing more precious than knowing God.

THE FISHING TRIP

LUKE 5

One day, Jesus came down to the lakeside in Capernaum. Huge crowds were following him, children were running around him, some people were shouting out questions, others were waving and trying to attract his attention. Everyone wanted to hear what he had to say. There were so many people crowding around him that Jesus could hardly stand up.

By the water's edge was a fishing boat. It belonged to Andrew and his brother, Simon (later known as Peter), who were washing their nets. Jesus called to them and asked them to untie the boat. "Let's sail out a little, so I can talk to all these people," he said.

Preaching from a boat? Simon had never heard of such a thing. And from his boat? He shook his head, amazed at this teacher from the hills who had such unusual ideas. But they sailed out – Simon, Andrew and Jesus. Jesus stood up in the boat and preached to the crowd for many hours.

Later, when the crowds had all gone home, Simon took up his oars to bring the boat back to the shore. Jesus shook his head gently. "Push the boat out!"

Simon was puzzled. "What for, Teacher?"

"We're going fishing."

"In the middle of the day?"

Simon and Andrew always went fishing at night, letting their nets down gently into the dark waters. Now Jesus was looking at Simon quietly and calmly, as if to say, "Obey me, Simon." The tough fisherman was troubled and confused. No one gave him orders like this; he did just what he wanted. But he shrugged his shoulders and sat down. He grabbed his oars and rowed out into the middle of Lake Galilee.

Two other fishermen, James and John, were rowing after them. They were amazed to see Andrew and Simon trying to catch fish in the hottest part of the day. Suddenly, they saw Andrew waving and shouting to them. He was leaning over the edge of the boat, almost falling into the water. Simon was standing up, clutching the nets that were stretching and breaking in his hands. They were full of fish, jumping and splashing and writhing, their silver scales flashing in the sunlight.

"James! John!" Andrew beckoned wildly to his friends. "We're sinking with the weight!"

The other fishermen grabbed the nets and loaded the rest of the haul into their boat, and then they rowed back to Capernaum slowly, pulling at their oars with all their might.

Simon waded into the water, leaving Andrew, James and John to unload the miraculous catch of fish. He did not look back at Jesus but sat down and put his head in his hands.

Jesus came and put his hand on Simon's shoulder.

"Lord, leave me alone!" said Simon.

Jesus looked at him with great kindness.

"Lord," said Simon, the tears rolling down his rough cheeks, "I am just a sinner."

He was ashamed that he'd been so slow to listen to Jesus.

"Don't be afraid, Simon," Jesus smiled. He turned to Andrew, James and John. "This is the day when I am going to make you a new kind of fishermen. From now on you will be catching people!"

A MIRACLE AT HOME

Simon became one of Jesus' closest friends, and there were many times when Jesus came to stay at his home.

One night, Simon's mother-in-law became very ill. She lay in bed upstairs, and she could hardly breathe. She was sweating, hot and then cold; her whole body was racked with pain. Her temperature was dangerously high, and there was no medicine that could help her.

When Jesus found out that she was suffering so badly, he went upstairs immediately. He sat beside her bed and commanded the fever to leave her at once.

She sat up, smiling, completely cured. She went downstairs, where everybody was eating a meal, and began to serve the food. The whole household was amazed. How could a man have power over illness? How could Jesus talk to a fever, as if it were an enemy or thief breaking into the house, and order it to leave immediately?

But this was just the beginning of many wonderful cures in the towns and villages of Galilee.

JESUS HEALS A LEPER

LUKE 5

The worst illness of all in those days was leprosy. It wasted the skin, destroying all feeling, creeping all over the body until fingers, hands and toes were lost, and faces were scarred and broken. It was a terrible curse to become a leper – no one would touch you or come near you; everyone ran away from you in fear. It was the loneliest and saddest life imaginable.

Lepers were forced to live away from other people, hiding in dark caves in the hills. If a leper came in search of food or water, he had to warn the whole world to keep away, crying, "Unclean! Unclean! Leprosy!"

One day, a leper heard about Jesus and his teaching. From a distance, he heard people singing and laughing, rejoicing because someone had been healed.

Healed… he thought. A man who can heal…? The leper looked down at his disfigured arm; he looked at his feet. Slowly, he dragged himself along, one wretched foot after another, hobbling towards the crowd.

Jesus was a long way away, but he could hear him saying, "Come to me… I will never turn anyone away…"

Not even a leper? Everyone turned lepers away, but the man kept edging forward until someone in the crowd noticed him and screamed, "Leprosy! Leprosy!" The people scattered in all directions, and mothers seized their children and ran for safety. No one was left in the street except Jesus, his followers and the poor broken figure who fell down before him, crying, "Lord, if you want to, you can make me clean!"

Jesus reached out and touched the man's arm. Everyone gasped in horror, but Jesus said softly, "I do want to. Be clean!"

Instantly, the man's skin became like a little child's: soft and perfect, without a single blemish. He touched his hand and fingers, new fingers which he could bend and feel; he stroked his arms, which were strong and whole. He ran his hands across his face, slowly, re-discovering his mouth, his nose, his eyes.

"Healed..." he said, hardly daring to believe the incredible miracle. "I... have... been healed."

Jesus told him not to tell anyone, only to show himself to the priest. "Offer a sacrifice and show your thanks to God in private," he said.

But the leper could not keep quiet, and soon the whole of Galilee heard about the extraordinary miracle.

FRIENDS AND ENEMIES

LUKE 5

Crowds of people came from far and wide to hear Jesus and to be healed of their illnesses. Blind people, deaf people, people who couldn't walk – they all came in search of the famous healer from Nazareth. But soon, those who wanted a cure for their bodies began to understand that Jesus wanted to touch their hearts as well. He spoke of God's love and forgiveness, and the need to live a new kind of life, full of love for others.

But not everyone was happy about Jesus. Some were afraid of his healing powers because they thought he would lead the people away from God. These Pharisees and teachers of the Law spent their lives trying to be good, obeying all God's laws. Many people looked up to the Pharisees because they were always praying and giving money to the poor and going to worship God whenever they could.

They had more than six hundred special rules which they followed – rules about keeping clean, avoiding the company of bad people, not doing any work on the Sabbath day. They were very strict, and some were proud of their own goodness. They did not like it when Jesus told them to be sorry for their sins, as if they were just like everybody else. And they did not like it when the crowds started to follow Jesus and listen to his stories instead of their preaching.

They were jealous of his power, and many of the religious leaders became his enemies.

THE PARALYZED MAN

MATTHEW 9, MARK 2, LUKE 5

One day, Jesus was teaching the people in a house in Capernaum. A great many Pharisees and teachers of the Law had come from all around to find out about this new teacher, and hundreds of other men, women and children were crowding through the streets, desperately trying to catch a glimpse of Jesus.

Four men came along that day, carrying their friend on a stretcher. He was paralyzed from head to foot and lay there staring at the sky hopelessly.

"Don't bother about me," he kept saying.

"No," his friends insisted, "we're taking you to Jesus. Perhaps he can heal you."

"Please let us through," they said, as they made their way through the crowds. "This man needs Jesus."

"We all need Jesus," someone grumbled. "Go away, come back another time!"

Just then, one of the paralyzed man's friends noticed the stairs up to the flat roof. "Yes...!" He waved to the others. "That's it, the only way to Jesus. We'll have to let him down through the roof."

The four friends were so determined to help the man that they climbed onto the roof and began to tear away at the mud and the straw.

Inside the house, Jesus was speaking. Suddenly, earth spattered down into the room, and everyone looked up, amazed, as a patch of bright blue sky appeared.

"What's going on?" shouted the owner of the house. "What are you doing?" But no one paid any attention to him because the paralyzed man was being lowered down with ropes, swinging into the room slowly and surely, right down to the floor.

"Friend," said Jesus, as if he had been expecting him. He smiled up at the four faces peering down from above, moved by their wonderful determination and faith.

He put his hand gently on the man's forehead. Everyone in the room fell silent. What would happen now? Would the man stand up? But Jesus said very simply, "Your sins are forgiven."

Sins? Forgiven? The Pharisees and teachers of the Law looked at each other in horror, not daring to say anything but all thinking the same: only God himself can forgive sins. How dare this man say such an outrageous thing!

The paralyzed man lay there looking up at Jesus, puzzled, but strangely at peace too. Forgiveness... yes, that was what he needed in his heart. That was the first thing, the deepest thing that he needed.

Jesus turned to the religious leaders and said, "Why are you thinking these thoughts?" They said nothing, but stared at him coldly. "Very well," said Jesus, "let me ask you a question. Is it easier to say the words, 'Your sins are forgiven,' or 'Get up and walk?'" Again, they were silent. Anyone could say these words, but who could heal a man paralyzed from birth?

"To show you that I have the right to forgive sins," Jesus said, turning back to the man who lay there rigid and helpless on his mat, "I tell you, get up, pick up your bed and walk!"

Immediately, the man moved. He rolled over. He sat up. A ripple went through the crowd, turning to shouts of wonder as he stood up and jumped in the air, throwing his mat up high. The man rolled up the mat and began to run through the crowd, pushing his way out, dancing. "Look at me – I've been healed, I can walk, I can run, I can dance. Glory to God!"

Everyone in the crowd said, "We have seen extraordinary things today," but the religious leaders left in silence, troubled and angry.

BREAKING THE RULES

LUKE 6

One Sabbath day, Jesus came into the synagogue and saw a man there who had a paralyzed arm. The man looked up at him as he passed, and Jesus stopped.

All the Pharisees and teachers of the Law were looking at him hard and thinking, Surely he knows that it is against the Law of Moses to do any work on the Sabbath day? He cannot perform a miracle on the day of rest!

Every Jewish family took the Sabbath day seriously, because

God had made it the special day of rest and worship, but the Pharisees had added many extra rules. They had long lists of what to do and what not to do on the Sabbath day. They were staring suspiciously at Jesus because they thought he was about to break their rules in front of all the people.

The man hid his arm, as if he were suddenly ashamed. Everybody was looking at him. He felt afraid, but Jesus looked down at him with great love. The eyes of the Pharisees were blazing with fury.

"Come and stand here," said Jesus. The man stood and walked towards Jesus.

"I'll ask you a question," Jesus said to the Pharisees suddenly, knowing these learned men would say nothing at all. "Tell me this: which is the way to keep the rules of the Sabbath? Is it best to do good or to do harm, to save life or to destroy it?"

They could not answer him. But everyone in the synagogue knew that the Sabbath was God's day, and that meant it was a day to do good things.

Jesus turned back to the man. "Stretch out your hand." The man obeyed, and his arm was healed at once. He bent it in all directions, flexed his muscles and curled his fingers. He touched his face, then clasped his hands, then stretched his arm straight out. Tears filled his eyes. He could hardly believe that something so wonderful had happened to him, but the religious leaders were filled with rage and began plotting how to destroy Jesus.

TWELVE CLOSE FRIENDS

MATTHEW 10, MARK 3, LUKE 6

One evening, Jesus went off alone to pray. He climbed a mountain overlooking Lake Galilee and stayed there all night beneath the stars.

When he came down in the early morning, he saw many of his friends gathered by the shore. There were fishermen and farmers, builders, carpenters, merchants and teachers; so many different faces looking at him, of all ages and types. They welcomed him, and he sat down among them beside the clear waters of Lake Galilee.

Jesus had many friends and followers, but now he needed to choose those who would leave their homes and travel with him everywhere. They would become his closest friends, telling the world about God's kingdom.

Jesus was silent, and the men all around him respected his silence. They knew that he was about to say something important. "Twelve of you will follow me wherever I go," he said. "You will be my chosen disciples."

"Simon," he said, slapping his hand on the rough fisherman's shoulder, "you first. And Andrew, James and John." Slowly, Jesus went around the throng of people, picking out his disciples. "Philip, Bartholomew, Thomas, Thaddeus. Simon from Cana, James, son of Alphaeus." He chose Judas Iscariot too, who would later betray him.

The man everyone was amazed to see chosen was Matthew.

"Matthew?" Simon and Andrew muttered under their breath. "Jesus can't be choosing Matthew to be one of us. A close friend?"

Matthew worked with the tax collectors who were always cheating people, and no one trusted him – except Jesus. He knew that Matthew's heart had changed.

A SOLDIER'S FAITH

LUKE 7

There was a Roman soldier who lived in the army barracks at Capernaum. He had heard about Jesus and the wonderful miracles that he performed, and when his servant became very ill, he believed that Jesus was the only hope.

The Roman soldier was an important man, a centurion, who had one hundred men under his command. He could have marched straight up to Jesus and demanded his attention: "I need help at once!" But the soldier respected the Jewish religion and was very humble.

I am a foreigner, a Gentile, he thought. I cannot ask Jesus for his help. I'll send my Jewish friends. So some Jewish elders of the synagogue came to Jesus and said, "Please help the centurion because he has shown great love to us and has even paid for our new synagogue."

"I will visit him immediately," Jesus promised, but when the centurion heard that the great teacher was on his way he sent a message: "Lord, don't take the trouble to come to my home yourself. I do not deserve to have you under my roof, which is why I have sent messengers to you. Just say the word! I am a soldier and I obey orders, while the men under me obey my orders! I simply say, 'Do this,' and men do it. If

I say, 'Come here!' they come at once."

Jesus was amazed that the man believed so deeply in his power, trusting him to heal the servant without even seeing him. "Look at the faith of this man!" he said to the disciples. "This man, who is a Gentile, has greater faith than anyone I have met in the whole of Israel."

When the centurion went into his servant's room, he found the man alive and well. He was completely cured of his illness.

THE STORY OF THE SOWER

LUKE 8

People reacted to Jesus in many different ways – some with great faith, some with a little faith. There were some who listened but then walked away and did nothing, and others who were troubled by his words.

One day, Jesus told a story. A crowd gathered around as he pointed to a farmer in the distance who was scattering seeds from a huge bag over his shoulder. They all stared at the figure who walked slowly up and down his field as clouds of tiny seeds fell to the earth.

"There was once a farmer like that who went out throwing seeds far and wide," said Jesus. "Some of the seeds fell along the edge of the pathway. They were trampled underfoot, and the birds came swooping down and gobbled them up. Other seeds fell on rocky ground and they grew up very quickly, but because they had no roots in the earth and no water, they dried up and died. Yet other seeds fell among thorns, and as they grew up the thorns twisted around them and strangled the life out of them.

"But other seeds fell into good, deep soil. They grew up ripe and strong, producing fields of crops that were a hundred times more than was sown!"

The crowd watched the farmer climbing silently up and down his field, scattering the seed to the winds, and wondered what Jesus meant by this parable.

THE HIDDEN MESSAGE

LUKE 8

The disciples gathered around Jesus that night until eventually one of them plucked up the courage to ask him, "Why do you always teach in parables? Sometimes we…" he hesitated, afraid to look stupid, "we don't know what you mean."

"I'll tell you the secret," said Jesus, "because you are my closest friends." The disciples huddled closer to him, eager to hear what he had to say.

"The seed is the word of God." He paused, and they nodded. "The hidden message of my story is all about what happens to the word of God in people's hearts.

"Those seeds along the pathway are the people who hear God's word, but the devil comes along quickly and snatches it from their hearts before they can believe and be saved.

"Those on the rocky ground are the people who hear the word and get very excited, but they have no roots at all.

They believe for a little while, but as soon as trouble and difficulty come along, they give up.

"Those that fall into the thorns are the people who hear the word but are soon distracted by worries, or thoughts of getting rich, or the pleasures of life and the craving for success. These desires choke God's word, and so nothing can grow.

"But the seed that lands in the good soil stands for those who have a fine and open heart. They hear the word, they take it in deeply, they act on it, and they produce a rich harvest because of their perseverance. They keep trusting in God whatever happens."

When he had finished speaking, Jesus gazed at each one of them in turn as if asking, "Which kind of soil is in your heart?"

COUNTING THE COST

LUKE 14

As the months went by, many people wanted to follow Jesus, but he kept warning them of the difficulties.

"You must count the cost before you even begin your journey," he told them.

It was easy to follow Jesus when he was performing miracles, when everyone loved him and praised him. Hundreds of people wanted to follow him and be near him now, but Jesus knew that a time would come when everyone, even his closest friends, would run away, fearing for their lives. He knew that one day he would have to suffer a cruel death.

"You must pick up a cross and carry it if you want to follow me," said Jesus.

A cross? People were puzzled. They had all seen criminals carrying their crosses, and they had seen the terrible deaths of those thieves and murderers, but what had all this got to do with Jesus, the healer and storyteller? He was wise and good. Surely it was the easiest thing in the world to follow such a leader?

"Anyone who is not prepared to lose his life cannot be my disciple," said Jesus.

The people looked mystified. No one understood these difficult sayings, so Jesus said to them, "If you set out to build a great tower, you have to work out the cost first." The people nodded slowly.

"You work out all the materials you need, the wages of the builders; then, when you have all the money, you start. But if you don't do this, and simply lay foundations and then run out of money – you'll look stupid. Everyone will pass by, laughing, 'Look how this builder couldn't finish what he'd started.'"

The crowd was silent. "Count your costs," Jesus repeated. "You must be prepared to give up everything to follow me."

JESUS' WORDS ABOUT HAPPINESS

MATTHEW 5, LUKE 6

One day, Jesus gathered all his followers on a hillside above Lake Galilee. There were many hundreds of people – men, women and children, sitting in the long grass. There were wild flowers on the hills around, and far below the fishing boats sailed across the calm waters.

In the great stillness of that bright summer's day, Jesus taught the crowd some words they would never forget:

"Happy are the people who know they are in desperate need of God, for theirs is the kingdom of heaven.

"Happy are those who mourn and weep, for they will find comfort.

"Happy are those who are meek, for they will inherit the earth.

"Happy are those who are longing to do good things, for God will answer their prayers.

"Happy are the people who are kind and merciful to others, for they will be shown mercy.

"Happy are the pure in heart, for they will see God.

"Happy are the people who work to make peace, for they will be called children of God.

"Happy are those who suffer for God's sake, for theirs is the kingdom of heaven."

The people sat listening in amazement. No one had said such surprising and wonderful things before. Jesus was talking of a very different way of life, which gave hope to people who were poor and suffering. These words of Jesus became known as The Beatitudes, which means The Blessings.

THE STORY OF THE TWO BUILDERS

There were many people who said, "I will follow Jesus," but did nothing about it. They claimed to be his disciples, but they did not show love to others or change their attitude in any way. "Why do you keep saying, 'Lord, Lord!'" Jesus challenged them, "when it means nothing? If you want to be my disciples, you must act on my words!"

He told this story about being a true disciple:

"Everyone who listens to my words and does something about them is like a wise man who built his house upon a rock. First he laid the foundations, digging deep down; then he worked carefully, slowly, surely, and built up the whole house layer by layer. At last, he had a solid building that was strong and secure on the rock.

"Then the winds and the rain came, battering the house; the flood rose high and lashed the foundations, and the house on the rock stood firm.

"But the person who hears my words and does nothing about them is like a stupid man who built his house on the sand. This man took the easy way, raising up the building very quickly on shallow foundations. Soon he had a tall house and he settled down, smiling and thinking, Now I'm safe and secure!

"But then the rains came pouring down, the rivers flooded their banks, rushing towards the house in a great torrent; the whole building tottered and broke apart and collapsed with a great crash! There was nothing left of that house but a pile of rubble.

"Don't take the easy way," warned Jesus, "take the hard way. Build your life on deep foundations and put my teachings into action."

THE STORY OF THE LOST SHEEP

LUKE 15

Some of the Pharisees and religious leaders disapproved of the way Jesus always welcomed people who were known to be bad. He even ate meals with people who were known to be cheats and wrongdoers. When they grumbled about this, Jesus answered by telling a story:

"Supposing a man had a hundred sheep, and one of the sheep went astray. Wouldn't he go looking for his lost sheep?"

People nodded in agreement. Every shepherd would search for his own sheep. There was no doubt about that.

Jesus went on, "A shepherd would leave all the other ninety-nine sheep on the hillside and search everywhere for the lost sheep until he found her. And when he found her, he would be so happy, he would lift the sheep onto his shoulders and carry her home to safety. Then he would call all his friends together and say, 'Come over and celebrate with me! For today I've found my lost sheep!'"

Jesus called out to the crowd, "In the very same way, there will be more happiness and rejoicing in heaven over one person who is sorry for their sins, than over the ninety-nine good people who do not need to repent!"

THE STORY OF THE LOST COIN

LUKE 15

Jesus told many stories about being lost and found. They were often about everyday situations like the woman who lost one of the valuable coins on her headdress.

"There was once a woman," said Jesus, "who lost a very precious silver coin. She looked all over the floor, but she couldn't find it. She looked in all her pots, under the mats, in the hearth, everywhere. She searched for many hours. As the sunlight faded from the sky, she lit every lamp in the house and swept out every nook and cranny.

"At last, hidden in a corner of the room, she saw the little silver coin. She shouted with joy. She picked it up and held it in her hand, running to her friends next door.

"'Come and eat with me,' she shouted. 'We'll have a party!' She called all her friends. 'I'm so happy because I have found my precious coin.' And so they all had a wonderful party!

"In exactly the same way," Jesus told his disciples, "the angels have a party in heaven when one sinner turns away from doing wrong things and comes back to God!"

THE STORY OF THE LOST SON

Jesus wanted people to understand more about God's love, so one day he told them a story about a person who was lost:

"There was once a man who had two sons. The eldest was very dutiful and worked hard on his father's farm, but the youngest said, 'Let me have my inheritance now – I want to go out into the world and enjoy myself!' So the father gave his son the money he would inherit when he died, and the young man went off to another country, determined to have a good time.

"He lived the high life, squandering all his money recklessly. He filled his days with wild parties, throwing his money at worthless friends, until he had nothing left. Then terrible famine hit the land, and soon the youngest son was in desperate need. His clothes were ragged, all his friends had disappeared long ago, and he was forced to take the lowest job in the land.

"The young man had to look after some pigs, feeding them and living in a hovel with them. He was so hungry he could have eaten the pigs' food, but no one gave him anything. One day he thought, Even my father's humblest servants have plenty of food, and yet here I am starving to death! I will go back to him and say, 'Father, I have sinned against God and against you. I am not fit to be your son any longer. Just take me on as a servant.' So the young man crawled out of the filth and began to stagger home.

"While he was still a long way off, his father saw him in the distance and ran to him.

"'Father –' the son began, but the old man kissed him and hugged him.

"'You're home,' he said, 'you're home!' He wept and clung to him.

"'Father,' the boy said, with tears streaming down his face, 'I have sinned against God and against you. I am not fit to be your son any longer.'

"His father did not let him finish. He waved and shouted to his servants, 'Quick, bring the best robes and dress him, put a gold ring on his finger and find sandals for his aching feet. Prepare the biggest calf for a great feast.' The servants gathered all around as the father led his son into the home.

"'Look,' he called out, 'my son was dead and he's come back to life! He was lost forever, but now he's been found!' Immediately, the celebration began.

"The elder son returned from the fields where he had been sweating and working all day. He heard music in the air, he saw lamps lit all along the house and around the courtyard. He watched the shadows of people dancing and jumping for joy.

"'What's this? A party?' he asked, and when he found out that it was for his good-for-nothing brother, he stamped away in a rage.

"His father came out to him. The elder son turned away. 'All these years I've worked for you, you've never given me a party! Now this son of yours who has wasted his whole inheritance on prostitutes turns up and is welcomed like a prince!'

"His father said to him softly, 'Son, everything I have is yours – everything! But I thought your brother had died and was lost forever. Now he is alive; he is found. Is it wrong for us to celebrate such wonderful news?'"

THE LORD'S PRAYER

MATTHEW 6, LUKE 11

One day, when they were alone with Jesus, the disciples came to him and said, "Lord, teach us how to pray."

They had been listening to his stories and wondering how they could follow his teaching in their lives.

Jesus sat down with them and said, "You don't need many words. Pray simply – don't babble on for hours, like those who think they will be heard for their endless chanting. Pray like this:

'Our Father in heaven,
May your name be kept holy.
Your kingdom come,
Your will be done,
On earth as it is in heaven.
Give us today our daily bread;
Forgive us our sins,
As we forgive those who sin against us.
Do not put us to the test,
But deliver us from evil.'"

Simon, James, John and all the others sat there, listening to every word, repeating the prayer quietly, trying to understand one of the greatest secrets of all. They knew that Jesus spent a lot of time alone, praying to his Father, and that prayer filled his whole life.

"You must pray and never give up," Jesus told them. "Be persistent!" He could see from their faces that they did not find it easy to pray – and to keep on praying.

"Listen," Jesus said. "Imagine you go to a friend's house in the middle of the night and knock on his door and say, 'Lend me three loaves of bread because an unexpected visitor has arrived at my house.'

"'Don't bother me now!' your friend shouts. 'I'm in bed and all my children are asleep!'"

The disciples laughed at the thought of the man turning over and refusing to answer the door.

"But you keep knocking," continued Jesus. "Bang, bang, bang! Eventually, the man has to get up and give you the bread, not because he's your friend, but because he can't stand the noise. You won't give up!

"That's how it is with prayer," Jesus said. "You must never give up. Ask and it will be given to you; seek and you will find; knock and the door will be opened!"

THE TWO PRAYERS

MATTHEW 6, LUKE 18

Jesus taught his disciples many other things about prayer. "Don't go around telling everyone how much you pray, or draw attention to yourself by praying loudly on a street corner. Go into your own room, shut the door quietly and pray in secret to your Father in heaven. He will see you there and reward you."

One day, Jesus told a story about a man who prayed in the wrong way, full of himself and his own goodness:

"There was once a Pharisee who went into the synagogue and he prayed like this: 'Thank you, God, that I am not like other people – greedy, dishonest, lying – and I am not like that tax collector over there who cheats everyone. I fast twice a week and I give a tenth of all my money to the temple.'

"Meanwhile, the tax collector lowered his eyes to the ground because he was so ashamed of himself. He could hardly bring himself to say anything. He was wringing his hands and weeping, 'O God, have mercy on me, a sinner!'

"Which prayer did God hear?" asked Jesus, as the disciples looked at each other, knowing there were times when they too were proud and thought that they were better than others. "I can tell you," Jesus said, "God heard that poor tax collector's prayer and forgave him, but the Pharisee went away without being forgiven."

A GIFT OF PERFUME

LUKE 7

A Pharisee in Capernaum invited Jesus to a meal, and while he was there a woman came rushing into the house. She had a very bad reputation, and everyone was shocked when she threw herself down at Jesus' feet. She began weeping and crying and wiping her tears away with her own hair.

"Can't he see what kind of woman this is?" said the guests in horror. Then she took out a jar of perfume, which was very valuable, broke the seal and poured it over his feet. The fragrance filled the whole room as the Pharisees looked on in disbelief. The woman was crying and covering Jesus' feet and ankles with her kisses.

The host of the banquet, a man named Simon, whispered, "If Jesus were a true prophet, he would know what sort of person is touching him like this!"

Jesus turned to him sadly. "Simon, I came as a guest to your house, but you did not wash the dust off my feet; yet look how this woman is washing me with her tears. You did not greet me with a kiss, but she is covering my feet with her kisses. You did not offer oil to anoint my hair, but look how she has poured a whole jar of perfume over me."

Simon knew it was true. He had offered none of the kind things which were given to travel-weary guests in those days. He sat there in embarrassed silence.

"She has been forgiven so much, and that is why she loves me so much," Jesus said. "But if you've only been forgiven a little, Simon, you will only love me a little."

The other Pharisees looked at Jesus with growing anger as he took the woman's hand. "Go in peace, now. All your sins are forgiven."

"Who is this man who claims to forgive sins?" they said. "What right has any man got to say this?" But Jesus ignored them, gazing after the woman as she walked calmly away from the house.

THE DYING GIRL

MATTHEW 9, MARK 5, LUKE 8

One day in Capernaum, a man struggled through the huge crowd that was around Jesus. "Please, please… let me pass… my daughter, my daughter…"

No one bothered at first. There were always people wanting to find Jesus.

But then someone noticed that it was a very important man in the town.

"It's Jairus," the word went around, "Jairus, a ruler of the synagogue!"

Jairus stumbled on, crying and mumbling, "My daughter... my little girl..."

The crowd parted respectfully. Many of the Pharisees and religious leaders in Capernaum were afraid of Jesus, and some hated him. But now Jairus, one of the most important men in the synagogue, was running up to Jesus and falling down at his feet.

He did not care what anyone thought. He knelt down in front of Jesus. "Master," he begged, "please come and lay your hands on my daughter. She's..." He shook his head, hardly able to speak. "She's... dying. But if you come now you can save her!"

Jesus looked down at the solemn, well dressed man who was kneeling in the dust so humbly, trembling and shaking his head. "I will come," said Jesus. "I'll come to your house at once."

Jairus stood up, mumbling, "Thank you, thank you." The crowd stared at him, amazed. Was this the same important man who stood up in the synagogue every Sabbath day? Suddenly they realized, Jairus was just an ordinary man, a father with a dying child. They watched as Jesus set off, following Jairus down the street.

THE WOMAN WHO TOUCHED JESUS

MATTHEW 9, MARK 5, LUKE 8

As Jesus moved slowly through the teeming crowds in
Capernaum, someone else was desperately creeping towards
him. She needed him too, but she could not reach him.

She was a poor woman who had been very ill for a long
time. Her illness was a shameful thing to her, and she was
embarrassed and afraid because, in those days, bleeding of this
kind meant that a woman had to hide away in her own home.
No one had been able to cure her in twelve years.

The crowd surged forward again, following Jesus to Jairus'
house. That was the moment when the woman saw Jesus. She
caught a glimpse of his face for a few moments, and she longed
to call out to him, but she was too afraid.

She edged her way ahead, pushing very slowly through the
people. No one noticed her, but at last she saw one robe,
among many others, and she knew it was Jesus. She struggled
forward one last time and, bending low, reached out and
touched the hem of his robe.

Instantly, she was healed. At that very moment, she felt all
the pain she had ever known lifted from her.

"Who touched me?" Jesus stopped. The crowd was
astonished. His question seemed so strange and stern.
Everyone denied touching him.

Simon was amazed. "Master, the whole crowd is pressing all
around you!"

"Someone touched me," Jesus said. "I felt the power go out
from me."

The woman knew that she could not hide any longer. She came out of the crowd, trembling, and fell down at Jesus' feet.

"Lord, I was afraid... I... please forgive me, I only wanted to touch you and..."

Jesus took her hand. "Daughter," he said, "your faith has healed you."

The woman stood up slowly, finding new strength and confidence in full view of all the people. Jesus said to her, "Go in peace," and she turned and walked happily away.

FROM DEATH TO LIFE

MATTHEW 9, MARK 5, LUKE 8

Jesus was on his way to Jairus' house to heal the girl who was dangerously ill.

They hurried through the crowded streets when suddenly two servants came from Jairus' house.

"Sir," they said, their eyes to the ground, "Sir..." They hardly dared bring their message. "Sir," they said, "don't trouble the Master any longer. Your daughter is dead."

Jairus sank to the ground. In the distance, outside his home, there was wailing and crying. Jesus said to him, "Don't be afraid. Believe, Jairus! And your daughter will be well."

Jesus led the way into the home, and when he saw the crying and the pitiful wailing of all the mourners he called out, "Stop! Stop all this crying!" They looked at him as if he were mad. "Don't be sad," Jesus told the mourners. "The girl is not dead; she's only sleeping."

Jesus took Simon, James and John with him and went with Jairus and the girl's mother to her room. The child lay there, quite still. Jesus took her hand in his and said softly, "Little girl, get up now."

The girl began to breathe. She opened her eyes and sat up suddenly. Her parents stood there, trembling, afraid of the great power they had seen and yet beginning to cry with joy. She ran into their arms, and they hugged her and kissed her.

"Give her something to eat," said Jesus, as if nothing unusual had happened at all. "She's hungry."

Later, he told them not to speak about this miracle, but the girl was the living proof of his power. The news spread through the whole land.

JOHN THE BAPTIST DIES

MATTHEW 14

The powerful rulers in the land became afraid of Jesus and his miracles. When King Herod Antipas heard what Jesus was doing in Galilee, he turned pale with fear. "This is John the Baptist, come back from the dead. John has risen again to haunt me!"

Herod had arrested John and kept him in the deep dungeon of his fortress at Machaerus. Then he was tricked into beheading him.

Herod had always hated John. The wild prophet down by the River Jordan had said many uncomfortable things about rich and powerful rulers, but the worst thing was that John had spoken out against Herod's new marriage. Herod did not like being called an adulterer, but he knew it was true. He had left his first wife and then taken Herodias from his own brother.

In her turn, Herodias had been determined to have John killed, and one day she found her chance. Her daughter, Salome, was dancing at a banquet for Herod and all his guests. The girl was beautiful and her dance was so exotic, thrilling and enticing that Herod called out, "I promise you any reward, even half my kingdom!"

Herodias took her daughter to one side and whispered, "Ask for the head of John the Baptist on a plate!" So the girl asked. Herod was suddenly very afraid, but he did not dare refuse because of his solemn promise before all the important guests. So John was beheaded that night, and his head presented on a plate to Salome.

When Jesus heard about this crime, he gathered his disciples together and went with them by boat to a lonely place across Lake Galilee. He wanted to go into the hills, to be alone with his sorrow, and to pray.

LOAVES AND FISH

MATTHEW 14, MARK 6, LUKE 9, JOHN 6

"Let's rest here," Jesus told his disciples, but even as he was speaking he saw hundreds of people running towards him. They had walked miles, following him along the shores of Lake Galilee.

One of the disciples sighed, "Can't they leave us alone for one day?"

But Jesus felt pity for them as he watched the thousands of men, women and children arriving. "They're like sheep without a shepherd," he said softly, and he began to teach the people and heal those who were sick.

It was getting late when Jesus turned to Philip. "Where can we buy some bread for these people to eat?"

Philip shook his head in amazement. "Master! This is such a lonely place, miles from anywhere! It would cost me the best part of a year's wages to give them all a few crumbs each!"

Jesus smiled at his disciples as they argued among themselves about how much it would cost and listed every difficulty. "Find out if anyone has any food," he said, and Andrew and Simon walked off into the crowd.

Food, thought Simon, to feed all this crowd?

Jesus knew exactly what he was going to do, but he wanted to test his disciples. Andrew was just about to give up when a small boy came up to him. "I've got five loaves and two fish," he said nervously. People laughed all around him.

"It's my dinner," said the boy.

Andrew called out, "There are five loaves and two fish here. But they won't go very far."

Jesus waved to the boy. "Bring them to me."

The boy stood up and carried his food very carefully to Jesus. There was silence in the crowd, because everyone could see that Jesus had taken the five loaves and two fish and was holding them very solemnly.

"Tell all the people to sit down," Jesus said. The disciples made the crowd sit down in fifties and hundreds. Then Jesus raised the loaves and the fish high up to heaven.

The little boy gazed up at his dinner as Jesus blessed it joyfully, thanking God the creator of heaven and earth. Then he divided up the food and kept handing out pieces until there was enough food for every single person on the hillside.

More than five thousand people ate and were satisfied, and when the disciples had finished collecting the leftover pieces of fish and bread, they had enough to fill twelve baskets.

WALKING ON WATER

MATTHEW 14

After the huge crowd had been fed, Jesus left the disciples and walked up into the hills. The disciples got back into the boat and sailed across Lake Galilee, but soon night fell and they were struggling, facing into a strong wind in the darkness.

They rowed on, strong, powerful oarsmen, ready for battle, and although their boat hardly moved against the wind, they kept their heads down. If they were afraid they did not admit it to any other man. The darkness folded closer. The spray stung their eyes. They rowed on blindly, digging their oars into the blackness, pulling, fighting. And the boat edged its way across the lake.

It was about three o'clock in the morning when one of them happened to look up for a moment, shaking his hair clear of the drenching sea, and he saw something. He motioned to his friends, but as he did so a terrible, chilling fear gripped him. The other disciples looked up slowly, one by one, as if drawn by the extraordinary sight, but no one spoke. They were speechless with fear. Suddenly, one of them cried out, screaming into the storm, "Ghost! It's a ghost!"

Terror gripped them, worse than any storm or any darkness they had known. Then the voice came. A voice so gentle and strong and familiar: "Don't be afraid."

Simon sat up slowly, in utter amazement. He knew, he was almost certain, who it was. He looked up and saw a figure standing on the dark, restless waves.

"Don't be afraid. It's me…"

None of the other disciples moved. They did not dare. They were frozen where they sat or crouched. They did not know what to think and could not utter a sound.

But Simon stood up slowly. "Lord," he said, "if it is you…" He hesitated, then breathed deeply. "If it really is you, then tell me to come to you across the waves."

Jesus stretched out his hand, and there was tenderness in his command, "Come on, then."

They all knew it was Jesus. Simon climbed onto the edge of the boat and, looking straight at Jesus, stepped off with one foot into the darkness.

He landed on the water as if he were stepping onto a solid pathway. The waves took his weight! He lifted his other foot off the boat and onto the sea. Now Simon was standing all alone, facing Jesus, his feet firmly on the water. He stepped forwards. A sudden squall carried the wind, lashing his face. For a moment, he lost sight of Jesus. He thought of the deep waters beneath him. He was sinking. He was sinking into the icy dark and the waves were breaking over his head. He could see nothing. He was going to drown. He screamed out, "Lord, save me!"

A hand seized his hand at that instant and pulled him up. Jesus lifted Simon before him. Now the fisherman was standing face to face with his master, and together they stood on the waves in complete safety. Jesus held him with both arms on his shoulders, saying, "O man of little faith, why did you doubt?"

Simon knew there was no blame, just that simple question which rang in his ears for many years to come: "Why did you doubt?"

Then Jesus climbed into the boat, leading Simon with him, and suddenly the wind died down. All the disciples gazed at Jesus. No one dared say anything for a long time. But then they said, "Surely you are the Son of God!"

PETER THE ROCK

MATTHEW 16

Jesus walked ahead of the disciples on the road north. Suddenly, they could see the city of Caesarea Philippi at the foot of Mount Hermon. The great houses and temples of the citadel shone in the glare of the sun, reminding them of the might of the Roman empire which stretched across the world.

Jesus did not look at the city, but raised his eyes to the top of the mountain where the snow lay, and beyond into the blue sky. He turned to his disciples and asked: "Who do people say that I am?"

"Some say that you're a prophet," they replied.

"John the Baptist come back from the dead."

"Elijah returning to the kingdom of Israel!"

"But you?" Jesus said, looking at them all intently. "Who do you think I am?"

The disciples looked at each other, but no one spoke.

311

Suddenly, Simon stepped forwards. "You are the Messiah, the Son of the living God!"

Jesus held out his arms to Simon and hugged him joyfully. "O Simon, son of John, no human being could have told you this – only my Father in heaven! You are Peter, the rock, and on this rock I will build my church." And then Jesus told his disciples not to tell anyone he was the Messiah.

As they continued along the road, they could see in the distance crosses where the bodies of condemned criminals were hanging. It was a dreadful but common sight in those days, and Jesus stopped again, as if touched by the shadow of death. He was struggling to speak. "One day... soon... I will go to Jerusalem. I will suffer many things at the hands of the chief priests and teachers of the Law, and I will be killed. But I will be raised to life on the third day."

"No!" Peter called out. "Never. This will never happen to you!"

"Get behind me, Satan," Jesus called out, and Peter looked at him in astonishment and confusion. "Simon Peter," said Jesus, "you're thinking like a man again. You must not stand in God's way."

THE TRANSFIGURATION

MATTHEW 17, LUKE 9

A few days later, Jesus took Peter, James and John with him up Mount Hermon. Soon they were lost in the mists, and the whole earth, with its teeming crowds of people, seemed far away. When Jesus reached the very top, he began to pray. Suddenly, his face shone like the sun, and his clothes became whiter than snow, and as he stood there, two figures appeared beside him in the brilliance.

Shielding their eyes from the blazing light, the disciples could not make out who the companions of Jesus were at first.

"Who are they?"

"I don't know, they look like the prophets from long ago!"

"What are they talking about?"

"Listen!"

Gradually, they could hear the conversation as the two radiant figures described the great events that would take place in Jerusalem and how Jesus would set people free through his death and resurrection.

Peter gazed at them in awe. "It's Moses…" he whispered, "and Elijah!" All three disciples did not know whether to speak or keep silent, to watch or to run away in terror.

"Lord," Peter called out, "it's good for us to be here with you. Why don't we make three tents: one for you, Moses and Elijah and…"

He had no idea what he was saying, he was so overcome, but then a great cloud of dazzling glory descended and wrapped around them. They were gripped with fear as they heard a voice saying, "This is my Son, the chosen one. You must listen to him!"

The disciples knew they had heard the voice of God, and they fell to the ground. When they opened their eyes, Jesus was standing there alone. The brightness had vanished, and they walked back down the mountain without saying a word to anyone about what they had seen.

WHO IS THE GREATEST?

MATTHEW 18, MARK 9

One day, the disciples were arguing about who would be the greatest in the kingdom of heaven. They thought that Jesus was going to be a powerful king who would rule the world. It was a heated, angry argument, because they each wanted to be the most important person in the kingdom.

But when Jesus came near them, they fell silent. At last, one of them spoke up. "Lord," he asked, "who is going to be the greatest in your kingdom?"

As they waited for Jesus to reply, the disciples shifted uneasily. Which one of them would Jesus choose? Who would bethe most famous and the most powerful person, next to Jesus himself?

There was a little child playing nearby. Jesus called the boy over and made him stand in front of the disciples. "I'm telling you the truth," said Jesus. "Unless you change and become like children, you will never even enter the kingdom of heaven."

"Never even enter…" The words shocked them. With wide eyes, the little boy looked at the grown men surrounding him. He knew nothing of their quarrels.

"Never despise these little ones," said Jesus. "For whoever humbles himself like this little child is the greatest in the kingdom of heaven. And whoever welcomes one little child in my name is welcoming me!" Jesus knelt down by the child and looked up at them all. "Whoever welcomes me is welcoming my Father in heaven who sent me."

A RICH YOUNG MAN

MATTHEW 19

As Jesus was talking to his disciples, a young man walked up to him. He was well dressed in expensive clothes.

"Teacher, I want to know…" the man cleared his throat. He had come with a very important question, and he wanted to choose exactly the right words. "I want to know what good thing I must do in my life to make sure I get to heaven."

"Good?" asked Jesus. "Only God is good. So why do you ask me?'"

The young man looked at Jesus earnestly. If anyone on earth could tell him the answer, surely Jesus could.

"Well, if you want to enter into eternal life," said Jesus, "then you must keep the commandments."

"Which ones?" asked the young man.

"Do not murder, do not commit adultery, do not steal, do not tell lies, respect your father and mother, and love other people as much as you love yourself."

"Oh," said the young man, "I've kept all these, but is there anything else I have to do?"

"There is one thing," said Jesus.

The young man looked at him, nodding seriously. He wanted to get everything perfectly right.

"Go and sell everything you have, give all the money to the poor, and you will have treasure in heaven. Then come and follow me."

When the young man heard this, he was shocked. He was extremely rich. He looked around at all the people, then at Jesus who was looking at him with great love. He lowered his eyes, then turned and walked away.

Jesus watched him walk into the distance. He felt a deep sorrow for the rich young man. "I'm telling you," he said to all the people, "it is easier for a camel to pass through the eye of a needle than it is for a rich man to enter the kingdom of heaven."

"Who can ever be saved?" the disciples said. It all seemed far too hard to them.

"It's impossible for people to save themselves," said Jesus, "but with God anything is possible."

A STORY OF THE DANGERS OF RICHES

LUKE 12

Jesus once told a story about a very rich man who was a landowner.

"One year the man had the best harvest in living memory.

"'My barns are too small!' said the man. 'There isn't room to store all the grain, so I'll pull down all the old barns and rebuild bigger ones. I'll collect all my goods together into great storehouses, lock everything up, and then sit back and relax. I'll say to myself, "Now you have plenty to look forward to! So eat, drink and be merry. Have a wonderful life!"'

"'You fool!' said God. 'This very night you will die. Then what use will all your riches be?'"

Later, the disciples remembered the parable, and they were reminded of the rich young man. As they sat by the campfire and thought about the story, they fell silent, gazing into the flames.

THE NIGHT VISITOR

JOHN 3

One night, Jesus was sitting with his disciples when a figure stepped from the shadows. He was a Pharisee named Nicodemus, an important man who was on the ruling council known as the Sanhedrin.

Nicodemus was afraid to come to Jesus in the daylight, in case anyone saw him and thought that he was a disciple.

"Rabbi," he said respectfully, "everyone knows that you are a teacher sent from God because of the miracles that you perform..."

Jesus looked steadily at the thoughtful figure who stood there so hesitantly. Nicodemus hesitated. "I mean... no one could do these things if God were not with him..." He looked over his shoulder, half expecting that he had been followed, but he was alone and safe for a while. Jesus beckoned to him to sit down.

"The truth is," said Jesus, "no one can see the kingdom of God unless he is born again."

"How can someone who is old be born again?" asked Nicodemus. Jesus seemed to be speaking in riddles and Nicodemus had so many questions.

"Human beings are physically born once in their lives," answered Jesus, "but they can be spiritually born as well."

Nicodemus frowned and rubbed his forehead as if the mystery were too difficult. Just then, the wind caught the leaves in the trees, and Jesus said, "Did you hear that? No one can see the wind or touch it; no one knows where it comes from or where it is going. That's how it is when someone is born of the Spirit."

"How is this possible?" asked Nicodemus, struggling to understand.

Jesus sighed softly. "You are a teacher of Israel and you don't even understand this?"

Nicodemus sat with him long into the night, almost until the birds greeted the dawn, as Jesus patiently taught him about the need to start all over again in order to be born into God's kingdom.

THE STORY OF THE GOOD SAMARITAN

LUKE 10

On another occasion, a teacher of the Law came to Jesus and said, "Teacher, what's the secret of getting into heaven?"

"You're an expert on the scriptures," said Jesus. "Tell me what you think."

"Well," argued the man, "Jewish Law says that we must love the Lord our God with all our hearts and strength and minds, and we must also love other people as much as we love ourselves."

"Correct," replied Jesus. "Do all that and you'll find eternal life."

"But, Teacher," said the man, "who *are* these other people?"

Jesus looked at the man, who was smiling and rather pleased with himself. "Let me tell you a story," Jesus said. "There was once a man going down the road from Jerusalem to Jericho. He was walking through the steep gorge all alone when suddenly robbers attacked him, took all his money, and left him for dead. Now along came a priest, but when he saw what looked like a dead body, he crossed to the other side of the road and walked on."

The crowd listened eagerly to Jesus' story, but the lawyer shifted uncomfortably. He guessed this story had a painful message for him. "Another important person from the temple came along," said Jesus. "He was also an expert in the Law, and he thought it was wrong to touch a dead body, so he moved on very quickly. Finally, a Samaritan rode along on his donkey."

The crowd gasped, because Samaritans were the most unpopular people. Jews and Samaritans hated each other, and they did not believe the same things about God. Why was Jesus bringing a Samaritan into this story? Jesus went on, "The Samaritan stopped and took pity on the man. He bandaged up his wounds and carried him on his donkey all the way to an inn. He gave money to the innkeeper and promised to pay for any expenses as he recovered."

Jesus stopped and looked at the crowd. He turned to the lawyer and asked, "Which of those three men was the true friend?"

"The one who showed such love," answered the lawyer quietly.

"You go then and do the same," said Jesus.

BLIND BARTIMAEUS

Mark 10, Luke 18

As Jesus approached Jericho, blind Bartimaeus heard the crowds pass. He heard the hundreds of feet running, the waves of sound surging past. "What's happening?" he murmured. "Where's everyone going? Wait…"

But no one waited, no one listened to the beggar beside the road. He was left behind in his dark solitary world. The clouds of dust made him cough. It was the biggest crowd he had ever heard.

Bartimaeus listened hard. Soon he picked out a voice a long way away. It was faintly calling, "Jesus!" Then someone else called out the same – people were cheering now. There was a roar. Bartimaeus leaped to his feet. He shouted out, "Jesus, Son of David, have mercy upon me!"

A man told him to keep his mouth shut. But Bartimaeus shouted even louder, "Jesus, Son of David, have mercy upon me!"

"Keep quiet!" said someone in the front of the crowd, angry that Bartimaeus was calling Jesus by this special name. David had been the greatest king of Israel, and his name could only be given to the greatest person of all – the Messiah, sent by God to save the whole nation.

As Bartimaeus' voice carried above the crowd, Jesus stopped suddenly. "Call him here," he said.

Voices echoed through the crowd, "Bartimaeus! Bartimaeus!"

"Go on then," said someone. "He's asking for you!"

The blind man walked forward slowly. When he came before

Jesus, he felt a gentle touch in the midst of his darkness. It was a hand on his shoulder.

"What do you want me to do for you?" asked Jesus.

"Lord," said Bartimaeus, "I want to see."

Jesus said to him, "Open your eyes. Your faith has healed you."

Suddenly, in an instant, Bartimaeus could see. There were people all around him and beyond them, fields, palm trees, the streets of Jericho. He turned round and round, and then back to Jesus, gazing in wonder. He stared in astonishment at the simplest things, as if he had just been born – his fingers, a blade of grass on the ground.

Jesus was smiling at him, laughing. Bartimaeus began to praise God, shouting for joy. He followed Jesus all through Jericho, jumping and singing.

A few minutes earlier, the crowd had simply ignored him. Now they were wild with excitement. No one in the whole of Jericho could believe that this was the same man, the blind beggar by the roadside.

ZACCHAEUS THE TAX COLLECTOR

LUKE 19

In Jericho, there was a man named Zacchaeus. He worked as a tax collector for the Romans, and he had cheated so many people, so cleverly and so often, that he had become very rich. People in Jericho would spit at his door when they passed. They thought he was worse than an ordinary thief because he stole from poor people. He had grown very rich on the sufferings of the Jewish nation, and so no one in Jericho thought of him as one of their own people. He was a traitor, the lowest of the low, more hated than the invading army of the Romans.

That day, Zacchaeus heard all the noise and shouting about Jesus. In fact, he had heard people talking about this miracle worker from Nazareth for some time, and he was very curious. He knew that Jesus would never talk to him, of course, but if only he could catch a glimpse...

Zacchaeus sneaked out into the crowds, but there were hundreds of people in the way. He was a very short man and so the people in front of him were like a huge wall. Suddenly, he saw a sycamore tree and, just like a child, scrambled up into the branches. From there, he could see Jesus coming.

But when Jesus came close to the tree, he stopped suddenly. He looked up. "Zacchaeus!" he said.

Zacchaeus could not believe that his name was being called. His mouth went dry. He began to tremble, because Jesus was looking straight at him.

"Zacchaeus," called Jesus. "Come down at once. I'm coming to your house today for a meal."

"My house...?"

"Yes, hurry up!"

Zacchaeus clambered down, not knowing whether to laugh or cry, he was so happy. He ran ahead of Jesus and ordered his servants to prepare a feast.

No one in Jericho could believe what was happening. What would Jesus want with a cheat like Zacchaeus? But Zacchaeus stood up at his feast to welcome the guests and, looking straight at Jesus, announced, "Lord... I will give half of all my possessions to the poor. And anyone I've cheated, I will pay them back four times as much!"

Jesus laughed and raised his hands in the air. "Today, salvation has come to this house! This is why I have come – to find and to save all those who are lost!"

MARTHA, MARY AND LAZARUS

LUKE 10

Jesus had known Martha, Mary and their brother, Lazarus, for a long time. They were very close friends, and he had visited them many times at their house in Bethany.

Martha and Mary were very different from each other. Martha was always hurrying around, organizing everyone, keeping the house clean and tidy. Mary was the opposite. She was quiet, a daydreamer, and her mind was often far away from cooking and cleaning. When Jesus came, all she wanted to do was sit at his feet with Lazarus and his friends and listen to his stories. Mary felt she could listen to Jesus talking forever.

And that's just how it seemed to Martha. When Jesus was there, Mary was never in the kitchen, never helping, always leaving her to do everything. One day, it was all too much for Martha. She just burst in angrily and said to Jesus, "Master, tell my sister to come and help me at once! I'm trying to do everything by myself!"

Mary's face reddened. She was on the edge of crying. It was true – perhaps she should have been helping Martha. Now she felt guilty.

But Jesus said nothing to Mary. He turned and looked at Martha for a while. There was silence.

"Martha, Martha," Jesus said. His words were gentle and yet very strong. "You're worried and anxious about so many things. There's only one thing that is important for you now."

Martha lowered her eyes. The furious anger seemed to drain away from her suddenly. All she could see was her younger sister sitting quietly at the feet of Jesus. All she could hear was her own name echoing, "Martha, Martha."

As she stood there, her worries about the meal seemed to fade. All the rushing around and the panic seemed so pointless. She joined the men who were crowding the room. She sat down at the very front with her sister, Mary, and her brother, Lazarus, and began to listen in silence.

A FAMILY TRAGEDY

John 11

When Jesus was on his way to Jerusalem for the Passover feast, a messenger came running up to him. "Master, Master, you must come…" The man was out of breath and desperately upset. He could hardly speak.

"What is it?" asked Jesus, clasping the man by the shoulders. "Tell me."

"It's your friend… Lazarus… He's dying. Martha and Mary are begging you to come now."

Jesus sat down, covering his face with his hands. He was filled with deep sorrow, but he did not move.

"Master... come now!"

Jesus stood up slowly. "Death will not be the end of this," he said quietly. "This illness will lead to the glory of God."

The messenger did not understand and begged him to follow, but Jesus turned away. The man returned to Bethany in despair and found Martha and Mary sitting beside their brother, weeping.

Lazarus was dead. Jesus gathered his disciples together and said, "Lazarus has fallen asleep. I'm going to wake him up."

"If he's only sleeping," said one, "then he's all right."

But Jesus explained, "My friend Lazarus has died."

They set out for Bethany, none of them daring to speak. How could Jesus have allowed such a good friend to die like that?

When Jesus arrived, Martha came running towards him. "O Lord," she sobbed, "if only you had been here, you could have saved my brother."

"Lazarus will rise again," said Jesus.

"Oh, I know," she wept. "I know he will rise again at the resurrection on the last day."

"I am the resurrection," said Jesus. "I am the life for those who put their trust in me."

Martha did not understand what he meant, but sent for Mary who came out of the house. When she saw Jesus, she fell down at his feet moaning and crying, "Lord, if you had been here, my brother would not have died!"

"Where have you buried him?" asked Jesus, full of love.

The two women took Jesus to the huge tomb, cut in the rock face. A great stone lay across, rolled into a deep groove.

When Jesus saw the grave and heard the weeping and crying all around him, he broke down and wept too. Then he said, "Roll the stone away."

"The stone? But, Lord…" cried Martha, "he's been in the grave for four days. There'll be a smell –"

"Believe, and you will see the glory of God. Roll away the stone!"

So some strong men from the crowd heaved and pushed and forced the great stone away until the darkness of the grave was opened to the air. There was a deep silence.

"I thank you, Father, for hearing my prayer," Jesus cried out suddenly. "You have heard it for the sake of all these people." Then he stepped forward calling, "LAZARUS, COME OUT!"

There was silence. Then a soft footstep. Then another. Slowly, steadily, a figure wrapped in strips of cloth walked out of the grave into the sunlight. The crowd gasped. Some screamed; others fainted. Others began to praise God and sing of his glory.

"Take off his grave clothes," said Jesus, "and let him go free."

PALM SUNDAY

MATTHEW 21, MARK 11, LUKE 19, JOHN 12

News that Lazarus had come back from the dead soon reached Jerusalem, and the priests, teachers of the Law and the religious leaders of the city were thrown into panic. "If Jesus goes on like this, everyone will believe in him; then the Romans will come and burn down our temple!"

The religious leaders were afraid of the people rising up in a rebellion against the Romans, with Jesus leading a great army. But Jesus was coming humbly, to bring peace. He did not choose a great stallion on which to ride down to Jerusalem or

tell his followers to carry swords. Instead, he
to find a little donkey that was tethered in a 1

"Tell the owners that the Master needs him,
them.

So the disciples brought the donkey to Jesus,
the gentle creature and rode down the steep path.
Mount of Olives. All around him, children carried palm
branches and sang at the top of their voices, "Hosanna to the
Son of David!" And the crowd of disciples and followers
shouted, "Peace in heaven and glory in the highest!"

It was just as if the angels had filled the sky once more above
the shepherds in Bethlehem, only now it was thousands of people
singing the same message of peace and goodwill. Jesus rode on,
the little donkey carrying him steadily down the rocky path into
the valley, and then up the steep hill to the gates of Jerusalem.

"Tell your followers to keep quiet!" some of the Pharisees
called to him angrily.

"If they keep quiet now," Jesus called back, "even the stones
would cry out, 'Glory to God!'" At last, he arrived in the city
itself, near the huge white temple towering up into the sky. He
climbed down off the donkey, then moved with the crowds
towards the temple.

A HOUSE OF PRAYER

MATTHEW 21

Jesus walked through the archway into the temple courts and
stopped for a moment in the dazzling sunlight. The crowd was

,g all around him, and children were shouting and
,g, but Jesus was silent.

He was staring at the hundreds of tables and all the traders
selling doves for the sacrifices; he was glaring at the money-
changers who were shouting out to the pilgrims and haggling
over the prices: "Best rates here!" "Good bargains!" "Low
interest!" "Change your money here!"

Everyone had to use the special temple coins, so the
traders were making huge profits from the poorest people.
Jesus was shaking his head in fury, and all the children
began to watch him in astonishment. First, he walked over to
a table piled high with bright coins. He grabbed it and
hurled it over.

"Hey, hey…" The merchant ran after him, but Jesus threw
over another table, then another. He seized a pair of cages with
doves in them and shook the birds free; he ran from one stall
to another, throwing the benches down and scattering coins
and weights onto the huge flagstones.

"It is written, 'My temple…'" his voice echoed around the
great building, "'… is a house of prayer,' but you have turned
it intoa den of thieves!"

All the traders, and the priests gathering in the
colonnades, watched Jesus angrily, but no one dared stop
him until he had finished. Everyone was afraid of him except
the children who began to sing again: "Hosanna to the Son
of David!"

One of the priests called out, "Listen to those children!
Can't you hear what they're singing?"

"Yes," said Jesus, "exactly as it says in the scriptures: 'From
the lips of children and babies, God has brought forth his
praises!'"

Saying that, Jesus walked away, out of the city, to Bethany. From then on, the religious leaders decided to find a way to get rid of Jesus.

A HARD QUESTION

Luke 20

One day, when Jesus was teaching in the temple, the religious leaders thought of a way to trick him into breaking the law so they could arrest him.

One of the religious leaders who was a highly trained lawyer – a very clever man – stepped forward. "Master," he said, "we know that everything you do and say is right. You are teaching God's way in all things!" The man smiled, and Jesus looked at him hard, knowing he was trying to trap him with a difficult question. The man continued, "Is it right to pay taxes to Caesar or not?"

The crowd gasped. This was a very dangerous question. If Jesus answered, "It is right," he would anger the people who hated the Romans, but if he said, "It is wrong," the Romans would arrest him as a rebel against Caesar. The lawyer stood there, clearly very proud of his cunning question, waiting for Jesus' reply.

"Give me a coin," said Jesus.

Someone handed him a denarius, a small Roman coin. Jesus held it up and it glinted in the sunlight.

"Whose head is on this?" he asked.

The lawyer was still smiling. "Caesar's!"

"Well then," said Jesus, "give to Caesar what belongs to Caesar and to God what belongs to God!"

Everyone was astonished at the wisdom of Jesus' answer, and the lawyer was forced to walk away in shame. The Roman soldiers watched the crowds leaving slowly, and Jesus walked out of the temple with his disciples.

He was safe for the moment, but in the shadows the religious leaders – priests, Pharisees and Sadducees – were plotting to arrest Jesus.

THE TRAITOR

MATTHEW 26, LUKE 22, JOHN 10

Every day in Jerusalem, hundreds of people gathered around Jesus to hear him speaking. He liked to talk in pictures about ordinary, everyday things.

"I am the good shepherd," he told them. The people knew what a good shepherd did – he looked after his sheep. But Jesus explained to them, "I am the good shepherd who gives up his own life to save his sheep."

The people did not understand why Jesus kept on saying, "I will give up my life," or "The Son of Man must suffer and die." They kept whispering to each other, "Surely he's the great leader who will free us from the power of the Romans? Why should he die?"

No one believed that the Messiah could be killed.

All this time the enemies of Jesus were trying to find a way of arresting him in secret.

"We'll have to take him by night!" one whispered.

"Everywhere he goes, there are hundreds of followers," said another.

"Sometimes he prays alone. We could find his special place on the Mount of Olives."

"It's dangerous. There are thousands of Galileans up there camping in the hills. There could be a riot and then the Romans will kill us all!"

Just then, as the religious leaders were whispering in the corner of the temple, a man stepped from the shadows. He looked over his shoulder nervously and then approached them. It was Judas.

"Aren't you one of the man's disciples?" they asked suspiciously.

Judas nodded. He cleared his throat. "How much money would you give me if I took you to Jesus?"

"You will take us to him?" They were astonished.

"There's a garden," said Judas softly. "A special place he goes to pray."

The chief priests paid Judas thirty pieces of silver, a huge sum of money. From then on, Judas waited for the right moment to betray Jesus.

THE LAST SUPPER

MATTHEW 26, MARK 14, LUKE 22, JOHN 13

The time for the Passover festival was drawing near, so Jesus and his twelve disciples went to an upper room of a house in Jerusalem to eat the Passover meal together.

Normally, Passover was a time for joy, celebration and laughter when people remembered how God had set his people, the Israelites, free from Egypt. But on this night, they all sat quietly around Jesus, who was very serious and sorrowful.

It was evening, and the lamps were lit. Jesus suddenly said, "One of you will betray me tonight."

"Surely it can't be me, Lord?" said Peter, outraged at the thought. "I'll never betray you."

"Nor will I!"

"Nor I – never!"

They all protested, every single one of them, including Judas.

"Surely you don't mean me, Teacher?" he said.

Jesus whispered, "As you say, Judas." Then he added, "Go and do what you have to do. Do it quickly."

Judas left the room immediately. None of the others realized what was happening.

"I will never betray you, never!" Peter banged the table. "Even if I have to die with you!"

"Peter," replied Jesus, "before the cock crows tomorrow morning, you will have said three times that you don't even know me."

Peter looked at Jesus, shaking his head in confusion. How could he – Peter, the rock – do such a thing, when he was one of Jesus' closest friends?

Jesus took the bread on the table and gave thanks to God. Then he broke it very slowly. The way he did it made all the disciples stare, because he seemed to feel the pain and the brokenness himself, as if a great sorrow were tearing him apart.

"Here." Jesus offered the pieces to his friends. "This is my body, which is given for you."

"His body…?" someone whispered. It was so hard to understand.

Then Jesus took the cup of wine.

"This is my blood, which is poured out for many for the forgiveness of sins. All of you must drink it."

They took the cup and drank, one by one, as Jesus spoke to them of how God had made a new agreement with humankind, promising to forgive sins and show his love to the world.

After they had sung a hymn together, they got up and left the house to go to the Mount of Olives.

THE GARDEN OF GETHSEMANE

MATTHEW 26, LUKE 22

Jesus and his disciples went out of Jerusalem, down the steep track into the valley of Kidron and then slowly up through the dark, moonlit trees of the Mount of Olives. When they reached the Garden of Gethsemane, Jesus turned and said, "Peter, James and John. Come with me – the rest of you stay here." His three closest friends followed him.

Meanwhile, Judas was standing in a courtyard with the temple guard. There were soldiers with helmets and spears, and a savage-looking band of men, all ready to march up the hill and seize Jesus by force.

"Be careful," their captain ordered. "Move in silence. No one must see you or hear you."

"I'll lead you to the garden where he prays at night,"

whispered Judas. "Then I'll walk up to him in the darkness and greet him with a kiss."

They planned the arrest down to the last detail, and then the troop of soldiers filed out of the courtyard and moved stealthily through the night.

In the Garden of Gethsemane, Jesus left Peter, James and John alone saying, "Keep watch for me." He knelt down in the shadows and began to pray to God desperately, begging him, "Father... Father! Please find another way. Let there be another way." He knew that he was soon to die a terrible death on the cross, and the sweat poured from his face like drops of blood.

After a while, Jesus got up and walked back to the three disciples who lay sprawled across the ground, fast asleep. He shook them gently. "Couldn't you watch with me for a single hour?" They were ashamed when they woke up, but as soon as Jesus went off to pray again, sleep overcame them once more and, one by one, they fell asleep.

"Father, let this cup pass from me..." Jesus lay on the ground, pleading once more with his Father in heaven to save him from death. But as he prayed he began to say, "Not my will, but yours... your will be done." Jesus whispered it into the darkness, utterly alone, while the disciples lay snoring beneath the tangled olive trees. "Your will be done."

Jesus went to the disciples and touched them again. "Wake up, the time has come," he said.

At that moment, Judas walked through the garden and went straight up to Jesus.

"Teacher!" he said, and kissed him.

"O Judas." Jesus looked at him with deep sorrow and love. "Would you betray your master with a kiss?"

Suddenly, the crowd rushed forward with swords, clubs and

spears and seized Jesus. Peter swung out wildly with his sword, slashing crazily, and cut off the ear of a young servant.

"No, no!" Jesus shouted. "This is not the way. Don't you think I could call on a huge army of angels to rescue me – if I chose?" He bent down, touched the young man's wound, and he was healed instantly.

Then the soldiers hustled Jesus away.

THE FIRST TRIAL

MATTHEW 26, LUKE 22

As soon as Jesus was arrested, all the disciples ran away, except Peter. He crept through the streets after the soldiers. He kept as near as he dared, keeping his face well hidden.

Peter followed the soldiers into a courtyard outside the house of Caiaphas, the high priest. The soldiers pushed Jesus through the great doors and into the house which was lit with flaming torches. Then Peter lost sight of Jesus.

From nearby, Peter could hear angry shouting, voices accusing Jesus of crimes against God and against the temple. He heard words like: "Blasphemer!" "Liar!" "Troublemaker!" "False Messiah!" He could hear the blows of soldiers hitting Jesus, and he sank down beside the charcoal fire that was burning in the courtyard.

Inside, Caiaphas strode around the marble floor which shone in the torchlight. "Are you the Son of God? Are you the Messiah? You must tell us!"

Jesus looked at him in silence for a long time, until the high priest became uncomfortable. "Well? I require you in God's name to tell us: are you the Son of God then?"

"It is as you say," said Jesus, without taking his gaze off the cold eyes of his accuser, "and one day you will see the Son of Man coming down in the clouds from heaven!"

There was an uproar among the religious leaders, and shouts of "Blasphemy!" "Sinner!" "Devil!"

Caiaphas called across the crowded chamber. "What more evidence do we need against this man?"

"He's guilty! Put him to death!" shouted the people.

"Take him away," said Caiaphas.

PETER DENIES JESUS

LUKE 22

While Jesus was being questioned, Peter was hunched by the fire in the courtyard, keeping well out of sight. He kept his head down and pretended to be one of the many servants warming their hands at the flames. Suddenly, the wind caught the fire and it burned brightly, lighting up his face.

"Hey!" a servant girl called. "This man was with Jesus of Galilee!"

Peter felt sick with fear. "Me?" He shook his head. "I don't know the man!"

The girl kept on staring at Peter, who turned his face away. Then another man shouted, "Yes, you were with him!"

"No, I was not!"

Later, another man walked right up to him and said, "I can

tell by your accent. You're from Galilee. You were with Jesus!"

Peter stood up furiously, swearing and shouting, "I have never even met the man!"

At that very moment, a cock crowed to herald the dawn, and Peter remembered what Jesus had said: "Before the cock crows in the morning, you will have denied three times that you know me."

A door banged against the wall, echoing in the stillness, and Jesus was pushed into the courtyard by the soldiers. They shoved him onwards but, as he passed, he looked straight into Peter's eyes, and Peter broke down and wept.

THE ROMAN GOVERNOR

MATTHEW 27, MARK 15, LUKE 23

The first light of dawn crept over the hills around Jerusalem and pale glimmers of light shone through the trees, but in the streets it was still dark. No one stirred, and none of the pilgrims from Galilee who were camped around the Mount of Olives guessed that Jesus had been arrested.

The soldiers chained Jesus and marched him through the streets in strict silence, keeping the shutters down on their lanterns. Behind them walked a crowd of chief priests and teachers of the Law in grim silence, thinking of how they could accuse Jesus in front of Pilate, the Roman governor. Pilate was a cruel man, and he had executed thousands of Jewish rebels in the past. He would show no mercy to Jesus if they could prove that he was an enemy of Caesar – but Jesus carried no sword, had no army, and did not tell anyone to fight the Romans.

Meanwhile, Judas went to the temple, carrying the thirty silver coins. "I have betrayed an innocent man!" he cried, but he could not undo what he had done. He ran to the temple sanctuary. He threw down his thirty pieces of silver. They spun through the air and clattered onto the cobblestones. Then he ran out of the city of Jerusalem, stumbling through the dawn mist to a lonely meadow. There, Judas, the disciple who had betrayed his lord and master, took a rope and hanged himself.

The soldiers arrived with Jesus at the gate of the fortress, where Pilate had been summoned to meet the priests and the city leaders with their mysterious prisoner.

"Jesus..." The Roman governor walked around the silent figure before him curiously. "What is this man's crime?" he asked.

"He tells the people not to pay taxes to Caesar," lied the religious leaders, but Jesus said nothing to defend himself.

"He says he is the Messiah, our king," one of the priests shouted out, pointing furiously.

"A king...?" Pilate studied him carefully. "Are you the king of the Jews?"

Jesus stood still and stared into Pilate's eyes. "These are your words," he said quietly.

Pilate was troubled and afraid. Something about this man was very disturbing, but he did not understand what it was – he certainly did not look like a criminal or a rebel who would lead an uprising.

"There is no case to be tried," announced Pilate.

Then all the enemies of Jesus started to shout out, "He has been stirring up the people all the way from Galilee to Judea. He is a dangerous rebel!"

Pilate raised his hand and they fell silent. "A Galilean? Then let him be tried by Herod, the ruler of Galilee. Take him away!"

THE TRIAL BEFORE HEROD

LUKE 23

King Herod had come to Jerusalem for the Passover and was staying in his magnificent palace. When he heard that Jesus was being sent to him, he was thrilled because he thought that this would entertain his guests. Perhaps he could persuade Jesus to perform a great miracle?

But when the prisoner was brought before him, tightly bound, standing silently in the great marble hall, Herod was disappointed. Jesus looked so ordinary, so weak. He had heard many stories about this brilliant teacher who healed the sick and even raised the dead.

"You're supposed to be a prophet… or some great magician," Herod said as he strode around him. "Well, show me your great powers then. Let's see a miracle or two!"

Jesus said nothing at all, even though the king kept asking him questions, urging him, walking around him and making sarcastic comments. "You're a king? So show me your powers!"

The priests shouted out their accusations again: "Liar!" "Blasphemer!" "Rebel!"

Then Herod called his servants and told them to dress Jesus in a rich, purple robe. "Let him look like a king!" he said with a sneer.

When Herod and all his courtiers had finished mocking Jesus, he was sent back to Pilate.

THE DEATH SENTENCE

MATTHEW 27, MARK 15, LUKE 23, JOHN 19

When Pilate heard that Herod could not find Jesus guilty of any crime, he was deeply disturbed.

Jesus stood before him once again, silently. His eyes seemed to gaze into Pilate's soul, and the Roman governor shifted away from the prisoner hastily. "Don't you realize that I have the power to crucify you or to set you free?"

"You would have no power over me if it hadn't been given to you from above," said Jesus, breaking his silence and troubling Pilate even more. From above? What did he mean?

Pilate did not believe in one God, but in many gods, and the only power he understood was the power of the Roman empire, of Caesar and his armies. Was Jesus talking of another power? Jesus was looking at him without fear of death, and it was Pilate who was feeling very afraid.

"I do not find this man guilty of any crime," Pilate shouted in desperation.

But by now a large crowd had gathered in the street below. "Crucify him! Crucify him!"

"Crucify your king?" Pilate leaned over the balcony. "Why do you want to kill your king?"

"We don't have a king," they shouted back. "Our only king is Caesar!"

"You are no friend of Caesar's," the religious leaders said, cleverly turning the blame onto Pilate, "if you do not sentence this man to death!"

Pilate looked at the crowd, at Caiaphas and the priests, then at the still, strong figure of Jesus.

Each year at the time of the Passover festival, the Roman governor would release a prisoner, chosen by the crowd.

"I can set Jesus free for you now!" offered Pilate.

But the crowd screamed out, "Barabbas, Barabbas, set Barabbas free!" Barabbas was a murderer and a rebel, who was in prison under sentence of death.

"Barabbas, the murderer?"

"We want Barabbas."

"Crucify Jesus, crucify him!"

"Crucify him!"

At last, Pilate could stand it no longer. In front of the crowd, he took a bowl of water, washed his hands and said, "Look, I am washing myself clean of all guilt! This man's death has nothing to do with me!"

Then he handed Jesus over to his Roman soldiers for crucifixion, ordering that a sign saying "The king of the Jews" should be put on the cross.

"Don't put that!" the chief priests protested angrily. "Just put, 'He said, "I am the king of the Jews."'"

"What I have written, I have written," said Pilate, and stormed away from them in fury.

THE CRUCIFIXION

MATTHEW 27, MARK 15, LUKE 23, JOHN 19

The soldiers took Jesus into their courtyard, shouting and jeering at him, pushing him and shoving him, spitting in his face. They stripped him and flogged him. Then they put his purple robe onto him and twisted a crown out of sharp thorns. They pressed it onto his head so the blood ran down his face and bowed down to him laughing, "King of the Jews! Hail, mighty king!"

All this time, Jesus stood there alone without saying a single word. Finally, the soldiers led Jesus out into the streets where they placed a heavy crossbeam on his back and whipped him forwards. Jesus struggled onwards, stumbling and falling. Then the soldiers seized a man from the crowds named Simon of Cyrene, who was visiting Jerusalem for the Passover festival. They forced Simon to pick up the cross and carry it instead of Jesus.

So Jesus walked on, followed by Simon with the cross, all the way to the place of execution, Golgotha, which was a skull-shaped hill.

In that lonely place outside the city walls, the soldiers crucified Jesus, watched by the priests and the religious leaders, and by the crowd which had followed the procession out of the city.

The followers of Jesus watched in horror as Jesus was nailed to the cross beside two thieves and hauled up with ropes.

They heard his cry as the cross fell into the socket. Then there was silence and the sound of the wind that was rising, hurling clouds through the sky. The three crosses stood, dark silhouettes against the fading light of the sun.

The priests turned to each other and said, "If he is the Son of God, let him come down now!"

"If he is the chosen one, the Messiah, why doesn't he prove his power?"

"Yes," said one of the thieves, grimacing in his pain, "why don't you save us too if you're the Son of God?"

"Don't you fear God at all?" asked the other. "We deserve to die for our crimes, but this man has done nothing wrong. He's innocent!"

Then he turned his face to Jesus and whispered, "Lord, remember me when you come into your kingdom."

Jesus looked into his eyes and said, "Today you will be with me in paradise."

Then Jesus saw Mary, his mother, standing there at the foot of his cross, and beside her was one of his closest friends, John.

"Woman," he said, struggling to breathe, "there is your son." And to John he said, "There is your mother."

John looked after Mary from that day onwards, taking her to live with him and his family.

At about twelve noon, the sun vanished into the rolling blackness of the clouds. Thick darkness came over the whole land, and all the people watching, including the soldiers, were filled with terror. It was as if the whole world had come to an end. Suddenly, Jesus cried out, "Father! Father! I am giving you my spirit!" With one last, agonizing breath, he shouted, "It is finished!"

His body hung down, dead, and at that moment a great storm shook the whole city of Jerusalem. The wind howled through the sky, rocks were split open, and the great veil which separated the Holy of Holies from the rest of the temple was ripped apart.

The centurion in charge of the crucifixion looked at Jesus in fear and amazement. "So this man really was God's Son!"

SECRET DISCIPLES

JOHN 19

Pilate had watched the storm and the darkness fall over Jerusalem and was sitting alone in his palace. He wanted nothing more to do with Jesus, nor did he want anyone to mention his name again.

At that moment, a servant ushered in two men. The first, dressed in fine clothes, was a rich merchant named Joseph from the town of Arimathea. The second was a Pharisee, Nicodemus. He was the one who had visited Jesus secretly by night.

Joseph spoke first. "We are disciples… That is… we did not follow Jesus openly, but now…" Joseph hesitated, then took courage, "We would like to give him a decent burial. I have a tomb, carved in the rockface of a garden outside the city."

"Your own tomb?" said Pilate, astonished.

"Prepared for the day of my own death," said Joseph, his eyes lowered to the ground. "I would like to bury him there."

"You want my permission to take down the body from the cross?" asked Pilate.

"We know that bodies of criminals are left to hang for many days but… please let us bury him."

Pilate shook his head in wonder. "Followers of a dead leader," he said. "What next?"

He swept away from them, calling out, "Have the body!"

THE BURIAL

MATTHEW 27, MARK 15, LUKE 23, JOHN 19

Joseph and Nicodemus walked out of the city and up to the hill of Golgotha, where the body of Jesus was still hanging upon the cross. Around him were women weeping: Mary Magdalene, Mary, the mother of Jesus, Salome, the mother of James and John, and others.

Slowly, and with the greatest care, the two men took out the cruel nails and lifted the body down. They wrapped Jesus in the linen shroud which Nicodemus had brought with him; then they carried the body to the garden where a tomb had been cut into the rock.

There, they laid Jesus down on the cold shelf of stone, in the darkness of the grave. The men heaved the great round boulder along its groove so that it rolled in front of the tomb and stood there, sealing the entrance.

Finally, the little band of mourners left the garden reluctantly, left Jesus behind – it seemed forever – and wandered down the long path into the city of Jerusalem.

THE EMPTY TOMB

Jesus' followers sat quietly, overwhelmed with sorrow. Their Lord and master was dead, nailed to a cross and then buried deep in the tomb.

The disciples, the closest friends of Jesus, were hiding in the upper room with the huge doors bolted. They were afraid, and they were bitterly ashamed that they had run away when Jesus had been arrested. Peter sat with his head in his hands, refusing to talk to anyone. He had denied Jesus, and now he wished that he, too, were dead.

Mary Magdalene wept alone, sighing, "My Lord… my Lord… he's gone, he's gone…"

Mary waited until the first light of day on that Sunday morning so she could visit the tomb and be near to Jesus once again. She had sat there through the long night, waiting for the daylight to come.

At the very first hint of dawn, Mary set off for the place where Jesus had been buried. She carried her precious spices and hurried to the garden.

When she arrived, the first rays of the sun were pouring through the trees, and the birds were beginning their dawn chorus. Everything seemed normal, except… the stone!

Mary gasped. She looked around, but she could see no one. Who could have rolled the huge stone away from the grave?

Jesus was gone. Immediately, she ran and told the disciples. At once, Peter and John ran to the garden and saw the empty tomb for themselves.

They walked in, Peter first of all, crouching down, touching the linen shroud that lay there, picking up the headcloth that was rolled up nearby.

The body had vanished. But could Jesus really be alive again? In wonder, Peter and John returned to the city.

Mary remained in the garden, crying. Then she stepped down into the tomb, and there she saw two angels sitting, one where the head and the other where the feet should have been. But there was no body, no Jesus, and in her confusion she did not know who these strangers were.

"Why are you crying?" they said to her.

She replied, "Because they have taken my Lord, and I don't know where they have put him." She stumbled back out into the garden and sat down, sobbing bitterly. She was crying so much that she did not see a figure come and stand beside her.

The figure spoke very gently to her. "Why are you crying?" he said.

"O sir," she said, "you must be the gardener here… If you have taken the body, please tell me where you have put him."

"Mary," said the figure.

She turned. She knew that voice. It was the voice of Jesus.

Jesus! It couldn't be… but he was looking at her, straight at her, with such love. She reached out her hands and clutched at his feet, calling out, "Master!"

"You don't have to cling to me now," he said. "Just go and tell all the disciples that you have seen me, and that I am on my way to my Father – and your Father – in heaven." So Mary ran back to the disciples and told them what she had seen and what Jesus had said.

THE EMMAUS ROAD

It was nearly evening, and two of Jesus' followers were walking on the road from Jerusalem to the little village of Emmaus. They felt desperately sad as they turned all the events of the week around in their minds.

"How could this have happened?"

"How could Jesus – the Messiah – have died the death of a common criminal?"

"How could such wonder and glory and hope – all those children waving palms, all the people singing, 'Hosanna!' – how could all that have ended in cruel death?"

The two walked on, hopelessly, weeping as they spoke.

But as they walked along, a stranger joined them on the road. They scarcely looked at him, although there was something a little familiar about the way he walked, and even about the tone of his voice.

"What are you talking about?" he said.

"Why – the terrible things that have happened in Jerusalem!" They shook their heads, hardly able to continue.

"Oh," said the stranger, "what things?"

"What things? Are you the only visitor who does not know what has happened in the city this week? The death of Jesus from Nazareth! We believed he was the Messiah, but..."

They explained how Jesus had been killed, how all their hopes had been dashed, how their whole lives had sunk into despair.

The stranger shook his head. "You foolish people," he said

gently, "don't you understand the scriptures? Don't you realize that the Messiah had to die…?"

They looked at him curiously. His eyes were deep in shadow, and the light of the setting sun seemed to blaze all around him. Who was he? Why did they think they had met him before, somewhere, somehow?

They walked on to Emmaus as the stranger went through all the scriptures, all the prophets, from start to finish, and explained to them how the Messiah, God's chosen one, had to give his life to save the world.

When they arrived at their home in Emmaus, they persuaded the stranger to come in and eat with them.

They sat down, and the mysterious guest took the bread, blessed it and broke it. And, suddenly, their eyes were opened. They saw that it was Jesus. They cried out in amazement, leaped from their chairs, but the place where he had been sitting was empty!

Jesus had vanished.

JESUS IS ALIVE!

LUKE 24, JOHN 20

The two disciples ran all the way back from Emmaus to Jerusalem, seven miles, to tell the others.

When they arrived, the doors of the house were locked and bolted because the disciples were still very afraid that they would be arrested by the religious authorities. Quickly, the two friends were allowed in, but the doors were bolted firmly again.

Safe inside, fear gave way to joy as the two friends told their story. Soon, they were all swapping stories, breathless with wonder. Jesus had appeared to Peter too, and as they shared what had happened in amazement, they did not know whether to laugh or cry, sit or stand, sing, pray, run or dance!

"The Lord has risen!" they shouted. "We have seen the Lord!"

Even as they were speaking, Jesus appeared in the middle of the room and said, "Peace be with you!"

No one moved. They were all afraid that he was a ghost, but Jesus said, "Touch and see! Does a ghost have flesh and blood?" Slowly, fearfully, they touched him, they held his hands, they looked at the scars left by the nails. They knew that it was really, truly, Jesus, standing right in the middle of the room, and the door was still locked and bolted!

There was one of Jesus' closest friends, Thomas, who was not there when Jesus came to the room.

When they told him the news, he said, "You may have seen Jesus, but I haven't."

The others did not know what to say, but Thomas stood up and said, "Unless I see Jesus for myself, unless I put my finger in the marks of the nails and my hand in his wounded side, I will not believe!"

One week later, the disciples were again meeting together behind locked doors.

"Peace be with you," said a voice. It was so close that it took their breath away. "Thomas," said the voice, firm and commanding.

Thomas stopped. He looked around very slowly. And standing right beside him was Jesus, holding out his hands. "Go on then. See for yourself. Touch the marks, feel my wounds!"

Thomas sank to his knees, his throat dry, his heart beating wildly. "My Lord," he whispered, "and my God!"

"Yes," said Jesus, "you believe because you have seen me, Thomas, but how happy are those who believe without seeing me."

BREAKFAST BY GALILEE

JOHN 21

Soon after the friends of Jesus had seen him alive again in Jerusalem, they returned to their homes in Galilee. One evening, Peter said, "I'm going fishing," and the others, including Thomas, James and John, said, "We'll come too."

They fished all night, but caught nothing. They just sat in the boat, dragging their empty net through the waters until the mist rose on the lake and the first light of dawn was breaking in the hills.

Now there was a figure standing on the shore, but they could not make out who it was. "Have you caught anything, my friends?" he called.

"Nothing!"

"Throw your net over the other side of the boat, and you'll catch something."

They threw their net over the other side, as if they were in a dream, not knowing who the man was but wondering… the voice was so familiar… the way he stood so calmly, gazing at them all…

Suddenly, the net was full of fish, scales flashing in the

sunlight, flipping and jumping, dazzling. A cascade of white and silver, so heavy that the men could scarcely haul the nets into the boat.

"It's the Lord," said John.

Peter leaped into the water, right up to his waist. He ran through the shallows while the others rowed the boat into the shore, dragging the net behind them.

They reached the figure, who was standing beside a charcoal fire, cooking some fish.

It seemed so ordinary. Jesus was standing there beside a fire, cooking breakfast. They stood there in silence like little children, suddenly unsure what to do or say.

"Bring some of the fish you've caught," Jesus waved to them. "Let's eat."

No one dared to ask, "Is it really you, Lord?" because they knew who it was. They knew it was Jesus as he handed around bread and fish. One by one, they sat down beside the fire to eat the meal.

The flames were fanned by the morning breeze, and the smell of fish and the scent of flowers in the meadows floated through the air. The men sat there all around their master, eating silently in wonder.

When they had finished eating, Jesus sat down beside Simon Peter. "Simon, son of John, do you love me?"

"Yes, Lord, you know I love you."

"Feed my lambs," said Jesus.

"Simon, son of John," Jesus continued, "do you love me?"

"Lord, you know I love you!"

"Look after my sheep."

Peter knew that Jesus was telling him to take care of those people who followed him and who would become his disciples, like a shepherd looking after his flock of sheep.

But Jesus had not finished with Peter yet. "Simon, son of John, do you love me?"

Peter was hurt when Jesus asked him the third time. "Lord, you know everything; surely you know that I love you!"

There were tears in his eyes and falling down his rough cheeks, because even as he answered for the third time he could hear the cock crowing in his mind, echoing, screeching. He remembered, with terrible regret, how he had denied knowing Jesus three times.

Now he had been given the chance to say three times, "I love you."

Jesus smiled and put both hands on Peter's shoulders. He looked deep into the fisherman's eyes as he said, "Feed my sheep!"

On that bright dawn beside Lake Galilee, Peter took courage. He knew he was forgiven and loved and ready to be a leader of the followers of Jesus.

"GO INTO ALL THE WORLD"

MATTHEW 28, JOHN 20, 21

In the weeks after Jesus rose from the dead, he appeared to his friends on a number of occasions. Often he came to one or two people, or a small group of disciples, but once he appeared to a crowd of five hundred of his followers. There could be no doubt that Jesus was alive.

He was the same Lord, the same Master who had told them

so many stories, healed the sick, spoken about the kingdom of God, and yet he was different. One moment he could appear among them, talking, laughing and encouraging them. Then he would disappear, and all they could see was the grass bending in the wind or his footprints in the dust. They were sometimes afraid, and their worship was full of fear and wonder.

One day, Jesus told the eleven disciples to gather on a hill above Lake Galilee. There, he appeared to them again. He held out his hands to them and said, "I have been given authority over all heaven and earth. Now you must go into all the world and make disciples from every nation. Teach others to follow me and baptize them."

They knelt before him humbly as he urged them, "Don't be afraid. I am with you forever, until the end of time!"

As his disciples listened, they gazed across Lake Galilee towards all the little villages and the great towns beyond. In silence, they imagined the whole world which lay before them and the great task Jesus had given them to do.

JESUS ASCENDS INTO HEAVEN

ACTS 1

Jesus' followers knew that one day he would finally leave them. He had said to them gently, "When I am gone, wait in Jerusalem until the Holy Spirit comes down upon you."

Now, as they gathered on the Mount of Olives near Jerusalem, the small band of Jesus' closest friends knew that the time had come for him to leave at last.

Jesus encouraged the disciples as he moved among them. "You will receive power from God when the Holy Spirit comes upon you," he reminded them. "You will tell the whole world about me. You will be my chosen messengers in Jerusalem and far beyond, to the very ends of the earth!"

As he spoke, a bright cloud wrapped itself around him, hiding him from their sight. His friends stepped back fearfully, and when the dazzling light faded into nothing, they looked up, gazing all around the hills. They could see no one at all, only the brightness of the sunshine.

Then two men dressed in white spoke quietly to them all: "People of Galilee, why are you standing here looking up into the sky? This Jesus, who has been taken from you into heaven, will one day return, just as you have seen him go!"

Comforted by the words of the angels, the disciples walked down the steep track to the city of Jerusalem, where they waited for the coming of the Holy Spirit.

They spent their time thoughtfully, choosing a disciple named Matthias to replace Judas. The twelve disciples were then joined by Mary, the mother of Jesus, other members of his family and the women who followed him. They all began to pray together and wait for the coming of the Spirit.

FIRE FROM HEAVEN

ACTS 2

The disciples were gathered in the upper room, where Jesus had first appeared to them after he had risen from the dead. It was the day of Pentecost, and Jerusalem was full of visitors who had come to celebrate the festival.

The disciples were all sitting together and praying, when suddenly the whole room began to shake. A mighty wind came roaring from the sky, thundering across the roof and surging through every window. The wild storm seized the disciples as if holding them, wrapping them all in its brightness and its power, and tongues of fire settled on their heads like flames.

Immediately, they began to speak in other languages. Words and phrases which they had never learned, but which the Holy Spirit poured into their hearts and minds, came tumbling from their mouths. They ran from the room and into the streets.

The crowds were astonished and fearful, because they could hear these ordinary, uneducated men speaking in their own languages. There were visitors from Parthia, Persia, Mesopotamia, Cappadocia, Egypt, Libya, Crete, Rome – Jews from every part of the Roman empire who were staying in Jerusalem for the festival.

"How can these Galileans speak in our languages?"

"How can they preach about the wonderful works of God in a foreign tongue they have never learned?"

Some started to shake their heads at the sight of the twelve men overflowing with joy and laughter. "They're drunk!" they said. Many people were shocked and bewildered at the extraordinary events.

GOD'S PROMISE

ACTS 2

Peter stood up and addressed the vast crowd. "Fellow Jews, from Jerusalem and all over the world, listen to me! None of these men is drunk. It's only nine o'clock in the morning! No, what's happening is something wonderful, which God promised hundreds of years ago through the prophet Joel:

In the last days, I will pour out my Spirit
*   on all people.*
Your sons and daughters will prophesy,
Your young people will see visions,
Your old people will dream dreams.
There will be signs in heaven and earth
*   in that great and glorious day,*
and everyone who calls on the name
*   of the Lord will be saved!"*

The crowd fell silent at the sight of the brave fisherman, whose voice was like the herald of a powerful king or some famous general addressing his troops. Every word that Peter spoke was full of life and beauty and strength. Suddenly, the man who had failed Jesus so badly had turned into a mighty preacher.

He told the crowds sternly how they – "God's people" – had crucified Jesus, but how God had raised him from the dead. Many were very moved and sorrowful and began to cry, "What shall we do?"

"Repent," Peter answered, "and be baptized so that your sins may be forgiven. And you will receive the gift God promised to you all, the gift of the Holy Spirit." He stretched out his hands to them, commanding them, longing for them all to know the love and forgiveness which was in his own heart.

On that day, the great day of Pentecost, three thousand people accepted Peter's message and were baptized.

The new followers of Jesus listened carefully to all that Peter and the other disciples told them. They often met together for prayer and for meals, when they remembered what Jesus had taught them and done for them. There were miracles, healings and signs of God's power. It was a time when the new disciples praised God and showed great kindness to each other. They shared their money and their possessions, making sure that the poorer disciples were well looked after.

Every day, seeing these wonderful things, more people joined them and became followers of Jesus.

A MIRACLE AT THE TEMPLE GATE

ACTS 3, 4

One day, Peter and John went to the temple to pray. As they walked through the great doors of the Beautiful Gate, a beggar began to rattle his bowl at them. "Have pity on me, sirs! Spare some change!"

All his life he had held out his bowl and called out the same words. Everyone knew him as the beggar at the Beautiful Gate. He could not walk, so each day his family carried him there and set him down beside the great bronze doors. He was surrounded by magnificence, dazzling whiteness, fine robes and the smell of incense, but in this place which they called beautiful, he felt ugly and ashamed.

"Have pity on me, sirs! Spare some change."

Peter stopped, full of love and sympathy. "Look at us!" he said.

The beggar, shielding his eyes against the sun, looked up into the faces of the two disciples.

"We haven't got any money," said Peter gently. "But what we do have we will give to you. In the name of Jesus of Nazareth, get up and walk!"

Peter grabbed the man by the right hand and pulled him up. At once, power flowed into his ankles and feet. The man started walking.

Pilgrims around the temple steps began to stop and stare.

"I can walk!" the man shouted. And then he began to run through crowds, leaping and shouting, "Thanks be to God! I've been healed!"

A crowd gathered, but Peter said to them, "There is no need to stare in amazement, as if we have healed this man by our own power. This has not been done by us, but through the power of Jesus Christ!"

At the mention of Jesus, the priests and Sadducees looked at them in alarm.

"Yes," said Peter, staring hard at them, "the man you rejected and killed! God has raised him from the dead, and we have healed by faith in his name."

At that, the temple guards came and arrested Peter and John and flung them into jail. They were released the next morning, with strict instructions not to mention Jesus' name again.

"We must obey God," they answered. "We cannot stop speaking about what we have seen and heard."

By now, there were thousands of new followers of Jesus in Jerusalem.

GROWING OPPOSITION

ACTS 5

The good news about Jesus spread all over Jerusalem. The high priest and the religious leaders were worried. It seemed that nothing could stop these followers of Jesus; once more Peter and his friends were arrested and put in prison. The next day, they were preaching in the temple courts after a miraculous escape from jail. The Sanhedrin, the council of religious leaders, met together.

"We've got to stop them!" shouted the high priest.

"How can we stop them?" one of the priests replied. "There are thousands of people listening to them all around the city."

"They blame us!" said the high priest. "They say we are murderers!"

An old Pharisee rose up shakily, and there was silence again. He was very learned and well-respected. His name was Gamaliel. "Listen," he said slowly, "many leaders have come and gone over the years. They have claimed to be prophets, messiahs, deliverers from the Romans! They have all been killed and their followers scattered, so we must wait and see. If this Jesus of Nazareth and his teaching is another empty dream, it will all come to nothing!"

All the members of the council nodded their heads. "But," said Gamaliel with great emphasis, "if Jesus is from God, then you cannot stand against him. How can you fight against God?"

There was a long silence. The high priest shifted uncomfortably. He did not like the advice of this old, wise Pharisee. He longed to see Peter and John arrested, tried and killed, but he knew that they were too popular with the people and he was afraid. What if the crowds turned against him? He would lose his power, his wealth and his important position. He could lose everything, even his life.

He longed for the day when the people of Jerusalem would turn against these followers of Jesus and see how dangerous they were. That day came suddenly, when a man named Stephen arrived in Jerusalem.

BRAVE STEPHEN

ACTS 6, 7

Stephen was one of seven men chosen by the twelve disciples to help share food among the poor widows of Jerusalem.

He was a great leader, a brilliant speaker who fascinated the crowds with stories about Jesus. Stephen performed many miracles by the power of the Holy Spirit, and soon the whole of Jerusalem was talking about him.

But Stephen's enemies were gathering. They heard him speak to others about how to worship God. Stephen told people they could worship wherever they were, as well as in the temple. He wanted everyone to know about the love of

Jesus, no matter where they lived or who they were.

And so his enemies spread lies: "Stephen is saying terrible things about God and Moses. He wants to tear up the ——— scriptures and throw them away!" Soon, some of the religious leaders began to turn against him, and one day a group of men crept up behind him and captured him.

They dragged Stephen off to the temple and threw him down in front of the high priest and all of the Sanhedrin, the council of religious leaders.

"Are these things true?" the high priest stared at him menacingly. "Do you hate God, Moses and the laws of the Jewish people?"

"My brothers, my fathers..." replied Stephen graciously, "listen to me. All through the history of our people, our great leaders have tried to show us the way to God, but the people have refused to listen!"

Stephen glanced at the men who had kidnapped him, and they stared back at him, burning with hatred. He carried on quietly, going through the whole history of God's people. He showed how, in the time of Moses and Joshua and through all the centuries, the Israelites had turned away from God, bowed down to idols and even murdered the prophets. "You're worse than your ancestors, because you have taken God's Messiah..."

The priests began to move towards Stephen furiously, but he would not keep silent. "You have refused to listen to Jesus Christ. You have captured and murdered him!"

At this, the whole Sanhedrin was in uproar. Men began to scream in fury at Stephen. They rushed at him waving their fists, but Stephen looked calmly high above their heads, high above all the terrible noise and hatred.

"Look!" he called out, his face radiant with joy. "Oh look! I can see the Son of Man standing at the right hand of God!"

Only Stephen could see the wonderful vision of the glory and majesty of Jesus standing in the presence of God.

His attackers blocked their ears, shouting, "Blasphemer!" "Liar!"

They seized him and dragged him through the streets, hurling him along and beating him until they had thrown him to the ground outside the city walls. There, they lifted up great stones and began to throw them down at Stephen, who cried out, "Lord Jesus, I give you my spirit."

He fell to his knees as the stones rained down upon his head and the blood poured from his wounds. The last thing he said was, "Lord, do not hold this sin against them... forgive them." Then he died.

Standing with the crowd of accusers, and looking after all the coats, was a young man named Saul. He strongly approved of the killing because he believed that Stephen was an evil man. Saul became the greatest enemy of all the followers of Jesus.

A REMARKABLE MEETING

ACTS 8

The friends of Stephen took up his body and buried him, weeping bitterly. But as they mourned their terrible loss, Saul was marching through Jerusalem with armed guards from the temple, smashing his way into the homes of every follower of Jesus. He interrogated and beat them and often hurled them into prison. Many hundreds of people escaped into the surrounding villages and towns, but even though they were being hunted down, they kept on preaching and teaching. They could not stop talking about the good news of Jesus wherever they went.

Philip, one of the most faithful followers of Jesus, went to Samaria and performed many miracles there. Hundreds of people believed and were baptized. One day, he was praying in the early morning when he heard a voice: "Philip, leave Samaria and go out into the desert! Go south down the dusty road that runs from Jerusalem." He knew it was one of God's angels speaking to him.

Philip obeyed, wondering what on earth this could mean. As he journeyed down the lonely track through the hot sands, he saw a cloud of dust approaching. It was a chariot and horses, richly equipped with all the trappings of a royal household.

"Go alongside the chariot," came the voice again. "Stay close and listen."

Philip walked beside the chariot as it slowed down in the deep sand. He could hear a man reading out loud, and he recognized words from the prophet Isaiah. He called out, "Do you understand what you are reading?"

The man called the chariot to a halt. He looked at Philip very curiously. He was a tall elegant figure, dressed in crimson and wearing the golden chains of high office. It turned out that he was the royal treasurer for Queen Candace of Ethiopia, and he was returning from a festival in Jerusalem where he had gone to worship God.

"Come and sit beside me," he said, intrigued by the dusty figure of Philip with his keen eyes and his confident stare. "Can you tell me what this means?"

He began to read the passage again – words about an innocent man being condemned to death: "like a sheep being taken for slaughter, he was dumb and said nothing to his accusers."

"Who is that?" asked the treasurer. "The prophet Isaiah or someone else?"

"I will tell you who it is," said Philip. "It's the man who died – and came to life again! It is Jesus Christ."

As the chariot sped onwards, Philip explained everything about the good news, and the man listened for many hours until he said, "Look – over there! Water! Why are we waiting? Stop the chariot by this river and let me be baptized at once!"

So the great government minister took off his crimson robe and royal chains and humbly walked down into the muddy stream, where Philip baptized him in the name of the Father, and the Son, and the Holy Spirit.

Then the Holy Spirit took hold of Philip and whisked him away, so that when the Ethiopian turned, Philip was gone. The treasurer climbed back into his seat, dripping wet, full of joy and wonder at the miraculous power of the God who had met him in so lonely a place.

A MIRACLE ON THE DAMASCUS ROAD

ACTS 9

Meanwhile, Saul was still threatening to find and murder all the followers of Jesus. He went to the high priest at the temple in Jerusalem and obtained a warrant to arrest any followers of Jesus in Damascus. Then he journeyed along the road to the north, through outposts and Roman garrisons.

As he drew closer to the great city of Damascus, dazzling light stronger than the sun suddenly shone all around him, and a voice called out, "Saul, Saul…"

The brilliant light and the voice that burned into his soul were the most terrifying things he had ever known.

"Saul!" Now it came like a whisper in his skull; it was so close, it seemed to penetrate his whole being and flood it with horror. "Why are you persecuting me?" the voice asked.

Saul could not speak for a moment. His companions could not see the light, but they could hear the voice.

"Who are you, Lord?" Saul whispered.

"I am Jesus," came the reply. "The one you are persecuting. Stand up now and go into the city. There you will be told what you must do."

The other men saw their leader get up, weeping and shaking his head. He stumbled forward, reaching out his arms.

Saul had been blinded by the dazzling light. Confused and troubled, his men led him by the hand all the way down the road, into the city of Damascus.

For three days and three nights, Saul could not see anything at all, nor did he speak or eat or drink. He sat in the darkness, alone in his room, utterly silent.

Then on the third night, a follower of Jesus named Ananias, who lived in Damascus, had a vision. Jesus was standing before him calling, "Ananias."

"Yes, Lord. I'm here," he answered.

"I want you to go to the house of Judas, in Straight Street. You must ask for a man from Tarsus, named Saul."

"Saul?" Ananias jumped up in terror. "The murderer of your people!"

"He's praying in his room right now, and he's had a vision too. He has seen a man named Ananias who will heal him from his blindness."

"Me, Lord? But… but…" Ananias was flustered. "This man… I've heard terrible reports of what he's done to all your followers, and now he's come to Damascus with an arrest warrant. He'll throw us all into jail!"

"I have chosen this man to speak in my name all over the world," Jesus said to Ananias. "He will speak to the Gentile nations and their rulers, as well as the people of Israel. He is my servant now and will suffer many things because of me. Go!"

So Ananias left his house and walked through the streets of Damascus until he came to the house where Saul was staying. When he saw the tormentor of the disciples sitting quietly on his bed, humbly reaching out to him, he was deeply moved, and he laid his hands on Saul's head with the words "My brother!"

Saul, too, was overcome, because he knew that Ananias had been sent by God.

"Brother Saul," Ananias said, "the Lord – Jesus, who appeared to you on the road – has sent me so you can recover your sight and be filled by the Holy Spirit."

As soon as Ananias' trembling hands touched Saul's head, the darkness melted away from his eyes, as if scales were falling away, and Saul could see once more!

That night, Ananias baptized Saul – the first step on Saul's extraordinary new journey. He had become the servant of Jesus, a man he had never known, a man he had hated, whose followers he had killed, but a man who had appeared to him in all his glory on the road to Damascus. It was an encounter that changed Saul's life forever.

KIND DORCAS

ACTS 9

After Peter left Jerusalem, he journeyed widely, teaching and healing in the name of Jesus. One day, he was in Lydda when two men came from nearby Joppa with a message: "Come and help us!"

In Joppa, there was a woman named Dorcas, who had died. She had been a true follower of Jesus, and many people were mourning because they loved her so much. She had made beautiful clothes for the poor widows of the area, working long into the night, and for years she had performed many works of great kindness.

When Peter arrived in Joppa, he was surrounded by women holding out their shawls and robes, beautifully and lovingly stitched by Dorcas. They were sobbing, helpless with grief.

Peter asked them all to leave so that he could be completely alone with the body of Dorcas. She lay there, cold and still, in the tiny upper room of her house. All around were half-finished gifts for the poor, needles, thread and rolls of cloth. It was a sad sight – a lovely, kind woman struck down in the prime of her life. Peter knelt down beside her bed, touched with all the sorrow of her friends, and prayed deeply to God. Then he turned to the body and called out, "Dorcas, get up!"

At once, she opened her eyes. She saw Peter gazing down at her with tenderness. She sat up. She breathed and stretched and yawned. Peter took her by the hand and helped her to stand up. When the people saw her, all the poor widows and her friends were overcome with joy, and shock. News about the incredible miracle spread far and wide, so Peter stayed in that region for a long time, telling everyone about the love and power of his master, Jesus.

ESCAPE FROM JAIL

ACTS 12

King Herod was very disturbed by all the reports of miracles in his kingdom. He had been glad when the Romans had executed Jesus, but now he was afraid. Peter, James and John, ordinary fishermen, had become great leaders with extraordinary powers. He had to stop these dangerous men before it was too late, or soon no one would bow down to him, Herod, mighty lord and ruler of Galilee!

Herod had James, the brother of John, arrested and beheaded. The disciples were heartbroken when they heard the news, but the enemies of Jesus were pleased with this crime, so Herod arrested Peter, too, and prepared to put him on trial. He would make an example of the ringleader and kill him. He wanted to stop these troublemakers once and for all.

Peter found himself in the deepest cell, chained and double-chained to two guards, with soldiers guarding all the prison gates. Peter's chains were huge and heavy, and all around him water dripped, while the guards stared grimly and silently into the darkness. That night, Peter quietly prepared to die.

A few streets away, the followers of Jesus gathered secretly in a house, praying and calling on the name of God. They prayed and begged God to save Peter, but they did not know how.

They cried out in desperation, "O God, hear our prayer. Save our brother Peter!"

Meanwhile, the prisoner had fallen asleep between his guards. He was curled up on the floor looking strangely peaceful, and the guards sat on either side of him, puzzled at his calm and carefree manner. Before long, they closed their eyes too.

At that very moment, light filled the whole cell, radiating into every corner, as an angel appeared and stood beside Peter. "Get up, hurry!"

Peter staggered up, dazed, as the chains fell from his hands and his feet. The two soldiers sat there, completely unaware.

"Put on your coat and your sandals," said the angel, "and follow me." Peter obeyed, but he was sure that he was dreaming as one door after another flew open. No one moved or flinched or noticed them as they passed through all the guard posts, until at last they came to the huge iron gate that led into the city. The gate creaked and swung open slowly, all by itself, and the angel led Peter all the way down the street, turned the corner, then vanished.

Feeling the cold night air on his cheeks, Peter suddenly knew that this was no dream. He ran through the streets until he came to the secret house and knocked on the door.

Inside, the followers of Jesus were still praying and begging God for help. A maidservant named Rhoda ran to the door and recognized Peter's voice. She was so happy and so shocked that she ran back to the others without opening the door. "It's Peter, it's Peter, it's him... it's Peter!" she stammered.

"You're out of your mind," they said.

"No, no... he's there, on the doorstep."

"It must be a vision."

But God had answered their prayers, and Peter was really and truly knocking at the door, whispering, "Let me in, let me in!"

Rhoda ran back and unbolted the door, and Peter walked into the middle of the room where the prayer meeting broke up in an uproar.

Peter held up his hand, and there was silence. "Tell the others that I'm safe," he said. Then he left the house while it was still dark and escaped from the city.

SPREADING THE GOOD NEWS

ACTS 9, 11, 13

Meanwhile, in Damascus, Saul joined the little band of followers – the people he had come to arrest – and began to tell them all that had happened. Among them was a merchant from Cyprus named Barnabas, a kind-hearted, cheerful man who showed great love and friendship to Saul.

Saul tried to tell some members of the Jewish synagogue in Damascus about his incredible vision, but soon they began to hunt him down, conspiring to kill him. His new friends helped Saul climb into a basket at night and lowered him down the city walls. So Saul, who had set out from Jerusalem proudly with an escort of soldiers, left Damascus very humbly in a basket.

Eventually, Saul went to Jerusalem. At first, Peter, James and John could not believe that he had become a true disciple. Many of Jesus' followers in Jerusalem thought Saul was a dangerous spy, but Barnabas stood up for him. He spoke to the apostles and convinced them that Saul had indeed met the risen Jesus Christ.

Because Saul had stopped his campaign of terror, there was peace for a while. The followers of Jesus grew in number, and for the first time, in the city of Antioch, the nickname "Christians" was given to them.

Meanwhile, Saul went back to his home city of Tarsus. It was many years later that Barnabas found him again and took him back to Jerusalem.

This time, the leaders of the church could see that Saul was truly chosen by Jesus himself, a special messenger – an apostle – to the world of the Gentiles. The Christians in Antioch sent Saul on a journey into the vast Roman empire, and Barnabas went with him.

They sailed first to Cyprus, Barnabas's home, where Saul became known by his Roman name, Paul. Although Paul was a Jew, he was also a Roman citizen. This meant that he had special rights and privileges that he knew would be useful as he journeyed throughout the Roman empire. So the two men moved on from Cyprus to Perga and to Pisidian Antioch in the heart of Asia Minor.

There Paul preached the good news about Jesus to many people, Jews and Gentiles alike. Some of these rejected his message, and they became furiously angry with him. Paul and Barnabas were forced to leave, but they kept their spirits up, believing that Jesus himself went with them every step of the way.

MISTAKEN FOR GODS!

ACTS 14

Paul and Barnabas journeyed on, visiting many different towns and cities, telling people the good news of Jesus and encouraging the followers who lived there.

In the town of Lystra, Paul began to speak to everyone he met. Many stopped to listen, but one man in particular was desperate to hear.

He was lame and had never walked a single step in his whole life. He sat there trying to hear this strange, wonderful story about Jesus who changed so many lives.

As Paul stood there boldly describing how his own life had been changed forever by the power of God, he saw the man leaning towards him, his mouth open in amazement, his eyes full of tears, longing for the love of Jesus.

"Get up," said Paul.

The poor bent figure stared at him, puzzled and afraid. Paul nodded and smiled, "Go on."

Now the crowd was silent. The lame man looked at Paul.

"Stand up now!" Paul called loudly.

Immediately, the man sprang to his feet. A gasp ran through the crowd. People moved back as the lame man took one step. Then another. Then a third, a fourth, a fifth.

All of a sudden, the crowd started shouting. "The gods, the gods!" the roar went up. "The gods have come down from heaven. They have come to Lystra!"

Paul and Barnabas were mobbed by hundreds of people rushing to touch them, falling at their feet to worship them.

They thought Barnabas was Zeus, father of the gods, and Paul was Hermes, messenger of the gods.

"No, no!" Paul and Barnabas shouted, tearing their clothes in anguish. "We are not your gods, we are not divine beings!" But even as they spoke, priests led oxen with garlands of flowers towards them.

"Let us sacrifice to the great gods of Lystra!" they shouted.

Paul silenced them with his hand. "We have not come to tell you about idols and myths and old stories! We are not gods, angels or spirits, but ordinary mortals with a message from the one true God. We have come to tell you of his love and about his Son, Jesus…"

But just then, some men arrived from the synagogue in Antioch. They blocked their ears at the sound of "Jesus" and rushed into the crowds.

"Don't listen to their lies!" they screamed. "Don't let these madmen trick you."

Before long, they managed to turn the crowds against Paul and Barnabas with their lies and accusations. Then the men from Antioch seized Paul, stoned him, dragged him out of the city and left him for dead.

Barnabas and some other believers knelt down beside Paul's body, certain that he was dead. Suddenly, the crumpled figure of the apostle opened his eyes and stood up.

"Come on," he said, brushing the dust off his clothes. "We have more work to do."

And with that, he walked back into the town and carried on telling the people of Lystra – anyone who would listen – about the wonderful news of Jesus.

Paul and Barnabas left the town and went through the region, visiting groups of Christians in many places before returning across the sea to Antioch in Syria.

PAUL IN PHILIPPI

ACTS 16

Once more, Paul set sail. This time his companions were Silas and Luke. They were heading for Macedonia, for Paul had seen a vision of a Macedonian man, begging for help. All the way, Paul's eyes were fixed on the horizon. The gulls wheeled and cried, circling the ship as it ploughed its white furrow through the waves, and as Paul stood on deck, he could still hear the voice of the man in his vision: "Please come and help us!" The ship made a straight run for Samothrace, and the three men journeyed overland to Neapolis and finally reached Philippi, the greatest city in the region.

After a few days' stay in the city, they decided to go outside the city gates where there was a special place of prayer for the Jewish people. It was the Sabbath day, and they knew that people would meet there to worship God. Down by the river, they found a group of women who had come together to pray.

Paul, Silas and Luke sat down and began to speak to the women about Jesus Christ and all that God had done through him. One woman was named Lydia. She listened to every word of this "good news" and kept asking Paul to tell her more. She believed in God, but she wanted to know everything about Jesus.

Lydia was the first person in the whole of Macedonia to become one of Jesus' followers. She was wealthy – she had a business in Philippi dyeing purple cloth – and she was well known in the city. She insisted that Paul, Silas and Luke come to stay with her. "If you consider me to be a true believer now," she said, "then you must stay in my house!"

She wouldn't take "no" for an answer, so they thanked her for her kindness, but each day they came out of the city and joined all those who came to pray, speaking about Jesus Christ to anyone who would listen.

A RIOT!

ACTS 16

In Philippi, there was a slave girl who was deeply disturbed. She was possessed by a spirit, and through this evil power she was able to tell fortunes and predict the future. Her masters made a great deal of money out of her.

When Paul, Silas and Luke arrived in the city, she began to follow them. Each day, she ran after them, shouting, waving and screaming at the top of her voice, "These men are servants of the most high God. They will tell you how to be saved!"

At first, Paul took no notice of the slave girl, but the loud interruptions became very difficult. One day, as she called out again, Paul was angry with the spirit which tormented her. He turned suddenly and said, "I command you, in the name of Jesus Christ, to come out of her!"

Immediately, the spirit left her. She sank down to the ground very meekly and quietly. She opened her eyes as if she had been awakened from a bad dream. She blinked and smiled. Now, the girl was completely normal, and the evil power had gone.

Her masters were furious. They raged at Paul and Silas, who had ruined their business. Now they had lost all their earnings from the poor slave girl, and they were out for revenge. They grabbed Paul and Silas and dragged them roughly away, hauling them into the market place to stand before the magistrates of the city.

"Look at these men!" said their accusers. "These Jews have come into our city and are breaking our Roman laws and causing trouble!"

The crowd surged all around, pushing and shoving and hurling insults. The magistrates ordered Paul and Silas to be beaten publicly. Then they were taken off to prison.

MAXIMUM SECURITY

ACTS 16

"Take these criminals," said the magistrate to the jailer, "and put them in the deepest part of the prison."

The jailer knew about Paul and Silas. Everyone had been talking about them for days. Now he had been told that they were very dangerous, so he took them to the inner cells and put their feet in the stocks. He slammed and bolted the door behind them.

Alone in the dark cell, Paul and Silas began to pray. Then

Silas began to sing, and Paul joined him quietly. Then, loudly, they both began to sing praises to God.

The other prisoners heard them through the walls. What could this singing mean? It was so strange. No one ever sang songs in that dark, fearful place, but they could hear these two strangers singing, and sometimes shaking their chains and laughing and praising God at the top of their voices.

That was when it happened, right in the middle of the night. A violent earthquake suddenly shook the whole of Philippi. The tremor shattered the foundations of the prison, the gates flew off their hinges, and the doors of the cells were left broken and hanging in clouds of dust.

The jailer woke up and stumbled into the darkness, coughing. All the prisoners were escaping, he was sure of it. They must be. He could see broken chains lying everywhere. He could hear men moving around. The jailer knew that this was the end for him, because if his prisoners escaped, especially these two dangerous criminals, he would pay for it with his own life. He unsheathed his sword and was about to fall on it when Paul called out, "Don't harm yourself! We're all here, every single prisoner!"

The jailer let his sword drop with a clatter. He shouted, "Lights! Lights!" Men brought flaming torches, and, in the gloom, he saw the smiling faces of Paul and Silas, sitting with the stocks and chains lying broken all around them. Nearby were all the other prisoners. Softly, Paul was singing another hymn to the amazement of them all. He and Silas clapped their hands and sang praises to the name of God.

NEW BELIEVERS

ACTS 16

The jailer had the men brought into his own home. He was trembling, in awe of the mighty power of God. He knelt down in front of Paul and Silas. "Sirs," he asked, "how can I be saved?"

"You must believe in the Lord Jesus Christ," they replied. "You and your whole family."

The jailer and his family all gathered around. Then Paul and Silas told them about Jesus and everything he had said and done. The jailer washed and tended their wounds from the beating they had received the day before. He gave them new clothes to wear. Then he and his family were baptized in the name of Jesus. They were all full of joy, and they invited Paul and Silas to eat a meal with them.

When morning came, Luke and the other disciples heard the news of how God had freed them and how the jailer had been saved, and they, too, sang praises to God. When they heard what had happened, the magistrates were afraid and sent messages to the jailer, insisting that Paul and Silas should be released immediately.

Paul said to the officers, "They have beaten us publicly and thrown us into prison without trial, even though we are Roman citizens. Do you think they can get away with this and send us off secretly? No! Let them come themselves and accompany us to the gates of the city in person!"

When the magistrates heard that Paul and Silas were Roman citizens, they were very afraid, realizing it was they who had broken Roman law. No Roman citizen could be punished without a fair hearing and a proper sentence. They knew they were in serious trouble.

Paul's stern response was a way of making sure that Lydia and the jailer, and the others in Philippi who had decided to follow Jesus, would be much safer from now on. And, sure enough, the magistrates came and apologized politely and asked them very respectfully to leave the city.

THE UNKNOWN GOD

Paul and Silas left Philippi and journeyed on through Thessalonica and Berea. Sometimes Paul spoke about Jesus and there were storms of protest in the synagogues; sometimes his message was welcomed both by Jews and Gentiles. Everywhere Paul went he made friends and enemies, but in most cities he left behind a little group of Christians.

The new disciples did not meet in fine buildings or in luxury. They often met in the poorest houses, crowding into little rooms where they listened eagerly to stories about Jesus and began to learn new songs and prayers. There were not many rich, clever or famous Christians; they were mostly ordinary folk who lived hard lives. Some of them were slaves, some were outcasts, beggars on the streets.

But one day, Paul came to the great city of Athens where the inhabitants considered themselves to be very intellectual. People did nothing but swap the latest fashionable ideas. Most of them thought that Paul's message about Jesus was crazy, an absurd story.

The people of Athens laughed at him. "Who on earth would believe in a carpenter named Jesus, come back from the dead?"

"Who is this Resurrection? Is she some foreign goddess?"

They had no idea what he was talking about.

Meanwhile, Paul had been looking around the city – the greatest city in Greece – and everywhere he could see huge statues, altars, idols, offerings of flowers and meat and wine, columns and niches with words inscribed to every single, imaginable god. It was like a vast market stall of gods and goddesses, an array of gold, silver and stone idols.

Paul was angry and disturbed. These people seemed to believe everything and nothing. They loved ideas, they loved philosophy, they loved talking, but they did not love God. All they did was collect new and exotic religions.

Paul stood up in the meeting place, high on the hill, and began to address the crowds: "People of Athens! I see that you are very interested in religion, and on my way here I saw an altar with the words: TO AN UNKNOWN GOD. Well, I have come to tell you about this God that you don't know." People began to listen. It was a good opening.

The altar to the "unknown god" had been put up because they did not want to miss any god or goddess by accident and so bring bad luck on the city.

"I've come to tell you about the one God you have forgotten," Paul went on. "You have missed the one true God who made heaven and earth. You cannot make statues of him or keep him in a temple. He doesn't need any help from you, because he made you all and every person on earth. He is greater than all this..." Paul swept his hands across the sea of idols and chattering philosophers.

The crowds listened quietly for a while, because there was

something about this stranger. His ideas were different, to say the least. But then Paul began to speak about Jesus again, and to talk about the Messiah returning one day to judge the world.

"God has proved that Jesus is his Son – his chosen one – by raising him from the dead!"

At this, the Athenians burst out laughing. Some of them cried with laughter at the stupidity and absurdity of a man rising from the dead.

"Away with this idiot!" they shouted, and they walked off, leaving Paul standing in the meeting place. But a few stayed and begged Paul to continue. That day, a man named Dionysius and a woman named Damaris became followers and believed in Jesus.

Paul left Athens knowing that he had become a subject of ridicule, but he didn't care. No mockery would ever change the vision of the risen Jesus he had seen on the road to Damascus.

PAUL IN CORINTH

ACTS 18

Paul arrived in the city of Corinth, where he was welcomed by a Jewish couple, Aquila and Priscilla. They had a tent-making business, and since that was Paul's own trade, he stayed with them and worked for them. He always worked hard to support himself wherever he went, so he would not have to depend on anyone else.

At first, Paul spent his time speaking in the synagogue on the Sabbath days, but soon he made fierce enemies.

"From now on," he said to some of the Jewish leaders who

hated him, "I will spend all my time with Gentiles."

Gradually, despite all the difficulties in the city where there was greed, wickedness, prostitution, crime and idolatry, and despite the dangers and many setbacks, Paul began to build up a small band of mainly Gentile believers.

One night, Jesus appeared to Paul in a dream, saying, "Don't be afraid; speak out! Never be silent! I am with you and no one will attack you or harm you here. There are many people in this city who belong to me."

From that day, Paul knew that he had to reach out far and wide, everywhere in Corinth – down at the docks, on the steps of the temples, in the market places and schools and courtyards. He preached the good news about Jesus alongside Silas and a young disciple named Timothy from Lystra and other fellow workers who joined him there. They stayed in Corinth for eighteen months.

Corinth was a very big, bustling, difficult city with many temptations, and after Paul left, the Corinthian church went through great problems. There were quarrels and jealousies. So Paul wrote letters to the believers in Corinth, just as he did to new followers of Jesus everywhere, challenging the new disciples and teaching them about real love.

FOLLOWING JESUS

The New Testament contains a number of letters, sometimes known as Epistles, about how to live as a follower of Jesus. Many of these letters were written to strengthen new churches and to encourage and challenge young Christians.

GOD'S LOVE
FROM ROMANS 8

Paul wrote to the followers of Jesus in Rome to remind them that God loves them – always and forever:

"I am completely certain that God loves us so much that nothing in the whole of the universe can separate us from his love – not dying, nor living; not angels nor heavenly powers; not the present, nor the future. Nothing in this world, or any other world, absolutely nothing can ever separate us from God's love which he has shown to us in Jesus Christ."

TRUE LOVE
FROM 1 CORINTHIANS 13

Paul wrote to the followers of Jesus in Corinth, where there were arguments and jealousy among the believers. He described true love: the love shown by Jesus to the world; the love which Jesus wants his followers to have:

"Love is patient and kind; love is not jealous or boastful; it is not proud or rude, always getting its own way. It is not touchy or resentful. It does not gloat over the bad things other people do; instead it is happy when there is goodness and truth.

"Love is caring, trusting, hopeful, and never gives up.

"Love never comes to an end."

NEEDING ONE ANOTHER
FROM 1 CORINTHIANS 12

Paul explained that following Jesus isn't simply a matter for individuals – each person belongs to the "body of Christ" and has a different role to play. He used this picture to show what he means.

"A foot can't say, 'Because I'm not a hand, I don't belong to the body,' and an ear can't say 'I wish I was an eye.' If the ear did not exist, then the body couldn't hear, and if the whole body were an ear, where would be the sense of smell? All the parts are different, but all of them make up the one body. God has put the body together, and given each part a different function. If one part suffers, the others suffer with it. If one part is praised, then the rest are happy for it. All of you make up Christ's body, and all of you have an important role to play."

BEING FRIENDS WITH GOD
FROM 2 CORINTHIANS 5

Paul wrote again to the people in Corinth, this time to remind them that, because of Jesus, people can enjoy being friends with God:

"When anyone becomes a follower of Jesus, he becomes a new person: the past is gone, and new life has come. Because Jesus died for us, we are friends of God and no longer enemies. And God tells us to share the message with others: God was in Jesus, making everybody his friends."

CHANGED LIVES
FROM GALATIANS 5

Paul reminded the Galatians that Jesus promised the Holy Spirit to his followers, and the power of the Spirit changes lives:

"God's Spirit makes us loving, joyful, peaceful, patient, kind, good, faithful and humble and gives us self-control."

TALKING TO GOD
FROM EPHESIANS 6

Paul had no doubt that praying was an essential part of following Jesus. This was his advice to the believers at Ephesus:

"Keep on praying and asking for God's help. Pray all the time, with the Holy Spirit leading you. Be always alert, and never stop praying for all God's people. And pray for me, too, so that I can always be ready to tell other people the good news of Jesus."

THE LORD OF CREATION
FROM COLOSSIANS 1

Paul wanted the believers at Colossae to know that Jesus Christ is the Son of God:

"Jesus Christ shows us what the invisible God is like. God's Son stands above the whole creation, and through him everything in heaven and earth, visible and invisible, all the powers and rulers of the universe, were created. Jesus Christ existed before anything else existed... and through his death on the cross, God made peace with heaven and earth."

THE NEW LIFE
FROM COLOSSIANS 3

Paul wanted to show people that when they are followers of Jesus, the Holy Spirit is at work, changing them for the better. He wrote to the Colossians about the characteristics of God's people:

"With great love and care, God chose you to be his people. So live like God's people, and show these qualities in your lives: be understanding and kind, be gentle and patient. Do not be proud or vain. Give other people the benefit of the doubt and forgive each other, because God has forgiven you. And more than anything, love each other so that you remain in harmony with each other."

HOW TO LIVE WELL
FROM HEBREWS 13

The letter to the Hebrews gives some practical advice:

"Keep on loving each other as part of God's family. Invite new people to your homes with kindness, and offer them a meal – some people have welcomed angels into their homes without realizing it! Pray for those in prison, imagining what it would be like for you, and pray also for those who are being treated badly for their faith.

"Keep your marriages special and be faithful to each other.

"And don't think about money all the time, but be satisfied with what you've got. Remember God's promise to look after us: 'I will never let you go.'"

ADVICE FROM JAMES
FROM THE BOOK OF JAMES

The letter of James is addressed to all God's people scattered over the whole world. Here he talks about rich people and poor people:

"My children, if you want to be true followers of Jesus, you must never treat some people better than others.

"Imagine a man coming into a place of worship wearing gold, jewels and expensive clothes, and a poor man walking in wearing shabby clothes. If you give all your attention to the rich man and say, 'Here's the best seat for you!' but say to the poor man, 'Stand at the back,' or 'You can sit on the floor beside me,' aren't you setting yourself up as the worst kind of judge? You are choosing the rich rather than the poor.

"Listen, my friends, don't you know that God has chosen those who are poor in the eyes of the world to become rich in faith?"

BE CAREFUL
FROM JAMES 3

James also warns believers to be careful about what they say:

"It only takes a tiny spark to start a forest fire. Your tongue is like that spark. If we let it, the tongue can spread lies and evil and bring about all manner of wrong… No one has ever been able to tame the tongue. We can use it to give thanks to God, and we can use it to curse another person, made in the image of God. This is wrong!"

TROUBLE IN EPHESUS

ACTS 19

Paul journeyed all over the Roman empire, spreading the good news about Jesus, and telling of God's love for the whole world. On his three great journeys, he braved every danger. Sometimes he was thrown in prison, sometimes he was beaten, often he went without food for many days. He faced threats from dangerous people and even from wild animals. Twice he was shipwrecked and nearly drowned, but throughout all these things Paul knew that God was looking after him. He knew that Jesus himself had chosen him as his apostle, so nothing could stand in his way. Paul was determined to keep on working and speaking about Jesus until he was too old, or until he was captured and killed.

On his last great journey, he had a very narrow escape. He came to the great city of Ephesus with its marble pavements and lavish buildings. The huge temple to the goddess, Diana, dominated the city. Paul began, as usual, by speaking in the synagogue. The people there listened to him, but eventually Paul made too many enemies and he was forced to begin speaking in the lecture hall of Tyrannus nearby.

Paul spoke in this hall every day for nearly two years, and hundreds of people from all over the city and the surrounding villages heard stories about Jesus Christ. Paul performed many miracles too. Soon the word went around that Jesus was more powerful than Diana, goddess of the Ephesians.

There was a local silversmith, Demetrius, who made a fortune by selling statues of Diana. He was furiously angry when he realized how popular Paul was, so he gathered all the craftsmen of the city together.

"Men," he shouted, "look what's happening to us! Our business is being ruined! This fellow Paul is going around saying that man-made gods do not exist. He says that Diana has no power at all!"

The tradesmen grumbled and shouted in agreement. "You're right!" said one. "If this goes on, no one will buy our souvenirs, our trinkets, our shrines, our gods and goddesses!"

"Diana is great," said Demetrius, pointing to a huge statue of the goddess. He grabbed one of his little shining statuettes. "Do you see this? Soon, it will be worth nothing. Our great, divine protector has been cheated of her glory."

Demetrius was a clever and powerful speaker, and soon he had the men whipped up into a frenzy of hatred. They ran through the streets, seizing people as they went. "Stand up for your religion! Stand up for the great goddess of the Ephesians – Diana!"

"Diana is great! Diana of the Ephesians!" the crowds called as they poured into the huge arena. And they began shouting for the blood of Paul and all the followers of Jesus.

In desperation, Paul tried to walk into the middle of the arena and challenge them all, but the other disciples grabbed hold of him. "No! It's too dangerous!" they shouted. They held him back from the seething, maddened crowds until the city clerk addressed the vast throng himself.

He raised his hand. "Citizens! Why are you screaming and shouting? These men have not robbed temples or uttered a word against Diana! If Demetrius has a grievance, he can go to court or speak to the Roman governor. But as for this chanting and bellowing, the whole city is in danger of being charged with rioting. The Roman garrison will march into the city and punish everyone. We could all be killed or end up in prison!"

So the clerk silenced the frenzy at last and dismissed the people, and Paul was able to leave the city quietly and safely.

THE ROAD TO JERUSALEM

ACTS 20

Paul had escaped death in Ephesus, but it had been very close. One day, he would not escape. He would have to face the same death as Stephen and James and a growing number of disciples who had been murdered by violent mobs or executed by the authorities. Would this be in Jerusalem like Jesus, with the crowds calling for his crucifixion? Or would it be in Rome? He did not know, but whatever happened, Paul was not afraid.

"For me to live is to be with Christ," he wrote to his friends at Philippi, "so to die is simply to have more of him. If I die, it's a great advantage."

Now Paul was set on returning to Jerusalem. He talked of this being his final journey. Paul's friends were anxious for him and sad for themselves.

At Miletus, Paul met up with his friends, the followers of Jesus from Ephesus. As they gathered on the shore, Paul said farewell to each one of the Christian leaders. They wept and clung to him, begging him not to go.

"I must," replied Paul. "I must return to Jerusalem."

"You will be captured and killed."

"It's true that in every city the Holy Spirit warns me of prison and suffering to come. But I must go. My life is worth nothing at all to me now," said Paul gently. "All that matters is finishing my task... being God's chosen messenger to the very end."

Paul's friends began to cry when he mentioned the word "end" and said to them, "You will never see my face again."

Paul did not speak for a while because he, too, was very upset. Then he encouraged them with many promises of God's love, and he warned them of dangers ahead. "Be good shepherds – look after your flock and keep them from harm!"

At last, he boarded the ship which would take him to the port of Caesarea, from where he would travel to Jerusalem.

The leaders of the church watched the ship pull away. They took courage and returned to their people.

ARRESTED!

Acts 21–24

Paul arrived in Jerusalem secretly, and the first thing he did was to visit the leaders of the church. They welcomed him, but deep down they were very shocked and troubled.

"You're in great danger," they told him. "A report is going around that you tell every Jew to turn away from his religion. You must do something to show that you are still a faithful Jew."

Paul agreed to go to the temple humbly, following all the Jewish customs, and show that he continued to worship God sincerely, for all the Jewish Christians in Jerusalem were very careful to follow the laws of Moses. But as soon as Paul approached the temple, people started shouting, "You're the one who teaches people to hate Moses!"

Then someone called loudly, "He has brought Greeks into the holy place!"

These charges were not true, but the crowds became furious. To bring a Gentile into the holy place of the Jews was a crime punishable by death. Very soon, the whole of Jerusalem was in an uproar, and the Roman commander sent in his troops. Paul was rescued from certain death.

"Let me speak to my people," said Paul, chained between two Roman soldiers. The commander agreed and called for silence.

Paul addressed the crowds: "Please let me defend myself – let me tell you the truth!"

Uneasily, the vast, angry crowd listened as Paul told them

the story of his life – how he had hunted down the Christians, how he had seen the great vision on the road to Damascus, how Jesus had said to him, "Go and speak to the Gentiles."

But when they heard this, they would not listen to him any longer. They thought that Paul was a blasphemer who wanted to destroy the Jewish faith, and they were ready to stone him to death.

The Roman commander was sweating as he looked at the violent mob and ordered his soldiers into positions on every gateway and tower.

"Take the prisoner away and flog him," he said, hoping to satisfy the people. But as the soldiers were preparing to whip Paul, he turned and asked, "Is it legal to beat a Roman citizen who has not had a fair trial?"

"A Roman citizen?" Suddenly, the soldiers were very afraid. A Roman citizen had the protection of the emperor, Caesar. If they did Paul harm, they could face death themselves.

"A Roman citizen…?" The commander looked at Paul anxiously.

"Yes," said Paul, "I am."

"I paid a fortune to become a Roman citizen," said the commander.

"I was born a Roman citizen."

From that moment, everything was different. Paul was sent by special armed guard to the governor Felix in Caesarea, who showed him deep respect. For two years, Paul lived there under arrest and was given great freedom. He carried on telling everyone about Jesus.

SHIPWRECK!

ACTS 25–27

When a new Roman governor arrived in Caesarea, Paul's
enemies in Jerusalem seized their opportunity. They sent
messengers, demanding that Paul be tried and punished in
Jerusalem. They expected to see him crucified like Jesus.

Festus, the new governor, summoned Paul. "Are you
prepared to stand trial before me in Jerusalem?" he asked.

"No," said Paul. "How can I have a fair trial in Jerusalem,
when the charges against me are lies? I appeal to the judgment
of Caesar in Rome!"

"Caesar?"

Paul nodded. Festus was astonished at his fearlessness. But
he simply said, "You have appealed to Caesar, and to Caesar you
will go!"

Paul was determined to go to Rome. He had survived
imprisonment, beatings, stoning, shipwrecks, cold and hunger
over many years. Now he was ready to face his last journey, by
land and sea, and he knew that God was with him. Luke and
other friends of Paul decided to travel with him. A Roman
centurion named Julius was put in charge of all the prisoners
on the voyage, and so they set sail.

The ship made its way up the coast and across to Cyprus.
The wind was against them all the way. In Myra they boarded a
grain ship bound for Italy. Clouds rolled across the sky and
powerful headwinds began to blow.

By the time they reached a port on the southern shores of
Crete, Paul, who was an experienced sailor, knew that they

were all in great danger. He spoke to Julius and to the commander of the ship. "Friends," he said, politely, "this voyage is becoming too dangerous. If we carry on, we will not only lose our cargo, but many lives as well!"

Julius ignored Paul's advice, listening only to the captain of the ship and the ship's owner, who were both determined to reach the port of Phoenix further along the coast.

As soon as they put to sea once more, a violent gale burst upon the ship from across the island. The boat was hurled up and down on mountainous waves, the sky darkened, and no one could see the sun or the stars for many days. Everyone – the ship's crew, the soldiers, the prisoners, all the passengers – everyone except Paul began to fear for their lives.

In desperation, the crew threw the heaviest cargo overboard. Then they began to throw the ship's tackle away, but it made no difference.

"We'll all drown!" they cried out as the biting winds and driving rain beat down upon the little ship, threatening to break it into pieces. At last, Paul stood up again.

"Friends," he said, shouting above the wind, "why didn't you listen to me? You would have been saved from this terrible trouble!"

Everyone was silent because they knew that Paul had been right all along. "Keep courage," he said. "No one is going to die. An angel of God stood beside me last night and said, 'Don't be afraid, Paul, for you will certainly stand before Caesar in Rome. Everyone sailing with you will be safe.'"

All the crew, the soldiers, prisoners and passengers listened as Paul lifted his hands up high. "Courage, everyone! God will do what he has promised, but we will be stranded on an island for some time."

The fierce storms continued for days. The wind howled and threw the boat from side to side. But Paul said, "Stay calm. Everyone must take some food. We will reach dry land soon!"

The people ate hungrily to gain strength. At last land appeared through the mists and the storms: a bay with a sandy beach.

Suddenly, the ship ran aground with a huge crash, and the vessel began to break up.

The soldiers began to panic, shouting, "We must kill all the prisoners before they escape to the shore!"

"No!" shouted Julius. "Paul must be delivered safely to Rome! Do not harm a single prisoner!"

So it was that, clutching driftwood, planks and pieces of wreckage, some floating, some swimming, every single person – two hundred and seventy-six people in all – arrived on the beach safe and sound.

TO ROME AT LAST

ACTS 28, 2 TIMOTHY 4

Battered by the storms, exhausted and terrified, the passengers staggered up the beach.

As the local people began to arrive, offering friendship and help, the shipwrecked passengers discovered that they had arrived on the island of Malta. During his stay on the island, Paul was able to speak about the love and power of Jesus and to heal many people.

At last, after three months, Paul, Luke, his other companions and fellow prisoners were taken on another ship to Puteoli, a port in Italy. From there, under guard, Paul journeyed to Rome. He was full of joy and quite unafraid. He knew that God had been with him all the way and would remain with him to the end.

Paul lived like a free man for a long time in Rome while awaiting his trial, and again he spoke about Jesus to every Jew and Gentile that he met.

Paul may well have been among those who were persecuted by the emperor Nero. The emperor began to hate the Christians in Rome, blaming them for a great fire which destroyed much of the city. Many thousands were thrown to the lions, burned at the stake or executed by the sword.

Paul knew that he was soon going to die, and in his last letter from a prison in Rome, he wrote his final message:

"It is time for me to leave this earth. I have fought the good fight to the very end; I have finished the race. Now there is waiting for me in heaven a crown of righteousness which the Lord – the only true Judge – will give to me on that final day. And not only to me, but to everyone who longs for his coming!"

A NEW HEAVEN AND A NEW EARTH

REVELATION 1, 21, 22

Over the years, many of Jesus' followers, including Paul, Peter and James, were killed because of their faith. Thousands of Christians had died, and the life of the Christian churches was very dangerous and troubled. People longed for Jesus to return to earth and save them from their suffering. One of these was John, who was sent to the island of Patmos as a punishment because he would not stop speaking about Jesus Christ.

John remembered Jesus' words, "I will always be with you, even to the end of the world." He knew that Jesus had never left him, even though he had vanished in bright clouds of glory, returning to heaven. John knew that the Holy Spirit was with him, and he prayed every day that Jesus would return to bring in a new era, a time of love and peace and an ending of all sorrow and suffering.

One day John heard a voice like the blast of a trumpet: "Write down my message and send it to the churches..."

John turned, and he saw a vision of Jesus – as a mysterious, dazzling cloud of light. The eyes of the figure burned like fire, his feet were like shining bronze, and his voice thundered like the roar of a great waterfall. In his hand he held seven stars. A two-edged sword flowed from his mouth like a sheet of flame, and his face was like the sun rising in all its glory.

So powerful and beautiful and terrifying was the vision that John collapsed. But the figure laid a hand on him gently and said, "Do not be afraid. I am the First and the Last. I am the Living One. I was dead, but now I am alive forever. I hold the keys of death and the afterlife, and you must write down everything that I tell you."

John wrote down everything that was revealed to him on the island of Patmos. He was allowed a glimpse of the future, the glorious and thrilling future that awaits the whole of creation:

"Then I saw a new heaven and a new earth; for the first heaven and the first earth had vanished, and the sea had disappeared. I saw the Holy City, the new Jerusalem, coming down from heaven like a beautiful bride dressed in gorgeous clothes for her husband. And I heard a loud voice, from the throne, saying, 'See this city! Here God will live with men and women. They will become his people, and God himself will make his home with them and be their God. He will wipe away every tear from their eyes; there will be no more death or mourning or crying out in pain, for the old world has gone forever.'"

Then the voice called to John, "See! I am making everything new."

John wrote down the very last words of the vision, calling out to God's people everywhere: "Jesus himself says, 'I am coming soon.' Amen! Come, Lord Jesus!"